That Other Gospel

UNDERSTANDING THE FIRST SERMON OF JESUS

Charles Cooper

Thorns and Gold Publishing
Winter Garden, FL

Thorns and Gold Publishing
P.O. Box 3285
Windermere, FL 34786

Printed in the United States of America

Ordering Information:
Quantity sales. Special discounts are available on quantity purchases by corporations, associations, and others.
For details, contact the "Special Sales Department" at the address above.

That Other Gospel: Understanding the First Sermon of Jesus/Charles Cooper.
—1st ed.
ISBN 979-8-9886537-0-7

For online resources, visit Kingdomalive.us

Book Layout ©2017 BookDesignTemplates.com

Contents

Contents

Dedication

**To my online Sunday evening Kingdom Alive Gathering
Past, Present, and Future!**

*Seek the Kingdom of God above all else, and live righteously,
and he will give you everything you need.*

—Matthew 6:33
(NLT)

Preface

Both scholars and laymen can and often do miss the importance of the chronological development of the New Testament and how that can influence our ability to properly interpret the Scriptures. Nowhere is this more important than in the Synoptic Gospels and the necessity to recognize the distinction between the primary pre-Easter message of Jesus and the primary post-Easter message of the apostles.

The resurrection of Jesus Christ changed the primary emphasis of the apostles' message. Pre-Easter, the dominant message was the "gospel" of the kingdom of God (GKG). Post-Easter, the primary emphasis became the "gospel" of Jesus Christ (GJC). These two "gospels" (one rewardific and the other salvific)[1] are not interchangeable, as we will show. The failure to recognize this critical fact results in confusion and systematic violation of the sound principles of Bible study that ensure incorrect interpretation.

Betz recognizes this problem and he summarizes:

> *How does the message of the earthly Jesus concerning the kingdom relate to the gospel of Christ which the Church preached after the resurrection? Are we here dealing with two distinct gospels: the first a Jewish one, a gospel of the Father, the second a specifically Christian one, in which the Son is central; the first, where Jesus appears as [a] brother to the Jews, the second, where Trinitarian dogma, irreconcilable with Jewish monotheism, is beginning to show its lineaments?[2]*

The difference is real. The failure to recognize the difference between the pre-resurrection message of Jesus and the post-resurrection message of the church can have profound consequences for the correct interpretation in the New Testament—the Synoptic Gospels, in particular. The habitual error of equating the two messages is an example of what is called "illegitimate identity transfer." Both scholars and students perpetuate this error, even though most have never heard of it by this name. As a result, this error dominates New Testament studies.

Bible translations are a major contributor to this problem as well. Because few believers have a background in biblical languages, they have to trust their favorite translation without understanding the major decisions made regarding how words and ideas were communicated from the original Hebrew or Greek manuscripts to create it. Take the noun εὐαγγέλιον (euaggelion), typically translated as "gospel."[3] Because the church now uses the term "gospel" to refer to the death, burial, and resurrection of Jesus Christ (the Gospel, capital G), it is systematically assumed that *any* appearance of this term in our English translations of the New Testament is shorthand for the same. This conclusion results in a serious misreading of the Synoptic Gospels.

In Mark 1:1, τὸ εὐαγγέλιον is likely an objective genitive[4] referring to the post-Easter church's message *about* Jesus Christ, not to the dominant message preached by the pre-Easter Jesus, himself. Thus, in Mark 1:1, τὸ εὐαγγέλιον refers to the contents and subject matter of Mark's narrative as a whole—the story of Jesus; the saving act of God in his Son, Jesus the Christ; and Jesus' words, deeds, death, and resurrection as they are expressed in Mark's written document and as they continued to be preached in Mark's own time.[5] Therefore to reflect the grammatical significance of Mark 1:1, we shall offer the translation, "The Gospel or Good News about Jesus Christ" to better reflect the intended meaning of the text.

However, Mark 1:1 is the only place in the Synoptics where this is the case. Failure to apply this critical distinction to every other occurrence of τὸ εὐαγγέλιον in the Gospels of Matthew or Mark (the only two Gospels where this specific term appears) is to commit illegitimate totality transfer. This is a second dominating error of many New Testament students. A rule of practice for good Bible study methodology requires every word to be contextually defined. Under no circumstance should one automatically assume the meaning of a term in any occurrence in the Bible without first examining the context to ensure an accurate interpretation. In fact, Mark's contemporary usage of τὸ εὐαγγέλιον at the very beginning of his biography of the Lord Jesus can be very misleading to a novice or careless New Testament exegete. This we will demonstrate in the following pages of this book.

Notes

[1] By adding the adjective suffix *fic*, which means "making" or "causing," we make a word that's opposite salvation. Rewardific refers to rewards earned by faithfully living as God demands. Merriam-Webster.com Dictionary, s.v., "-fic," accessed December 5, 2023, https://www.merriam-webster.com/dictionary/-fic.

[2] Otto Betz, *Jesus' Gospel of the Kingdom*, p. 54, in The Gospel and the Gospels, Peter Stuhlmacher (William B. Eerdmans Publishing Co., Grand Rapids, 1991).

[3] Τὸ εὐαγγέλιον does not occur in the Gospel of Luke or John. This fact alone should signal caution on the part of New Testament studies as much as most see John's Gospel as the most salvific focused in the New Testament.

[4] In New Testament Greek, the genitive case functions to restrict another noun. In the sentence, "The wife of Rob came home later than usual." The genitive "of Rob" restricts the noun "wife." We are talking about a specific wife. Students of New Testament Greek quickly learn that there are many different relationships expressed by the genitive case. Specifically, there is the objective vs. subjective genitival usage. The subjective genitive occurs when the noun in the genitive case is the name of the subject of the action. The objective genitive case is the name of the object of the action. Is Jesus Christ the object of the Gospel or is he the subject of the Gospel? In other words, is the Gospel about Jesus Christ (objective); or is the Gospel the message Jesus Christ preached (subjective)? In some cases, it can be both.

[5] We must keep in mind the fact that Mark wrote his Gospel at least 25 to 30 years after our Lord departed from the earth. During this time, several NT words acquired additional nuances. Thus, there is a need to exercise care and not read new developments back into words used by Jesus during his earthly ministry. A check of the term τὸ εὐαγγέλιον reveals that over time, the original meaning of "the good news" additionally could mean "the good news about Jesus Christ = the Gospel," "a written biography of Jesus Christ," and in the most recent modern period, "to tell the truth."

CHAPTER 1

The Forgotten "Gospel": The Good News Jesus Preached

lbert Einstein is widely credited with saying, "The definition of insanity is doing the same thing over and over again but expecting different results." While we might expect an insane person to engage in this type of behavior, sane people do, as well. Their *behavior* might not be insane, but it can be considered foolish and unwise. Let's take the salvation debate as an example.

In 1988, John F. MacArthur, Jr. published a book entitled *The Gospel According to Jesus*. It sparked a debate that continues to this day concerning the question: "How does one obtain the righteousness of God?" Two camps—one dubbed "lordship salvation" and the other "easy believism"—have traded book for book and article for article since then.

Each has taken the moral high ground, claiming to represent the biblical view of salvation.

"Lordship salvation," represented by Dr. MacArthur, holds that in order to receive eternal life, one must accept Jesus Christ as both Savior and Lord. The other holds that one can accept Jesus as Savior, while not understanding the deep truth of his lordship; thus, one may be saved but live without the fruits evidencing a life transformed by the Holy Spirit. Both camps come to the Bible with presuppositions and set about proving them true.

Despite the flurry of books and articles on the subject, the debate remains unresolved, in the eyes of some believers. Why? Because both camps keep saying the same thing the same way, expecting to convince the other. If the goal is truth, perhaps a fresh look is in order. That is the purpose of this book, and we will start with an analysis of the underlying exegetical errors of the lordship salvation view that prevent this debate from being resolved. Those errors revolve around the use of the term so closely associated with salvation, "the gospel." For examination purposes, we will craft our discussion around Dr. MacArthur's views on the subject since they are so well known. Our goal is not to attack Dr. MacArthur. It is simply to use his writings to facilitate that discussion.

After his first book, MacArthur went on to write other "Gospel According to" books. In 1993, he wrote *Ashamed of the Gospel: When the Church Becomes Like the World*. In 1993, he published *Faith Works: The Gospel According to the Apostles*, republished in 2000 as *The Gospel According to the Apostles*. In 2017, he published *The Gospel According to Paul*. In 2018, he added *The Gospel According to God*. Each is victimized by the same error—the failure to properly contextualize "the gospel" in each occurrence of the term in the Synoptic Gospels.

DEFINING "THE GOSPEL"

One would be correct in assuming that any discussion of the English translation "the gospel" should begin with a look at the Greek term on which that translation is based. This would ensure an accurate reflection of the original intent of the text. Yet, in this debate, that seems to be missing. In referring to the works of both John MacArthur and William Dubose, Jeremy D. Myers concludes that these "authors nowhere define what they mean by "gospel.""[1]

Rather, there seems to be an underlying assumption that each instance of the English translation "the gospel" refers to the death, burial, and resurrection of Jesus for the atonement for sin. Myers draws a similar conclusion when he writes,

> *Throughout these books (as well as most others about the gospel), the gospel seems to be defined as "the essentials of what must be explained in evangelism" or "the facts that must be believed in order to receive everlasting life.*[2]

We draw this conclusion because no concise, biblically based lexical definition of "the gospel" is given in the "Gospel According To" series. A lack of precision in this area is the Achilles' heel of MacArthur's position.

Take, for example, Mark 1:1, which opens the book with, "The beginning of the gospel of Jesus Christ, the Son of God." One must ask, "What meaning does Mark intend by the phrase 'the gospel of Jesus Christ'?" In the modern church, the term "gospel" has come to refer to one of three things: the death, burial, and resurrection of Jesus

(DBRJC) for the atonement for sin (or the Gospel, capital "G"); the four written biographical accounts—the gospels of Matthew, Mark, Luke, and John; and lastly, to tell the truth ("You can take that as gospel"). Yet the Greek term τὸ εὐαγγέλιον (*to euaggelion*) can also mean "the glad tidings" or simply "the good news," about anything.

What is often overlooked is that many of these nuances were acquired over a very long period of time. If a nuance developed after the time that the text was written, can that nuance then be read legitimately back into the earlier text? This is a critical question underlying this debate. Notice the chart below:

The Good News

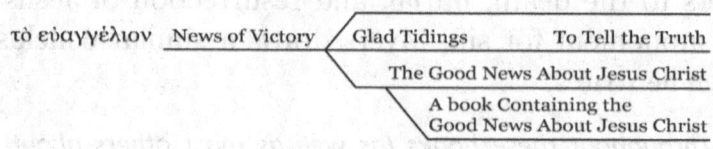

At what point during the development of the New Testament did the definition of "the gospel" narrow to refer to Jesus' atoning sacrifice only? When did the Greek noun become the exclusive shortened way of referring to the DBRJC for the atonement of man's sin? Serious error results when one assumes that at the beginning of Jesus' public ministry, everyone using the term "gospel" (John the Baptist, then Jesus, and the subsequent apostles) did so with this intent. To ensure an accurate interpretation of Mark 1:1 and any subsequent usages of the term, this question must be answered.

These are questions that Dr. MacArthur does not address. In the introduction to *The Gospel According to Jesus*, the revised and expanded anniversary edition, the very first line is a question: "What is the Gospel?"[3] Given that the New Testament is a translation of Koine Greek, we expect MacArthur to follow this question with a lexical definition of the Greek term and give some attention to the history of its use. Where in the diachronic development of this noun did new nuances occur? How was the term used in the Old Testament era? How was it used during Jesus' earthly ministry? Did the term add additional nuances over time or did it remain static? Did it have a predominant nuance at a particular point in time? In the New Testament, why is *euaggelion* translated as "good news" or "glad tidings" in some instances and "gospel" in others, and still yet others "good news"? Are there textual rules that govern when a particular translation is appropriate?

The English term "gospel" occurs more than 360 times in *The Gospel According to Jesus*. Yet, McArthur does not address any of these complexities. In addition to "the gospel," MacArthur does use the nuanced phrases "the gospel of Christ" and "the gospel of the kingdom," but he does not point out any distinction between them.

The same problem extends to MacArthur's other writings, as well. In *The Gospel According to God*, for example, we find 101 occurrences of the term "gospel." In examining these instances, which also include "the gospel of Christ" (GC) and "the gospel according to God" (GG), Dr. MacArthur likewise does not distinguish between them. For the reader, the takeaway is that he does not see such distinction as necessary.

A HISTORICAL PERSPECTIVE

While Dr. MacArthur does not demonstrate knowledge of the history of the noun *to euaggelion*, we will do so in this book. One consistent method of discovering the possible nuances of New Testament Greek terms is to attempt a diachronic study. This typically begins with the Hebrew Masoretic text, then the Greek translation of the Old Testament, the Septuagint.[4]

When one takes this approach, one quickly discovers that the noun *euaggelion* does not occur in the Greek translation of the Old Testament at all. The Greek noun is not found in any writings before the letters of the New Testament. While scholars dispute whether Paul wrote 1 Thessalonians or Galatians first as the very first book of the New Testament canon, both have the Greek noun in them. The noun only occurs in the gospels of Matthew and Mark, which many agree were written possibly after the letters of Paul.

While we would be right in examining the use of the noun *to euaggelion* in the Gospels in which it occurs, it is also useful to examine the times in which it is not. Notably, *to euaggelion* does not occur in the Gospel of John. This alone should cause all to proceed with caution. If the most "gospel" of the Gospels, which focuses on salvation more than any other, does not utilize *to euaggelion* to describe the message of Jesus Christ in toto, the question is why? The term does not occur in the Gospel of Luke, either. This strongly suggests that the use of this term, in the technical sense, to refer to Jesus' death, burial, and resurrection as atonement for mankind's sin was not yet in use. Indeed, the term was not used this way by the church until after Pentecost, which we shall prove in the next chapter.

If this use of "to euaggelion" did not start until after Pentecost, this casts tremendous doubt that it was used this way during Jesus' earthly ministry. Or that his audience would have understood it that way. To his audience, our Lord was still Jesus of Nazareth, introducing the good news (τό εὐαγγέλιον) from God about his kingdom. Before Pentecost, we must exercise *extreme care* when defining the term any other way.

Euaggelion = gospel (generic noun = "good news")

To euaggelion = the gospel (singular noun pointing to a *specific* set of good news = "*the* good news")

Understanding the historical development of *euaggelion* is critical to correctly interpreting the Synoptic Gospels. Evidence proves that MacArthur does not understand this fact. The term "gospel" occurs more than 330 times in MacArthur's book *The Gospel According to Jesus*. Yet, not once does he give a clear, concise lexical definition of what it means. We count no less than 25 other transliterated Greek terms with definitions in MacArthur's book. Yet, *euaggelion* is not among them. Why?

Nor does Dr. MacArthur trace the historical development of the usage of this term. Rather, he appears to apply the post-Pentecost definition of *to euaggelion* to every instance translated as "the gospel," even when it is used before Pentecost. MacArthur acknowledges the challenge in his own position when he writes, "While Jesus' gospel was not yet fully completed until His death and resurrection, the elements of it were all clear in His teaching."[5] MacArthur appears to be trying to resolve his theological problem with this statement, but we might ask, "All clear to whom?" It certainly was not the case with the Twelve, which we shall see shortly.

Saying that the elements of the Gospel were "clear" in Jesus' teaching is perhaps one of the most egregious statements MacArthur makes. On the contrary, the necessity of Jesus' death, burial, and resurrection was hidden from his disciples. In fact, the very first time Jesus told them about what was about to happen, Peter rebuked him (Matt. 16:21–23). Given Peter's response, there is no way that he understood the need for Jesus to die. When one understands that this incident occurred a little over six months before our Lord's death, MacArthur's claim is shown to be preposterous. How could Peter understand *euaggelion* to refer to Jesus' death, burial, and resurrection when he did not believe that Jesus would have to die at all?

Even after Jesus' resurrection, the truth of the modern Gospel was still unclear to the Twelve. On the third day after our Lord's death, Luke 24:13–21 reports,

> *That very day two of them were going to a village named Emmaus, about seven miles from Jerusalem, and they were talking with each other about all these things that had happened. While they were talking and discussing together, Jesus himself drew near and went with them. But their eyes were kept from recognizing him. And he said to them, "What is this conversation that you are holding with each other as you walk?" And they stood still, looking sad. Then one of them, named Cleopas, answered him, "Are you the only visitor to Jerusalem who does not know the things that have happened there in these days?" And he said to them, "What things?" And they said to him, "Concerning Jesus of Nazareth, a man who was a prophet mighty in deed and word before God and all the people, and how our chief priests and rulers delivered him up to be condemned to death and crucified him. But we had hoped that he was the one to redeem Israel. Yes, and besides all this, it is now the third day since these things happened. (emphasis added)*

Cleopas makes clear that with the death of Jesus of Nazareth, the apostles' hopes of Israel's redemption were dashed (v. 17). In the eyes of the two on the road to Emmaus, the death of Jesus had no benefit for National Israel. The idea that they understood Jesus' death as having a spiritual benefit for all mankind requires reading later developments back into the text.

While both the lordship salvation and the easy believism camps are quick to condemn and castigate one another, both are guilty of committing the same errors. They assume conclusions never proven by Scripture.

THE "GOSPEL" IN THE PARABLE OF THE SOWER

We see MacArthur making the same error in the parable of the sower.[6] In his exposition, MacArthur transfers the meaning of "the Gospel" to the phrase "the Word of God." He writes,

> *Now alone with the disciples and other inquisitive believers (Mark 4:10), the Lord took what seemed like a simple, obvious story and used it to unveil the magnificent reality of the kingdom. The seed he spoke of was not [a] literal seed, but rather the gospel: "When anyone hears the word of the kingdom . . . " (v. 19). The seed is the message about the King and his kingdom. Luke 8:11, a parallel account, is even more explicit: "The seed is the Word of God." Thus the sower is anyone who plants the seed of the gospel by the Word of God (cf. 1 Peter 1:23) in the heart of an individual. The prototype of all sowers is the Lord himself. (emphasis added)[7]*

For the uninformed reader, this transfer of meaning might go unnoticed, but for the careful exegete, it should not. Is MacArthur justified in reading the modern Gospel into this parable as equivalent to the Word of God, i.e., the DBRJC as we now understand it?

It is normally considered good hermeneutical practice to recognize the importance of context. Words, phrases, sentences, paragraphs, chapters, individual books, sections of books, and the complete Old and New Testaments are the circles of context. One first discovers the nuance or nuances of individual words from the lexicon. Second, one looks at how the author uses the word throughout his writings. Next, one looks at how other writers used the term. Lastly, if possible, one may look at how the term was used outside the Bible. The circles of context are an interpreter's best friend.

Instead of allowing the historical context to guide his interpretation, however, MacArthur perpetuates previous hermeneutical errors. He transposes the "seed" in this parable with the Gospel. In the selected text above, his purpose appears to be to make a case for his position. Yet, we don't see the same careful exegesis as in his past writings. This leads to errors in interpretation.

Dr. MacArthur is guilty of at least two errors regarding his interpretation of the parable of the sower: *illegitimate identity transfer* and *illegitimate totality transfer*. These two errors are central to our discussion.

WHAT IS ILLEGITIMATE IDENTITY TRANSFER?

In an attempt to correct common errors routinely made by biblical scholars in the area of linguistics, James Barr published a book entitled *The Semantics of Biblical Language*. In it, he lists several methodological errors. Among them are *illegitimate identity transfer* and *illegitimate totality transfer*.

Barr defines illegitimate identity transfer as occurring when "the identity of the object to which different designations are given does not imply that these designations have the same semantic value."[8] In other words, an illegitimate identity transfer concludes that because two words *refer* to the same thing, the two words must *mean* the same thing. However, just because A and B point to the same object or event does not automatically mean A = B.

An excellent example occurs often concerning Hebrews 11:1. Since the text clearly says, "Now faith is ...." Many automatically assume that Hebrews 11:1 is a lexical definition of the term "faith" and read this meaning into every other occurrence of the term in the New Testament. Yet, a check of the Greek lexicon does not include Hebrews 11:1 as the definition of the Greek noun πίστις [*pistis*].

In MacArthur's interpretation of the parable of the sower, he sees the phrases "the seed," "the Word of God," and "the word of the kingdom" referring to the same thing—DBRJC. In this, MacArthur is not alone. Many New Testament scholars make this hermeneutical error, and they pass it on to their students. Rather than allowing each occurrence of the term to be defined by its immediate context, they assign the same meaning to every occurrence, whether this meaning is contextually appropriate or not.

The parable of the sower is found in the accounts of Matthew, Mark, and Luke. One should not offer a conclusion about the meaning of the text until all three accounts are evaluated independently and then correlated. In Matthew's account, the seed is explicitly identified as "the word of the kingdom" (Matt. 13:19), more appropriately translated as "the word about the kingdom [of God]." In Mark's account, the seed is "the word" (Mark 4:14), which reflects Mark's apocopated style. In Luke's account, the seed is "the word of God" (Luke 8:11). Thus, we see three different phrases that define the *seed*. Is the "seed" the same in all three accounts?

For Matthew and Mark, the answer is yes. Scholars generally agree that Matthew gives an expanded view of what

Mark typically apocopates. Thus, "the word" for Mark is the same as "the word about the kingdom [of God]" for Matthew. Regarding the latter, Hagner concludes,

> *The beginning of the interpretation of the parable identifies what is sown by the sower as* τὸν λόγον τῆς βασιλείας, *"the word of the kingdom." This phrase is used in the Gospels only here and is the equivalent of Matthew's* εὐαγγέλιον τῆς βασιλείας, *"gospel of the kingdom," i.e., the essence of Jesus' preaching about the dawning of the kingdom in and through his ministry (4:23; 9:35; 24:14).[9]*

Mark explicitly states that the core message of Jesus from the beginning of his public ministry was "the gospel of God," or the good news that, with the revelation of his identity as the Messiah, the kingdom of God was being ushered in on Earth. There is no other way to conclude that "the word about the kingdom" refers to the post-Pentecost understanding of the death, burial, and resurrection of Jesus than to assume it at this point in the chronology of our Lord's earthly ministry.

Luke, however, defines "the seed" differently than the other two Gospel writers. For Luke, the "seed" is "the word of God." In the ESV's translation of Luke's Gospel, the phrase "the word of God" occurs five times (3:2; 5:1; 8:11, 21; and 11:18). Except for Luke 3:2, the Greek term λόγος (*logos*) is used for "word" in the phrase "word of God." In Luke 8:11, 21, instead of the choice of ῥῆμα as in Luke 3:2, the author uses λόγος (*logos*). Some argue that ῥῆμα suggests a particular message of God, while λόγος looks at the entire scope of God's message.[10] Thus, it is very tempting to read into the phrase "the word of God" a meaning derived from later usage in the New Testament. This is clearly what MacArthur does.

However, sound exegesis begins with the immediate context. Luke 5:1; 8:11, 21, and 11:28 put the phrase "the word of God" in the mouth of Jesus. No serious New Testament scholar can argue that when Jesus used this term during the earliest months of his earthly teaching, the Jews heard and understood this as referring to the DBRJC. Yet, this is precisely what MacArthur wants us to believe.

Instead of defining the meaning of "the seed" from the immediate context, MacArthur falls to the temptation to transfer meaning from other, unrelated passages. John indeed says that Jesus is the Word. However, one should resist the urge to transfer that meaning into the parable without confirming such a conclusion. Matthew adds the genitival qualifier "of the kingdom," which is unique to his account. Unlike Lenski, who adopts the position that "the word of the kingdom" is best regarded as a subjective genitive;[11] we adopt the view that an objective genitive is best: "the word about the kingdom."

The first occurrence of the phrase, "the word of God" in Luke 5:1 occurs in the Lord's selection of the first group of men who would constitute the Twelve Apostles – Peter, James, and John. This account occurs in both Mark and Luke. If we compare Luke 5:1 with Mark and Luke's chronological accounts, what Luke 5:1 calls "the word of God," Mark identifies as "the word," (Mark 2:2). In all cases, "the word" concerns the good news of the kingdom of God.

The parable of the sower does not begin with the customary introductory formula "the kingdom of heaven is like" or "the kingdom of God is like." However, Luke's account makes clear that the parable is about "the secrets of the kingdom of God" (Luke 8:10). Thus, Nolland is correct when he concludes,

Matthew adds "of the kingdom" to Mark's "the word" in order to establish a link with his language of proclaiming the gospel of the kingdom in 4:23; 9:35; 24:14. [12]

By importing the notion of "the Gospel" (DBRJC) into the parable of the sower, MacArthur commits an illegitimate identity transfer. The "good news about the kingdom of God" (pre-Easter) is not the "good news about Jesus Christ" (post-Easter). There is no thought of Jesus' death, burial, and resurrection this early in Jesus' ministry. Nor does Luke's phrase "the word of God" support MacArthur's claim that the word is the Gospel. We conclude that MacArthur refers to Luke's account only because the phrase "of God" appears there. He offers no proof that the phrase "the word of God" refers to Jesus personally or to his death, burial, and resurrection. It would be more than two-and-one-half years later before Jesus would introduce that concept. [13]

Luke uses the phrase "the word of God" three times in his account of our Lord's public ministry. The first occurrence is in Luke 5:1. He informs the reader, "On one occasion, while the crowd was pressing in on him to hear the word of God...." It is a juvenile attempt at biblical interpretation to conclude that the meaning of "the word of God" here refers to the modern Gospel without any attempt to define it contextually. At this early stage in our Lord's ministry, there is no historical proof that the Jewish people associated the death, burial, and resurrection motif of Jesus with "the word of God."

At the end of Luke 4, the writer tells us explicitly what "word" Jesus was preaching: the word about the kingdom. Jesus told the people, "I must preach the good news of the kingdom of God to other towns as well; for I was sent for this purpose" (Luke 4:43). "The good news about the kingdom of God" has nothing to do with Jesus' death, burial, and resurrection at this point.

Luke 8:21 puts the phrase "the word of God" into the mouth of the Lord Jesus again. He states, "My mother and my brothers are those who hear the word of God and do it." Just before Luke reports this encounter between Jesus and his mother and brothers, we have the parable of the sower given and explained, in which "the word of God" is explicitly identified as "the good news about the kingdom of God." So, the "word of God" that Jesus was referring to wasn't the Gospel as we understand it today. It was the gospel about the kingdom of God.

Similarly, the third and final appearance of the phrase "the word of God" occurs in Luke 11:28, where the Lord retorts, "Blessed rather are those who hear the word of God and keep it," in response to a woman who shouted, "Blessed is the womb that bore you, and the breasts at which you nursed" (Luke 11:27). In contrast to the woman's praise for the mother of Jesus, Jesus puts the praise on those who are obedient to "the word of God." There is no contextual reason to see this phrase as referring to anything different from the previous references. "The word of God" here refers to "the good news of the kingdom of God."

In both cases, "the word of God" requires obedience, but nothing contextually calls for this obedience to be faith in the work of Christ at Calvary. At this point in the Lord's earthly ministry, the explicit command of God is "to repent and believe the good news [about God's kingdom]" (Mark 1:15). Jesus is calling for obedience to the revealed will of God at the time (Mark 3:35). MacArthur and others are guilty of importing an idea into the text that the original author does not intend.

WHAT IS ILLEGITIMATE TOTALITY TRANSFER?

A second hermeneutical error that victimizes MacArthur's work is illegitimate totality transfer. Barr defines "illegitimate totality transfer" as "the error that arises when the 'meaning' of a word [understood as the total series of relations in which it is used in the literature] is read into a particular case as its sense and implication there."[14] Andy Woods similarly summaries Barr's definition as "a hermeneutical error that arises when the meaning of a word derived from its use elsewhere is automatically read into the same word in a foreign context."[15]

In what may be considered a definition of "the Gospel," MacArthur writes,

> *Paul's epistle to the Romans is an exposition of the gospel in almost point-by-point fashion. In the first verse of the epistle, Paul describes himself as one "set apart for the gospel." The gospel was the foundation of Paul's ministry, and in Romans he gives a clear and thorough presentation of it. He writes about God's wrath and human sin (chapters 1–3), justification and imputed righteousness (3–5), sanctification and practical righteousness (6–8), election and Israel's rejection of Christ (9–11), and then makes practical applications of various gospel truths in chapters twelve through the end of the epistle. The gospel is his theme throughout, and one of Paul's reasons for writing Romans seems to be to demonstrate the centrality of the gospel to all Christian life and ministry.*
>
> *When we speak of "the gospel" we tend to think of an evangelistic message—and surely the gospel is that. But it is not only a four- or five-point outline of salvation truths. The gospel—in the sense Paul and the apostles employed the word—includes all the revealed truth about Christ (cf. Rom. 1:1–6; 1 Cor. 15:3–11). It does not stop at the point of*

conversion and justification by faith, but embraces every other aspect of salvation, from sanctification to glorification. The gospel's significance therefore does not end the moment the new birth occurs; it applies to the entire Christian experience. And when Paul and the other New Testament writers spoke of "preaching the gospel," they were not talking about preaching only to unbelievers (cf. v. 15).[16]

We may give MacArthur the benefit of the doubt that his representation of the content of "the Gospel" for Paul and the other New Testament writers is correct. However, there is not a single sentence of proof that, at the time Jesus walked the earth, he taught any one of these concepts in connection with his own life in a way that his audiences understood. *Spiritual* salvation, justification, sanctification, and glorification as defined by Paul would never have been in the thinking of those who heard the Lord's teachings pre-Easter. To read Paul's post-Easter theology back into Jesus' pre-Easter teachings violates every norm of hermeneutical excellence. Yet, this is exactly what MacArthur and others do.

What the Greek phrase τό εὐαγγέλιον (*to euaggelion* = the good news or glad tidings) meant during the ministry of Jesus must be contextually defined. Otherwise, Jesus can be made to say anything. MacArthur does not seem to recognize the historical development of the usage of this term by the New Testament writers and the church fathers.

Part of the blame for MacArthur's error derives from his reliance on modern translations. The Greek noun *euaggelion* occurs 77 times in the New Testament.[17] Sadly, most modern translations, including MacArthur's preferred New American Standard Bible, foster an error when translating *euaggelion* as "the gospel" each time.

There is a compound error here, which we will discuss in two parts.

First, the translators create confusion by translating *euaggelion* as "gospel" rather than simply "good news." This error prejudices the reader to interpret this as the DBRJC. Second, they consistently translate the generic noun *euaggelion* as if it were the singular noun *to euaggelion*. Remember that, in Greek, *euaggelion* is a generic noun referring to "good news" of any type. ("Good news! It's Friday!" "Good news! The ice cream truck has arrived!") The Greek *singular* noun points to a *singular* set of good news that is widely or universally recognized by the intended audience. ("Did you hear the good news?") When you say "*the* good news," the audience may or may not know what you are referring to. The noun, *euaggelion* occurs 77 times in the NT. Of the 77 occurrences, the singular articular noun, *to euaggelion* occurs 13 times (four times in Matthew and nine times in Mark).[18] Yet modern translations consistently translate the generic noun (*euaggelion*) as if were the singular articular noun (*to euaggelion*), whether it actually is or not.

As you will see, there is no historical basis to translate either one of these terms—*euaggelion* or *to euaggelion*—as "gospel" or "the gospel."[19] Nor is there a historical or textural basis to translate the generic *euaggelion* as if it contained the singular article sense. Combine the two and you have a one-two punch of error upon error and confusion upon confusion. Thus, with this "one, two punch" of sloppy translation, modern translators point readers to a conclusion that the original author does not intend.[20]

Put plainly, if *to euaggelion* is translated as "the gospel" in Matthew and Mark's gospels, it should have quotation marks or some other indicator to alert the reader to its special use at each occurrence. To avoid confusion about the meaning of *to euaggelion* in the context of Jesus' earthly ministry, the translators of the Gospels would have better served their readers by using simply "the good news" or "glad tidings" instead. However, because many NT scholars do not see Jesus' ministry in proper historical-chronological sequence, errors about what the people understood about who or what Jesus did or said continue to abound.

"SON OF MAN IS LIFTED UP"

We see confirmation of this conclusion in John 12:1. Here, the text informs the reader that "[s]ix days before the Passover, Jesus therefore came to Bethany, where Lazarus was, whom Jesus had raised from the dead." In less than a full week, our Lord would be put to death. Thus, chapters 12–19 of John's Gospel focus on the Lord's final week before his death on the cross. So less than six days before the Lord Jesus died, the crowds heard him say,

> *"Now is the judgment of this world; now will the ruler [Satan] of this world be cast out. And I, when I am lifted up from the earth, will draw all people to myself." (John 12:31–32)*

It is critical that the reader understand that, when Jesus said this, it was less than six full days before his death. In an editorial comment, John reported, "He said this to show by what kind of death he was going to die." This editorial comment of John is his reflection on our Lord's comment thirty-plus years later. We are convinced that John did not know this fact contemporaneously at the time. John is saying that the Jewish crowd listening to the Lord's statement understood what he meant by the phrase, "And I, when I am lifted up from the earth."

We cannot emphasize enough that this is the first time that Jesus has spoken of his imminent death to a group larger than his original Twelve. John writes,

> *So the crowd answered him, "We have heard from the Law that Christ remains forever. How can you say that the Son of Man must be lifted up? Who is this Son of Man?"*

The response of the crowd is hugely insightful. First, they understood the phrase "the Son of Man must be lifted up" to mean death. Thus, if Jesus is "the Son of Man," which he claims; and if "the Son of Man" is another way of referring to the Messiah, which the Jews seem to have accepted; then Jesus' statement that "the Son of Man must be lifted up" is a contradiction of their understanding of the Old Testament Scriptures. At the time, the commonly accepted doctrine among the Jews was that the Messiah would come as a political and military leader who would free the Jews from the oppression of Rome. This expectation did not include the death of the Messiah. Scholars recognize that the idea of the Messiah dying was not a part of the standard theological teachings of the Jewish faith.

Regarding the Jewish response in John 12:34, Edwin A. Blum writes in *The Bible Knowledge Commentary,*

> *The crowd was puzzled. If the Messiah is the Son of Man, then He should be here forever, they reasoned. Daniel 7:13–14 spoke of the Son of Man's everlasting dominion. Perhaps the people wondered if He was making a distinction between the Messiah (Christ) and the Son of Man. Did He use the term "Son of Man" differently than its sense in Daniel 7:13? They seemed to understand that Jesus was predicting His death,*

but they could not see how that was possible, if He was the Messiah.[21]

George R. Beasley-Murray, in the *Word Biblical Commentary*, adds,

The crowd voices a difficulty which the representatives of Jesus were to face from Good Friday onward. The "Law" (= the OT, supremely represented by the Law) says that the Messiah remains "forever" . . . For most Jews the perpetuity of the kingdom of God included the continuance of the Messiah. . . The crowd therefore asks, "How can the Son of Man-Messiah be 'lifted up,' and so removed from the earthly scene by death?" Their further query, "Who is this Son of Man?" means, "What sort of a Son of Man is this, of whom such an unheard of fate is spoken?"[22]

The apparent contradiction between what the crowd believed about the Messiah and what Jesus taught about himself is evident. MacArthur's notion that the death-burial-resurrection motif was taught and understood from the very beginning of our Lord's ministry is contradicted by the facts. Up to the very day of Jesus' death, the people did not believe the Messiah must die in order for their sins to be forgiven. The Jewish populist did not see the death of the Messiah as a necessity to bring freedom to the Nation. As we shall see, neither did the Twelve, who had objected strenuously to our Lord's prediction of death six months earlier.

Thus, whatever else τό εὐαγγέλιον might have meant at the initiation of our Lord's ministry and whatever it might have come to mean after his death, we are certain that only an accurate historicity of the phrase ensures a correct interpretation of both Matthew and Mark's Gospels. When we consider that context, it becomes clear that translating τό εὐαγγέλιον as "the Gospel" any earlier than moments before Jesus left the earth to return to heaven creates the temptation to commit illegitimate totality transfer and, thereby, come to a false interpretation of the dominant message of Jesus before Calvary.

Notes

[1] Jeremy D. Myers, "The Gospel is More Than "Faith Alone in Christ Alone," *JGES* Vol. 19, no. 37 (2006), 32.

[2] Ibid.

[3] John F. MacArthur, *The Gospel According to Jesus*. Zondervan. Kindle Edition, 25.

[4] By looking at the Greek terms used to translate the Hebrew Old Testament, scholars can understand the possible nuances of Greek terms. However, one must exercise care because words can acquire new meanings that may not be reflected in the previous usage record.

[5] John F. MacArthur, *The Gospel According to Jesus*. Zondervan. Kindle Edition, 373.

[6] Matthew 13:18 says, "Hear then the parable of the sower." Thus, we identify this parable by this designation.

[7] MacArthur, J. F. (1997, 1988). *The Gospel According to Jesus: What Does Jesus Mean When He Says "Follow Me?"* Includes index. (Electronic ed.). (Grand Rapids, MI: *Academic and Professional Books*, Zondervan Pub. House).

[8] James Barr, *The Semantics of Biblical Language* (London: SCM Press Ltd, 1983), 217–218.

[9] Donald A. Hagner, *Matthew 1–13*, Vol. 33A, Word Biblical Commentary (Dallas: Word, Incorporated, 1993), 379.

[10] Darrell L. Bock, Luke: 1:1–9:50, Vol. 1, *Baker Exegetical Commentary on the New Testament* (Grand Rapids, MI: Baker Academic, 1994), 285.

[11] R. C. H. Lenski, *The Interpretation of St. Matthew's Gospel*, Minneapolis, MN. (1961): Augsburg Publishing House, 518.

[12] John Nolland, *The Gospel of Matthew: A Commentary on the Greek Text, New International Greek Testament Commentary* (Grand Rapids, MI; Carlisle: W.B. Eerdmans; Paternoster Press, 2005), 539.

[13] This is a point that I will prove beyond a shadow of a doubt later.

[14] James Barr, *The Semantics of Biblical Language* (London: SCM Press Ltd, 1983), 218.

[15] Andy Woods, "A Case for the Futurist Interpretation of the Book of Revelation," *Chafer Theological Seminary Journal*, Vol. 13, No. 1 (2008): 6–7.

[16] John F. MacArthur, *Ashamed of the Gospel: When the Church Becomes Like the World*, Wheaton, Ill.: Crossway Books (1993), 121.

[17] This count depends on the 28th edition of Nestle-Aland Greek New Testament.

[18] This count depends on the 28th edition of Nestle-Aland.

[19] With the possible exception of Mark 1:1, as we will discuss shortly.

[20] This conclusion I will prove shortly.

[21] Edwin A. Blum, "John," in *The Bible Knowledge Commentary: An Exposition of the Scriptures*, ed. J. F. Walvoord and R. B. Zuck, Vol. 2 (Wheaton, IL: Victor Books, 1985), 318.

[22] George R. Beasley-Murray, John, *Word Biblical Commentary*, Vol. 36 (Dallas: Word, Incorporated, 1999), 215.

CHAPTER 2

Τό Εὐαγγέλιον Ἰησοῦ Χριστοῦ: The Good News About Jesus Christ

S ome type of theological battle line exists in just about every area of Christian theology. While the continual existence of some battles is easily explained, the one regarding salvation remains a mystery to this author. Considering that among true Christians, no question is more fundamental than how to obtain the righteousness of God (spiritual salvation), it remains challenging to understand why all parties will not gather and refuse to quit until a consensus is reached.

If forgiveness of sin is possible and Jesus Christ forgives sins based on his death at Calvary, then why can't a person simply ask Jesus for forgiveness? Why can't a person believe God's promise and it is accounted to him as righteousness? Is this not what is taught in the biblical example of Abram? The Bible declares, "And he [Abram] believed the LORD, and he [God] counted it to him as righteousness" (Gen. 15:6). In the context of Genesis 15, God made Abram a promise. Abram believed that promise and God gave him full credit for it, i.e., spiritual salvation. If Abram's salvation came by faith in the promise of God, why would it not be so for us?

Yet, the 1990s began with two battleships: lordship salvation versus easy believism trading salvos back and forth. The longevity of this debate, however, did not begin in the 90s. Dr. Darrell L. Bock offers an excellent summary of this historical debate when he writes,

> One side of the debate argues that Jesus must be confessed only as Savior, and not as Lord (i.e., Master of one's life). The gospel involves faith in Jesus' redeeming work as the God-Man. To add a confession of lordship to the gospel is to run the risk of destroying the grace focus of the gospel, for how much lordship is enough to qualify as saving faith? According to this view the term "Lord" refers to Jesus' divinity. This side can be called the Jesus-is-Savior view....

The second side in this debate argues that Jesus is to be confessed as Lord (Master) as well as Savior. The gospel involves a call to repentance as well as to faith. To confess the lordship of Jesus is not a mere confession of deity; rather it is a confession of total submission to the personal Lord, a commitment to obey in every area of life. In this view, to offer Jesus as Savior only is "easy believism." One does not choose to make Jesus Lord, He is Lord of all. If He is not Lord of all, He is not Lord at all. To leave saving faith to anything less than a confession of Jesus as Lord ignores the discipleship teaching of the Scriptures and forgets that the basic definition of "Lord" is "master," "ruler," or "owner." This view can be called the Jesus-is-Lord view....[1]

We are convinced that had both sides consulted an excellent linguist when the debate first arose, those salvos never would have been exchanged, to begin with. The debate would have been stopped in its tracks. Both camps began with an assumption that τό εὐαγγέλιον, which can be transliterated *to euaggelion* and translated as "the good news," "glad tidings," or "the gospel," always refers to the DBRJC, even during the time of our Lord's public ministry. This assumption is profoundly and fundamentally incorrect. [2]

The decision to translate τό εὐαγγέλιον as "the gospel" of Jesus Christ is a translator's choice, for nothing in the Greek language itself demands this conclusion. When trying to discover the meaning of a written text, one should try, to the greatest degree possible, to set the meaning of that term in its historically appropriate context. Take, for example, the modern English term "awful." The Old English term "awe" originally referred to "fear, terror, or dread." Over time, however, the term developed the connotation of "very unpleasant." Certainly, being full of fear and dread is very unpleasant, but the modern sense of the word is very different from the original. One would have little trouble understanding the term "awful" in a current newspaper, but if one were to encounter the term "aueful" in a Shakespearean sonnet, one would need contextual information in order to understand the intended meaning.

This same issue arises with *to evangelion*. Being that the term "the gospel" is so central to the salvation debate, we would expect to find a credible presentation of the history of the word as part of that debate. Instead, we find that discussion entirely missing on both sides. Both the lordship salvation (Jesus-is-Lord) and easy believism (Jesus-is-Savior) camps read modern usage or meaning of the term from the post-Easter writings of New Testament authors back into the pre-Easter biblical accounts of the ministry of Christ.

UNDERLYING ASSUMPTIONS FUEL THE DEBATE

The reason many Bible teachers do this is because of another underlying assumption: that salvation from sin is the dominant message of Matthew, Mark, Luke, and John. In this view, every pericope in the four Gospels focuses on the doctrine of salvation. While the text might speak about how one enters the kingdom of God, how one inherits eternal life, or for that matter how one is "saved," it is important to remember that, in a historical context, those terms can have either a spiritual or temporal meaning. Based on context, they can refer to spiritual life and salvation or to physical life and deliverance. Rather than letting the historical context determine the interpretation, however, most Bible readers conclude that these terms are always related to spiritual salvation.

Many NT scholars force this assumption on every passage in Matthew, Mark, or Luke. Edmund K. Neufeld concludes:

> While the different terms are not identical, they are often used interchangeably in the Synoptic Gospels. The Rich Young Ruler story illustrates this effectively. With no apparent change in referent, Matt 19:16–30 uses "have eternal life," "inherit eternal life," "enter the kingdom of heaven," "enter the kingdom of God," and "be saved." Similar variation can be seen in Mark 10:17–30 and Luke 18:18–30. In addition, Mark 9:46–47 uses both "enter life" and "enter the kingdom of God" to contrast "thrown into hell."[3]

Clearly, the assumed fact that these terms are interchangeable is driven by the underlying assumption that the story of the rich young ruler is soteriological (or related to the doctrine of salvation) rather than rewardific (related to the doctrine of sanctification). Once this assumption is accepted, errors in interpretation will multiply. Many conclude the meaning of the passage without any attempt at specific or contextual exegesis. Thus, they either ignore or fail to see the contradiction produced by interpreting the story as soteriological. Who believes that for a wealthy person to be saved, he or she must give up every last penny? Who believes that keeping the Ten Commandments will save a person spiritually? Even among those holding to a works salvation view, neither of those conclusions would seem tenable. Taking the story of the rich young ruler as soteriological creates more problems than it solves.

PRODUCING ERRORS OF IGNORANCE

Among many New Testament scholars, there is an awareness that Matthew, Mark, and Luke lack explicit teaching on salvation. Salvific nomenclature is minimal. This is the case even in the Gospel of John. George A. Turner adds,

> All agree that the theme of salvation is expressed in analogies—light, life, knowledge, bread, water, truth—rather than in forensic terms as in Paul.[4]

The lack of explicit "forensic" (or technical) language caused much confusion among the Jews who heard our Lord's teachings.[5] This unrecognized fact leads to speculation on the part of many students of the New Testament and disagreements about what themes, concepts, and words have salvific significance.

Recognizing the small amount of data in the Gospel of Mark that is explicitly salvific in nature, one author states,

> *Thus, while the Gospel [of Mark] contains very little direct teaching about salvation, it shows salvation in action as Jesus calls human beings into a relationship of discipleship to him.*[6]

Again, a false conclusion was drawn because every word in Mark's Gospel is seen through the lens of spiritual salvation. Depending on implicit references in Matthew, Mark, and Luke cause other errors, as well. Absent explicit data, Edmund K. Neufeld, working with the texts of Matthew, Mark, and Luke, concludes that works obtain salvation. He writes, "The Synoptics normally attach eternal life to obeying Jesus, and occasionally to trusting him."[7] Due to their presuppositions about the meaning and significance of Jesus' words, this is the most logical conclusion. This assumption, based on a false understanding of the teachings of Christ, forms the basis for both lordship salvation and Arminianism. Both are false conclusions based on biblical ignorance.

Many scholars recognize a paucity of explicit references to the Lord's death, burial, and resurrection in Matthew, Mark, and Luke. They also know that, prior to his crucifixion, Jesus never said explicitly that his death would be necessary so that men's sins could be forgiven. Other than the three explicit predictions of his death that we shall look at shortly, there are hints but no overt discussions of its necessity for man's spiritual salvation. There is certainly no evidence that the Jewish crowds or the Twelve understood this. Only by looking back at the statements of our Lord with the help of after-sight do we understand the intent of many of his sayings.

One clear example is found in Matthew 12:40, which highlights an exchange between Jesus and the scribes and Pharisees:

> *"For just as Jonah was three days and three nights in the belly of the great fish, so will the Son of Man be three days and three nights in the heart of the earth."*

In neither Matthew, Mark nor Luke is the reader given any clue regarding the audience's understanding of our Lord's reference to Jonah. There is no evidence that the Jews understood the significance of his prediction at the time. Nor is there an explanation for why the Son of Man must die.

Of the 77 occurrences of *evangelion* in the New Testament, twelve occur in Matthew and Mark.[8] With few exceptions, modern Bible versions translate this term as "gospel." However, there is nothing about *evangelion* that mandates this as the best English translation. No ancient church father spoke or wrote in English. Writings were either Aramaic, Greek, Latin, or Hebrew, and there are no grammatical clues to suggest when "the glad tidings," "the good news" or "the gospel" is the correct option. Most modern translations reflect the translators' convictions about context. In fact, historical context tells us that *to evangelion* was not even used to refer to Jesus' death, burial, and resurrection for the remission of sin until after Pentecost, possibly a twenty-plus-year-gap. Thus, prior to Pentecost, we would expect translators to agree that "good news" is the best option. It is our conclusion that, in most modern translations, the decision to translate *to evangelion* as "the gospel" (implying *the* Gospel, capital "G") was a decision guided by later developments of the term's usage. This usage is then read back into their renditions of the Gospel accounts.

Greek Chart

Greek :   τὸ εὐαγγέλιον

Transliteration :   το euangelion

Translation :   "the good news"

Peter Stuhlmacher has done one of the most thorough studies of the term εὐαγγέλιον. He begins his summary with these words:

> New Testament research has not yet succeeded in constructing an understanding, one established and universally recognized by scholars in the field . . . of the history of the word "gospel."[9]

Stuhlmacher's work is commendable, but it perpetuates the confusion. Our English term "gospel" is a matter of translation. It is a necessary but *secondary* step in the process of interpretation. The primary step occurs before translation. This is determining the meaning of the original term—in this case, εὐαγγέλιον. Thus, Stuhlmacher should have written, "New Testament research has not yet succeeded in constructing an understanding . . . of the history of the word" εὐαγγέλιον. Thus, in order to arrive at the proper interpretation, two issues need clarification. First, what is the history of the articular Greek noun τὸ εὐαγγέλιον? When was it first used? How was it used at that time? When did it become a technical term for the

DBRJC? If it did not come to have this meaning until after Pentecost, then how can we legitimately read that definition into Jesus' teaching before then?

Second, when did one of the options in translation become "the gospel"? Being that τὸ εὐαγγέλιον, or *to evangelion*, has historically meant "the good news" or "glad tidings," when did "the gospel" become the third possible option?[10]

When trying to understand the diachronic history of a Greek term, New Testament scholars typically start with the LXX, or Septuagint, the Greek translation of the original Hebrew text produced in the third through the first century before Christ. As a translation of the Hebrew Masoretic text, scholars can discern much regarding the meaning of both Hebrew and Greek by looking at what words were chosen to reflect the intent of the more ancient Hebrew text. Scholars can also discern whether any nuances developed after the LXX was finished.

Regarding the articular noun *to euangelion*, the LXX gives us very little insight. Kittle says, "The NT use of *euangélion* clearly does not derive from the LXX,"[11] because the singular noun does not appear in the LXX at all.[12] What is the significance of this fact? If we date the completion of the LXX to the first century before Christ, then we must acknowledge that, as a word, *to euangélion* arose just before our Lord's birth or during his lifetime.

While a plural form of the noun has been found prior to the writings of the New Testament,[13] there is no evidence of a singular usage before this time.[14] Again, this is important. Before this time, we have proof of several sets of good news. However, there is no evidence that there was a (singular noun) "good news" that, by its very nature, was unique and set apart from all other forms of good news.

While the LXX does not have the singular noun, it does have the verb form of *evangelion,* which is *euangelizō* ("to preach the good news"). Barrow concludes:

> *The verb occurs frequently in the LXX, rendering* בשר *with meanings varying from the news of a victory to the glad tidings of Messianic restoration and glory. The books of Samuel and Kings have it nine times, Psalms three times, Joel and Nahum once each, and Isaiah six times. It also occurs once in 1 Chronicles in a parallel to one of the passages in 1 Sam. The six occurrences in Isaiah are the most important for us; they are all in the latter portion of the book and refer to the coming deliverance of God's people, the reign of God, and the future glory of Zion.* [15]

The verb *euangelizō* occurs 54 times in the New Testament, with almost half occurring in Luke/Acts (25 times). In these instances, Luke is quoting from Messianic passages in the book of Isaiah. [16] Luke could have chosen to quote from the Hebrew text. Instead, he chose to quote from the LXX, which translates the Hebrew verb *basar,* which means "a fortunate announcement" or "good news." Luke then adopts this as the most accurate verb to describe what Jesus was doing—proclaiming "the good news."[17]

It is important to note that, in the Gospel accounts (including Luke's), the only instances of *euangelizō* come from the writers themselves, never from the mouth of Jesus. By the time Matthew, Mark, and Luke penned their Gospels, *to evangelion* was already in use in the modern sense of Jesus' sacrifice at Calvary. They would have been aware of this definition when they were writing. However, considering that (1) Jesus, himself, never used the term,[18] and (2) there is no OT evidence that the singular noun (interpreted as *the* one and only Gospel) was in use at that time, we would argue

THAT OTHER GOSPEL • 35

that this term should be translated in the Gospels in the ordinary, natural, customary sense *as it was being used at that time*: "the good news." There is simply no historical basis for *to evangelion* to be translated as "the gospel" in either Matthew or Mark's accounts.[19]

The refusal of MacArthur and others to recognize this fact has caused a three-decade-long debate that was baseless from the very beginning.

MUST THE MESSIAH DIE?

That "the Gospel" in its modern sense is not in view in Matthew nor Mark's Gospels is confirmed by the contemporary context in which Jesus was speaking. The crowds to whom Jesus spoke did not understand that Jesus would die. Certainly, they did not understand that he *had* to die. How could Jesus be teaching the Gospel in the modern sense of his death, burial, and resurrection without explaining this unique sense to them? There is not a single example of our Lord teaching on this specific topic to either the multitudes or his disciples.

To get around this problem, MacArthur argues that the crowds were unbelievers. In this view, the reason the crowds didn't understand the Gospel wasn't because Jesus didn't teach it. It was because their unbelieving status prevented them from understanding or accepting it.

MacArthur writes,

> John's Gospel gives us a clear snapshot of what the people who actually heard Jesus teach and saw his miracles were thinking. In John 12:32 the Lord said to them, "And I, when I am lifted up from the earth, will draw all people to myself." He was referring to his crucifixion (v. 33). Incredulous, the crowd answered him, "We have heard from the Law that the

> *Christ remains forever. How can you say that the Son of Man must be lifted up? Who is this Son of Man?" (v. 34). A dying Messiah was incomprehensible to them since they saw no need for his death to atone for their sins.* [20]

Certainly, it is true that, in the larger context, the idea of the death of the Messiah was not the Jewish understanding of the Old Testament Scriptures. However, as one reads MacArthur, it is very easy to get the impression that, from his perspective, *only* unbelieving Jews were ignorant of the necessity of this sacrifice. As we will show shortly, this simply isn't true. The grammar allows this definition, but the historical context does not. MacArthur's defense might explain why the so-called unbelieving crowds did not understand Jesus' predictions of his death, but it fails to explain why the Twelve didn't either. Are we to believe that the disciples were saved yet were ignorant of the one fact necessary to be saved? MacArthur's explanation fails the sniff test.

Few, if any, first-century Jews could have articulated the spiritual benefits of the death of the Messiah, including Jesus' disciples. If the disciples didn't understand Jesus' teachings that way, why would anyone else?

WHEN DID JESUS START TEACHING ABOUT HIS DEATH?

As we explore this idea, it's important to restate that Jesus did not teach about his death explicitly until the very end of his ministry. The Lord Jesus spoke of his death in unambiguous language on three separate occasions in the Synoptic Gospels of Matthew, Mark, and Luke. In all cases, he started making these statements only a few months before his actual crucifixion. If the modern Gospel were truly in view throughout Jesus' entire earthly ministry, it is all the more remarkable that John's Gospel (the most focused on "salvation" of all of the Gospels) does not contain any of these accounts.

Please notice in the chart below where, in the chronology of our Lord's earthly ministry, he began to predict his death, burial, and resurrection explicitly.

Death, Burial, and Resurrection Predictions		
Matthew	Mark	Luke
First Prediction of Death		
16:21-23	8:31-33	9:21-22
Second Prediction of Death		
17:22-23	9:30-32	9:43-45
Third Prediction of Death		
20:17-19	10:32-34	18:31-34

Let's see what we can learn by looking at each one of these predictions. As we do, it is important that one does not allow the placement of the first explicit prediction in each Gospel account to prejudice the reader regarding the historical timing of the prophecy. At first glance, based on the mid-book location of these predications, one might conclude that the predictions occurred near the middle of the Lord's ministry. However, a closer look shows that the first half of each Gospel writer's book (Matthew, Mark, and Luke) covers approximately the first three years of

Jesus' ministry, while the second half covers approximately the final six months. The fact that each writer decides to commit more than half of his book to the final six months of the Lord's ministry shows us just how important that time was.

We will start with Matthew 16:21–23, which reports,

> *From that time Jesus began to show his disciples that he must go to Jerusalem and suffer many things from the elders and chief priests and scribes, and be killed, and on the third day be raised. And Peter took him aside and began to rebuke him, saying, "Far be it from you, Lord! This shall never happen to you." But he turned and said to Peter, "Get behind me, Satan! You are a hindrance to me. For you are not setting your mind on the things of God, but on the things of man." (emphasis added)*

There are four critical details the readers should notice here.

FIRST: THE TIMING OF THE PREDICTION

The phrase, *from that time,* is a critically crucial temporal mark and has received much scholarly attention. If Jesus began teaching about his death, burial, and resurrection *from that time,* this means that he was not teaching it before then. Kingsbury has written extensively on this unique phrase and its significance for the interpretation of the chronology of Matthew. In one place, he concludes:

> *That Matthew, by combining the phrase apo tote with the verb archomai, has succeeded in creating an expression that strongly denotes the beginning of a new phase in the "life of Jesus."*[21]

This truth is easily demonstrated by the context of the fourth chapter of Matthew. Matthew 4:17 states, "From that time Jesus began to preach, saying, 'Repent, for the kingdom of heaven is at hand.'" Whatever else our Lord said or did before John's imprisonment, it did not include public preaching of the message of repentance in light of the imminent coming of the kingdom of God. The grammatical precision of Matthew's phrase will not allow that possibility.

Regarding this critical phrase, David R. Bauer, in an outstanding presentation regarding the structure of Matthew, writes that Matthew "1:1, 4:17, and 16:21 are general headings which are expanded in the material that follows in each case."[22]

By way of summary, Bauer continues that Matthew

> 4.17 is parallel in form to 16.21: 'From that time Jesus began to show his disciples that it was necessary for him to go to Jerusalem and to suffer many things from the elders and chief priests and scribes, and to be killed, and on the third day to be raised'. Both passages contain the preposition 'from' + the adverb 'that time' + the phrase 'Jesus began' + the infinitive ('to preach and to say' in 4.17; 'to show' in 16.21) + a summary of the content of the message (direct discourse in 4.17; object clause introduced by 'that' in 16.21).
>
> This parallelism is all the more significant when one considers the unique literary character of the formula. The phrase 'from that time' (ἀπὸ τότε) occurs on only two additional occasions in the New Testament: Mt. 26.16 Lk. 16.16. Yet the phrase in 4.17 and 16.21 is not utterly distinctive; in the other two passages it is linked with Jesus, nor does it contain any reference to 'begin'.
>
> In addition to the parallelism between 4.17 and 16.21, another feature distinguishing the use of the phrase 'from

that time' in 4.17 and 16.21 from that found in 26.16 is its asyndetic character. Matthew 26.16 is connected to its preceding context by means of 'and' (καί), but no such connective is found in 4.17 and 16.21. The asyndeton is all the more remarkable when one examines the liberal use of connectives in the material surrounding each of these verses. The asyndetic character of the phrase 'from that time' in 4.17 and 16.21 distinguishes the use of the phrase in these two passages from that of 26.16 and underscores the formulaic character of this phrase in 4.17 and 16.21.[23]

Bauer's conclusion regarding the significance of the phrase "from that time" is correct in our opinion. He states,

Although there are differences between the use of the phrase 'from that time' in 4.17 and 16.21, and in 26.16, the meaning of the phrase is generally the same in all the passages where it is used; it marks the beginning of a new period of time.[24]

The reader should not miss this. In Matthew 16:21, the Lord Jesus declares explicitly to his disciples that his death was imminent. This is the first time Jesus made this explicit prediction to any group, particularly his inner circle—the Twelve.

DON'T MISS THIS CRITICAL POINT

A. T. Robertson posits that this prediction by the Lord Jesus (Matt. 16:21, cf. Mark 8:31, Luke 9:21) occurs less than one year before his crucifixion.[25] Fred R. Coulter similarly places it as occurring between "Passover 29 AD to Passover 30 AD."[26] McGarvey and Pendleton also place our Lord's first prediction between the third Passover and our Lord's arrival in Bethany,[27] a week before his death.

Matthew places this first explicit prediction of our Lord's death immediately following Peter's explicit declaration that Jesus is "the Christ, the Son of the Living God." Matthew 16:13 places Peter's confession at the time "when Jesus came into the district of Caesarea Philippi." Caesarea Philippi, at this time, would have been about 105 miles northeast of Jerusalem. It is thought by many that this is the farthest point Jesus went from Jerusalem. By making an explicit reference to the time and place of Peter's confession, Matthew helps his readers to understand that Jesus has moved into the climatic period of his earthly ministry.

We are convinced that no more than six months passed from this explicit prediction until his death on Calvary. Why is this point so important? There are several illusions that Jesus gives about his death before his last six months on Earth, but none were clear enough to form the basis of the death-burial-resurrection motif for the forgiveness of sins that came later. Jesus did not disclose the facts of his death, burial, and resurrection, nor the reason for his death, until after his resurrection. Therefore, there is no basis to see the term *to evangelion* as a reference to these things before that time. Any such conclusion requires reading later developments back into Jesus' words during his earthly ministry.

SECOND: THE CONTENT OF THE PREDICTION

If the first statement, "from that time," speaks to the timing of when Jesus started preaching about his death, burial, and resurrection, the second statement, "began to show," demonstrates the content.

The clause "Jesus began to show" explains the actions of our Lord as he started the second and final phase of his earthly ministry. The verb chosen by Matthew, δείκνυμι (*deiknymi,* or "to show"), is distinct from the one in Mark's account, which is translated as "he began to teach them." Lowe and Nida suggest that the sense of Matthew's verb is "to make known the character or significance of something by visual, auditory, gestural, or linguistic means— 'to make known, to demonstrate, to show.'"[28] The emphasis seems to be "to show and tell" rather than merely verbal telling.

With this conclusion, Bauer agrees. He recognizes the dual focus of Matthew 16:21 and gives an excellent summary of the importance of the verb δείκνυμι when he writes,

> *It speaks not only of the journey of Jesus to Jerusalem and his passion, but it also speaks of the presentation Jesus makes to the disciples of the necessity for this journey with its passion and resurrection. We note that Matthew does not say that Jesus "taught" or "instructed" his disciples regarding his passion, but rather that he "showed" (δείκνυμι) them . . . A glance at the concordance reveals that, in the New Testament, the word never means simply "teach." Rather, this term means "present" or "show," which may include verbal description, but in the New Testament always includes more than simply speech. The term is used in Mt. 4.8, where the devil presents Jesus with a panoramic vision of the kingdoms of the world; and in Mt. 8.4 Jesus instructs the former leper to show himself to the priest, thus demonstrating his cleansing. If we place "show" in 16.21 within the context of the flow of the narrative throughout 16.21–28.20, it becomes evident that Jesus shows his disciples the necessity of his passion not only by what he says but also by what he does, especially by himself undertaking the journey to Jerusalem.[29]*

As the Lord Jesus turns his daily walk south toward Jerusalem, we are not privy to his moods, attitudes, or emotional state in their entirety between the first announcement of his soon-coming death and the event itself. However, the night before his death presents our Lord in great distress. It shows his understanding of the level of suffering he was about to endure, a level of suffering beyond any human being's comprehension.

Again, the first explicit declaration of his imminent death spoken in Matthew is marked by four necessitates expressed as infinitives. He **must**: (1) go to Jerusalem; (2) suffer many things; (3) be killed; and (4) be raised. Combined, these four necessities display for the Twelve the divine imperative operating in the Lord's life.

Δεῖ (*dei*), the Greek verb used here, is consistently translated in most modern versions as "must." Scholars recognize δεῖ as an impersonal verb form. Students of Scripture may not appreciate an essential distinction in the meaning of this word, but Bennett correctly captures the point when he states,

> This verb has posed a problem to theologians and Biblical scholars alike, chiefly because as an impersonal form δει does not specify the cause of the necessity which determined the fate of the Son of Man.[30]

Looking back through the lens of history, it is easy for us to supply a context that allows us to see the implicit hand of God at work here. However, there is no evidence that the twelve disciples got it. In fact, we see just the opposite. Even after the resurrection of our Lord, it can still be said of the disciples,

"O foolish ones, and slow of heart to believe all that the prophets have spoken! Was it not necessary that Christ should suffer these things and enter into his glory?" (Luke 24:25–26)

It was necessary for the Messiah to suffer because the prophets had predicted it. The prophets predicted it because this was God's will.

A Handbook on the Gospel of Matthew indicates:

> *Quite frequently, as here, must is used in the Gospels of a necessity imposed upon a person in the fulfillment of the divine will (see 17:10; 24:6; 26:54). Some translators have even used a phrase like "that God required that" or "that it was God's will that" to convey the full force of must.* [31]

Balz and Schneider add, "In the NT statements with δεῖ are normally understood more or less as divine decrees." [32] The lexical meaning of the term and its contemporary understanding by the disciples suggests confusion. There is no textual basis for the claim that the disciples understood this divine necessity. Perhaps Nolland is closer to the truth when he writes, "The kind of necessity that stands behind δεῖ ('it is necessary') is not yet clearly visible, but it will gradually become so." [33]

It is nowhere implied or explicitly indicated by Jesus the purpose of the events predicted in Matthew 16:21 (parallels: Mark 8:31, Luke 9:22). This is a fact that the reader must keep in clear focus. At this point, Jesus does not say that his death is necessary to forgive sin. Jesus does not say why he must die, only that he must.

The death of Jesus must occur in Jerusalem. This reality lies in front of our Lord, and he holds it in constant remembrance. This is evidenced by Luke 13:33–34:

"I must go on my way today and tomorrow and the day following, for it cannot be that a prophet should perish away from Jerusalem. O Jerusalem, Jerusalem, the city that kills the prophets and stones those who are sent to it!"

The irony is not lost. That any prophet sent from God should be killed in Jerusalem because his message is unpopular shows the rebellious heart of the people. It also shows their lack of understanding that killing the prophet does not stop the will of God.

The second imperative is that our Lord must *suffer many things.* In Jesus' first prediction of the coming troubles, he does not delineate the elements that will contribute to his suffering.

The third imperative is that our Lord must *be killed.* Louw and Nida define the Greek verb *apokteinō*: "to cause someone's death, normally by violent means, with or without intent and with or without legal justification— 'to kill.'"[34] While the Lord had spoken of "the cross" several times, it is unclear whether the disciples understood his references as metaphorical or literal. There is no evidence from the Lord's prediction that his death would come from natural causes.

The fourth and final imperative is that *on the third day (he) be raised* from the dead. In this context, being raised from the dead is a clear implication. As we read this prophetic prediction now, it seems so clear what Jesus was saying. Yet, we must pay attention to the text and the reaction of the disciples. We must not allow our familiarity with this passage to force unwarranted conclusions.

Remember what MacArthur writes,

Incredulous, "the crowd answered him, 'We have heard from the Law that the Christ remains forever. How can you say that

the Son of Man must be lifted up? Who is this Son of Man?'"
(v. 34). A dying Messiah was incomprehensible to them since
they saw no need for his death to atone for their sins.

MacArthur concludes that the crowd did not believe
Jesus because they were unbelievers. Yet, let us notice the
response of Peter and the Twelve to this same prediction.
They didn't believe Jesus either.

THIRD: PETER'S RESPONSE TO THE PREDICTION

Let's look at Peter's response as it is recorded in
Matthew 16:22. It portrays complete and total surprise.
One is hard-pressed to explain Peter's response if this is
not the first time he heard it. Peter's response also
suggests that he had no historical understanding of the
need for the Son of God to die. Nor can anyone conclude
that Peter received this message from Jesus as "good
news." The text said that Peter *rebuked* the Lord. Peter's
reaction is every bit evidentiary of the worst news he had
ever heard.

It is clear that Peter did not know *why* Jesus had to
die. His ignorance can only be explained by the fact
that Jesus had not yet disclosed this information to
the Twelve or, even if he had, that God had blocked
Peter's mind from understanding it. Nor did
explaining the reason behind Jesus' death remove
Peter's confusion. Typically, in a situation like this,
New Testament methodology would be to insert an
indication of (an explanation by way of) prophetic
fulfillment. That did not happen here. That the
Messiah must die is prophetically detailed in the Old

Testament, but no attempt is made to clear up Peter's confusion with a scriptural explanation.

Peter's language is emphatic. "To rebuke" (*epitimaō*) means "to express strong disapproval of someone— 'to rebuke, to denounce.'"[35] Οὐ μὴ (*ou mā*) is the most emphatic way to express negation in the New Testament. In a sense, Peter tells the Lord that in no way and under no circumstance must he suffer death. At this point, Peter sees no God-ordained reason for the Son of God to die. If Jesus pervasively preached his death and resurrection for the forgiveness of sin, Peter clearly must have been absent the whole time.

It is not simple revulsion, along with sincere regret and concern, that we see in Peter's behavior. Peter expresses the widespread belief among all Jews at the time: "We have heard from the Law that the Christ remains forever. How can you say that the Son of Man must be lifted up?" Peter expresses the majority opinion among all Jews at this point in Israel's history—that the Messiah's death was not part of the equation.

FOURTH: WHO HEARD THE PREDICTION?

Both Mark and Luke include this first prediction of our Lord's death, burial, and resurrection in their accounts. There are textual details included in Luke's account that Matthew and Mark do not give. Notice in Luke 9:21–22:

> *And he strictly charged and commanded them to tell this to no one, saying, "The Son of Man must suffer many things and be rejected by the elders and chief priests and scribes, and be killed, and on the third day be raised."*

The context of Luke 9:21–22 makes clear that only the twelve disciples were with the Lord Jesus when he first predicted his death. No one but the Twelve heard it, and Jesus "strictly charged and commanded them to tell this to no one" (Luke 9:21). Notice that, after telling the Twelve about his imminent death, Jesus called the crowd to come to him (Mark 8:34). The crowd did not hear Jesus' prediction. To this point in Jesus' ministry, no one had heard him publicly and explicitly state that he must die or why his death was necessary.

OUR LORD'S SECOND EXPLICIT PREDICTION OF HIS DEATH

Regarding Jesus' second explicit prediction of his imminent death, we place it no more than two months before the crucifixion. Matthew 17:22–23 states:

> As they were gathering in Galilee, Jesus said to them, "The Son of Man is about to be delivered into the hands of men, and they will kill him, and he will be raised on the third day." And they were greatly distressed.

Notice the additional information in Luke 9:43–45 regarding the Lord's second prediction:

> All were astonished at the majesty of God. But while they were all marveling at everything he was doing, Jesus said to his disciples, "Let these words sink into your ears: The Son of Man is about to be delivered into the hands of men." But they [the Twelve] did not understand this saying, and it was concealed from them, so that they might not perceive it. And they were afraid to ask him about this saying. (emphasis added)

The context makes clear that Jesus is only speaking to his twelve disciples. Luke's account of the second prediction is short and to the point. However, he does add explanatory details. First, Luke adds that "They [the Twelve] did not understand." Luke uses this grammatical construction to express their ongoing ignorance. In fact, Luke explains why they didn't understand: "It was concealed from them so that they might not perceive it." The word used here, *parakalyptō*, is a verb that Luke uses only once in the New Testament, and it means "to hide."[36] God purposely hid the meaning and significance of the Lord's prediction from the minds of the Twelve. Luke concludes with the final fact, "They were afraid to ask him about this saying."

The reader is not given the reason God prevents the Twelve from understanding. Perhaps he knew their hearts and how easily they could be impressed to desert the Lord before these frightening events started to unfold. Fear of persecution and perhaps one's own death is a powerful deterrent.

Please get the points. First, only the twelve disciples heard the prediction. Second, they did not understand what they heard. Third, God blocked their minds so they would not understand it. Fourth, they were afraid to ask Jesus what he meant. Result: complete ignorance! In light of these facts, it is, therefore, entirely inappropriate to ascribe any notion of the DBRJC to Matthew, Mark, or Luke—pre-Easter.

THE THIRD EXPLICIT PREDICTION OF DEATH

The third prediction is recounted in Matthew 20:17–19, where we find:

And as Jesus was going up to Jerusalem, he took the twelve disciples aside, and on the way he said to them, "See, we are going up to Jerusalem. And the Son of Man will be delivered over to the chief priests and scribes, and they will condemn him to death and deliver him over to the Gentiles to be mocked and flogged and crucified, and he will be raised on the third day."

As best we can tell, this prediction occurs two weeks before the Lord's death. Again, the passage clarifies that "he took the twelve disciples aside." No one other than the Twelve heard what Jesus said. It would be post-Easter before the Twelve would understand or divulge this information.

It is in this third declaration that we learn that the method of our Lord's death would be crucifixion. Both Jews and Gentiles would have a hand in this matter. Luke 18:31–34 offers more insight. Luke writes,

Taking the twelve, he said to them, "See, we are going up to Jerusalem, and everything that is written about the Son of Man by the prophets will be accomplished. For he will be delivered over to the Gentiles and will be mocked and shamefully treated and spit upon. And after flogging him, they will kill him, and on the third day he will rise." But they understood none of these things. This saying was hidden from them, and they did not grasp what was said. (emphasis added)

Again, please notice the textual details. First, only the twelve disciples heard the prediction. Second, they did not understand what Jesus meant. Third, the reason they did not understand is that God had hidden the meaning from them. At this point, it should be clear in the reader's mind that the purpose of the Lord's death had not been communicated. This, perhaps, explains why they desert him once his trial begins.

These three accounts should dispel any notion that the "gospel about Jesus Christ" was common knowledge during the whole ministry of Jesus. This is just not true. Only the Twelve heard the Lord's explicit prediction of his imminent death, and God would not allow them to understand it until after the resurrection, ten days short of Pentecost, specifically.

Luke confirms this conclusion:

> As they were talking about these things, Jesus himself stood among them, and said to them, "Peace to you!" But they were startled and frightened and thought they saw a spirit. And he said to them, "Why are you troubled, and why do doubts arise in your hearts? See my hands and my feet, that it is I, myself. Touch me and see. For a spirit does not have flesh and bones as you see that I have." And when he had said this, he showed them his hands and his feet. And while they still disbelieved for joy and were marveling, he said to them, "Have you anything here to eat?" They gave him a piece of broiled fish, and he took it and ate before them. Then he said to them, "These are my words that I spoke to you while I was still with you, that everything written about me in the Law of Moses and the Prophets and the Psalms must be fulfilled." Then he opened their minds to understand the Scriptures, and said to them, "Thus it is written, that the Christ should suffer and on the third day rise from the dead, and that repentance for the forgiveness of sins should be proclaimed in his name to all nations, beginning from Jerusalem. You are witnesses of these things. And behold, I am sending the promise of my Father upon you. But stay in the city until you are clothed with power from on high." And he led them out as far as Bethany, and lifting up his hands he blessed them. While he blessed

them, he parted from them and was carried up into heaven.
(Luke 24:36–50, emphasis added)

That Jesus had to open their minds to understand the connection between his death, burial, and resurrection and repentance for the forgiveness of sins is clear from Luke 24:45. *Anoigō*, the verb meaning "to open," is the single divine action necessary for the Twelve to understand both the meaning and significance of these events. That it is God's power to do so was never in question. This confirms that the imposed limitation on the disciples' understanding was not accidental but the will of God.

What may be missed by the reader is the fact that this explicit explanation of the events of his death, burial, and resurrection for the forgiveness of sin, and their necessity, occurred on the very day our Lord left the earth to return to the Father in heaven. Therefore, to suggest that the phrase *to evangelion* was invested with the meaning of the DBRJC prior to our Lord's departure is an abuse of Scripture. Jesus never referred to his death, burial, and resurrection as "the Gospel." The twelve disciples never understood the death, burial, and resurrection of Jesus as "the Gospel" prior to our Lord's death either.

Matthew 26:1 explicitly states,

When Jesus had finished all these sayings, he said to his
disciples, "You know that after two days the Passover is
coming, and the Son of Man will be delivered up to be
crucified."

Two days before his death, the Lord Jesus stated for the last time, "The Son of Man will be delivered up to be crucified." Matthew does not record the disciples' immediate reaction to this declaration. Mark, Luke, and

John also report the events two days before Passover, but none repeat his declaration. There is no evidence that the Twelve understood the Lord's prophetic statement. In fact, they will run away from him at this critical hour and deny that they know him. Their actions make it difficult to believe that they understood and accepted the necessity of the Lord's death, burial, and resurrection as essential for human salvation.

To what conclusion are we forced? No occurrence of the phrase to evangelion as reflected in modern translation as having been explicitly spoken by the Lord Jesus can refer to his death, burial, and resurrection prior to the resurrection. Thus, we can without reservation declare MacArthur's whole argument in his book null and void. By confusing the gospel of the kingdom of God (the coming of the kingdom) and the gospel about Christ (the gospel of salvation as a result of Jesus' death, burial, and resurrection for the forgiveness of sin), MacArthur and many others perpetuate a problem that never should have existed. Spiritual salvation requires faith. Sanctification requires faithfulness. The failure to recognize this fundamental distinction continues a firestorm of man's own making.

Instead of celebrating the significance of the events culminating in the trial and eventual death of Jesus, the Twelve see no spiritual or eternal value in Jesus' death. Matthew 26:56 concludes, "All the disciples left him and fled." This is hardly the behavior of men who saw and appreciated the prophetic fulfilling significance of the DBRJC.

In the Gospel of John, on the very day Jesus was raised from the dead, John offers this editorial comment, "For they [meaning Peter and John] did not yet understand the Scripture that Jesus must rise from the dead" (NET).

NEW CALVINISM[37]

John MacArthur is not alone in asserting that the Synoptic Gospels have a dominant focus on the issue of spiritual salvation. This is also considered a significant pillar of New Calvinism. This includes popular teachers like John Piper, Don Carson, Tim Relier, Al Mohler, and C.J. Mahaney."[38]

New Calvinists maintain that "the Gospel" is the primary controlling purpose of God and the central message of the Bible as a whole and specifically of Matthew, Mark, Luke, and John. George Gunn argues in his study of New Calvinism that "One of the most significant catchphrases of New Calvinism is 'gospel-centered.'"[39] They are correct that Matthew, Mark, and Luke are 'gospel-centered'; however, they incorrectly identify which "good news" is the focus.

Notes

[1] Darrell L. Bock, "Jesus as Lord in Acts and in the Gospel Message," Bibliotheca Sacra 143 (1986): 146–147.

[2] Nowhere in Matthew, Mark, or Luke should the phrase *to evangelion* be translated as "the gospel." The lone exception is Mark 1:1, where most translations read similarly to the NET: "The beginning of the gospel of Jesus Christ, the Son of God." This is the only verse in Matthew, Mark, or Luke that refers to "the gospel of Jesus Christ" in our modern sense. The reason it can be translated that way is because it is written in retrospect, nearly three decades after the events Mark records. By the time Mark records the events themselves, *to evangelion* should be translated as "good news," since this is the historical sense in which that term was used. But when Mark was writing the introduction to his Gospel more than three decades later, the use of that term had changed. At that time, it had come to be identified with Jesus' death, burial, and resurrection for the remission of sins. Thus, Mark 1:1 is, at best, an editorial comment that reflects the historical development of the term post-Pentecost. Many scholars agree with Nolland, who states that "v. 1 is intended to function as the heading to the whole book." Ref: R. T. France, "The Gospel of Mark: A Commentary on the Greek Text," *New International Greek Testament Commentary* (Grand Rapids, MI; Carlisle: W.B. Eerdmans; Paternoster Press, 2002), 50.

[3] See Footnote 1 in Edmund K. Neufeld, "The Gospel in the Gospels: Answering the Question 'What Must I Do to Be Saved?' from the Synoptics," *Journal of the Evangelical Theological Society* 51, no. 2 (2008): 266.

[4] George Allen Turner, "Soteriology in the Gospel of John," *Journal of the Evangelical Theological Society* 19, no. 4 (1976): 270.

[5] This conclusion I will prove shortly.

[6] Brenda B. Colijn, "Salvation as Discipleship in the Gospel of Mark," *Ashland Theological Journal*, vol. 30 (1998), 11.

[7] Edmund K. Neufeld, "The Gospel in the Gospels: Answering the Question 'What Must I Do to Be Saved?' from the Synoptics," *Journal of the Evangelical Theological Society* 51, no. 2 (2008): 293.

[8] Based on the 28th edition of Nestle-Aland. Matthew 4:23, 9:35, 24:14, 26:13; Mark 1:1, 14, 15; 8:35, 10:29, 13:10, 14:9, and 16:15.

[9] Peter Stuhlmacher, "The Theme: The Gospel and the Gospels," in *The Gospel and the Gospels*, ed. Peter Stuhlmacher, trans. Joh Vriend (Grand Rapids, Eerdmans, 1991), 1.

[10] English translations of the Bible are just a little over four hundred years old. The decision to translate *teo evangelion* as "the gospel" date back well beyond the original 1611 King James Bible (Gospel of Christ, Gal. 1:7).

[11] Gerhard Kittel, Gerhard Friedrich, and Geoffrey William Bromiley, *Theological Dictionary of the New Testament, Abridged in One Volume* (Grand Rapids, MI: W.B. Eerdmans, 1985), 270.

[12] Millar Burrows, "The Origin of the Term 'Gospel,'" *Journal of Biblical Literature*, 44 (1925), 21.

[13] See 2 Kings 4:10.

[14] There is repeated use of the feminine noun in 2 Samuel 18:19–27.

[15] Millar Burrows, "The Origin of the Term 'Gospel,'" *Journal of Biblical Literature* 44 (1925), 22.

[16] That Luke points out the significance of Isaiah 61:1 in the ministry of Jesus will require close examination later. The verb occurs in Isaiah 40:9(2); 52:7(2); 60:6; and 61:1. Barrow is convinced that Isaiah is the main source for the Christian use of the term εὐαγγέλιον. Ibid.

[17] Overwhelmingly, the LXX is the source of most quotes taken from the Old Testament by Jesus, the Gospel writers, and Paul, Peter, and John. Perhaps it was because the Greek language was the common language of ordinary people in the Roman Empire.

[18] That Luke and John never used the term is an argument from silence. However, Matthew and Mark use the term but never in direct statements of Jesus. To some degree, this is also an argument from silence.

[19] The date of the writing of Mark's Gospel is a clue to the historical development of *teo evangelion* as a technical term for the death, burial, and resurrection of Jesus Christ. Clearly, by the time of its writing, the term had acquired a technical status. However, this is not a license to put this meaning into the mouth of Jesus.

[20] MacArthur, John F., *The Gospel According to God*, Crossway. Kindle Edition, 90–91.

[21] Jack Dean Kingsbury, *Matthew: Structure, Christology, Kingdom* (Minneapolis, MN: Fortress Press, 1989), 8.

[22] David R. Bauer, *The Structure of Matthew's Gospel: A Study in Literary Design* (London: Bloomsbury Academic, 1989), 73.

[23] Ibid., 85.

[24] Ibid.

[25] Robertson, A. T. (2009). *A Harmony of the Gospels* (Lk 9:7–9). Logos Bible Software.

[26] https://www.churchathome.org/pdf/A%20Harmony%20of%20the%20Gos pels.pdf (last accessed 8/23/23)

[27] John William McGarvey and Philip Y. Pendleton, *The Four-Fold Gospel* (Cincinnati, OH: The Standard Publishing Company, 1914), 414.

[28] Johannes P. Louw and Eugene Albert Nida, *Greek-English Lexicon of the New Testament: Based on Semantic Domains* (New York: United Bible Societies, 1996), 339.

[29] David Bauer, *The Structure of Matthew's Gospel: A Study in Literary Design* (New York: Bloomsbury Publishing, 1989), 105–105.

[30] W. J. Bennett, JR., "The Son of Man Must ... ," NovT 17 (1975), 113.

[31] Newman, B. M., & Stine, P. C. (1992). *A Handbook on the Gospel of Matthew*, United Bible Societies, 527.

[32] Horst Robert Balz and Gerhard Schneider, *Exegetical Dictionary of the New Testament* (Grand Rapids, MI: Eerdmans, 1990–), 279.

[33] Nolland, J. (2005). *The Gospel of Matthew: A Commentary on the Greek Text* (W.B. Eerdmans; Paternoster Press), 686

[34] Johannes P. Louw and Eugene Albert Nida, *Greek-English Lexicon of the New Testament: Based on Semantic Domains* (New York: United Bible Societies, 1996), 234.

[35] Ibid., 435.

[36] Ibid., 344-345.

[37] Myron A. Penner writes, "The New Calvinism is a trans-denominational theological movement, the central features of which are the 'five-point Calvinist' understanding of human depravity, atonement, and grace coupled with complementarian, male-headship theology." Myron A. Penner, "The Rise of New Calvinism Among Canadian Mennonite Brethren," *Direction* 42/2 (2013), 148.

[38] Vic Froese notes, "and maybe John MacArthur." Froese uses the term "maybe" because MacArthur is also a critic of New Calvinists, especially of Driscoll. Vic Froese, *New Calvinism: A Selected Bibliography, Recommended Reading*, 251.

[39] George Gunn, *New Calvinism: A Theological Evaluation*, 2015, 38.

The Gospels

The Gospel of God | The Gospel of Christ

Pre- | E | Post-
| a |
Rewardific | s | Salvific
Faithfulness | t | Faith
Temporal | e | Eternal
Outside Darkness | r | Eternal Fire

CHAPTER 3

Τὸ Εὐαγγέλιον Τοῦ θεοῦ: The Good News from God

I n the previous chapter, we looked at the articular genitival noun *to evangelion* and asked whether it was ever used in the Gospels of Matthew or Mark to refer to the death, burial, and resurrection motif of Jesus Christ (DBRJC) as we understand the Gospel today.[1] Our research proved that, with the lone exception of Mark 1:1, there is no historical, contextual, theological, or grammatical basis for this claim.

The failure on the part of a majority of New Testament scholars forces them, as Myers correctly concludes,

Either there are numerous different gospels with each author [Peter, Paul, James, and John] having one or more gospel, or there is one large, diverse, multi-faceted, all-encompassing gospel for the entire NT (which essentially is the entire NT). This second approach sees the NT term gospel as a non-technical way to refer to any and all good news connected to Jesus Christ.[2] (emphasis added)

Sadly, and with negative consequences, Myers and many others take the second option. It is our conclusion that the New Testament speaks of two "gospels" only: the gospel of Christ and the gospel of the kingdom of God.

Mark 1:1 has the only occurrence with the modifier *of Jesus Christ* in the four Gospels. The only other occurrence of the articular genitival noun with a modifier in Mark's Gospel occurs in Mark 1:14, i.e., "the gospel of God," which fosters several major questions. First, is "the gospel of God" the same as "the gospel of Christ"? Second, does it, in any way, refer to his death, burial, and resurrection for the remission of sin? Or is it another gospel entirely? The majority view is that "the gospel of Christ" (GC) and "the gospel of God" (GG) are two ways of saying the same or very similar things.

Yet, we repeat, a study of the history of the noun *evangelion* and its utilization in the New Testament reveals that it does not refer to the DBRJC in the Gospels of Matthew or Mark. The false conclusion that it does has caused many (including MacArthur)—[3] to misinterpret Matthew, Mark, and Luke regarding the dominant message of Jesus Christ during the inauguration of God's final plans to set up a kingdom for his Son on earth in fulfillment of Scripture.[4]

By promoting the good news about Jesus Christ as the dominant message of the Synoptic Gospels, the good news from God has effectively been forgotten. In 2017, James W. Sheets, Jr. published his master's thesis entitled, "The Kingdom of God: The Missing Gospel within the Gospels." In the introduction to this important essay, Sheets laments,

As one surveys the spectrum of doctrinal diversity, taking note of the similarities and contrasts represented, it isn't long

before a conundrum becomes apparent, namely, that while there are a variety of differing beliefs concerning the nature of the Gospel, the biggest chasm is not limited to the soteriological systems themselves. The most challenging theological gulf lies between the "shared" foundational understanding of the streams of the Church and the resultant and unavoidable misapplications of what much of the modern Church teaches contrasted with what Jesus taught as seen in the narrative of the four evangelists—Matthew, Mark, Luke, and John.

The canonical [G]ospels, filtered through the reduced theological perspectives superimposed upon them in much of modern reading, has often resulted in a misunderstanding and application of the truth and power of the historical Gospel message proclaimed by Jesus during His earthly career—the Good News (Gospel) of the Kingdom of God. The four canonical Gospel narratives present the truth concerning who Jesus was, who He believed and said that He was, the things He did and many times the purpose behind why He did them, what He said and why He said it, why He died and what He expected to happen as a result of all that.

Though the in-breaking of the eschatological Kingdom of God, through the person, life, and work of the Lord Jesus Christ, is at the core and is "part and parcel" of the Gospel narratives, they have been "misplaced" by much of the Church for a significant part of church history. It would be fair to say that the Gospel of the Kingdom is the "missing" Gospel within the Gospels.[5]

With a few clarifications, Sheets' assertions are fundamentally correct. It is very easy to be confused given that Sheets uses the term "gospel" with three different nuances of which the average reader is unaware.[6] The missing "gospel" of God has been forced to be subservient to the Gospel of Jesus Christ instead of vice versa as Scripture intends. The loss of the essential differences between the GC and GG forces students of the synoptic biographies of Jesus to look for one thing—spiritual salvation—at every turn.

To this, we would add Steven R. Service's conclusion in his work, "The Lost and Forgotten Gospel of the Kingdom: A First Century Hebraic Perspective." He writes,

> Although the contemporary Judeo-Christian world has come to identify the meaning of "gospel" narrowly with the "story of Jesus' death, burial and resurrection," this is most assuredly not what writers of the Gospels were referring to as they used the term. This is why: The Gospels make it clear, because of His disciples' inability to bear the understanding that He intended to die a sacrificial death, that Jesus said nothing explicit regarding His impending crucifixion until the very end of His earthly ministry. If this point is accurate, then the "gospel" Jesus preached at the start of His ministry, could not have possibly had anything to do with the "story of His death, burial, and resurrection." The "gospel" He and others preached, in the 1st century A.D., must have been something completely different than the common definition that has been accepted by religious leaders for more than a millennium.[7]

Service is on the right track, but he falls victim to the same error so prevalent in today's scholarship. The term "gospel" is prejudicial and leads away from a correct interpretation unless one forces the reader to see the basic meaning of "good news" that must be contextually defined. Service states, "The realization that the 'gospel' had come in several instances before Christ unveils a serious chronological problem."[8] The incorrect translation of *to evangelion* as "the gospel" at every occurrence is the trap that leads Service to this conclusion. He like so many others will continue to struggle with the correct interpretation of the New Testament as long as GC controls the dominant message of the New Testament.

This is even though the Greek word for salvation, *sōtēria*, does not occur in Matthew. It appears only once in the disputed ending of the Gospel of Mark. It occurs four times in the Gospel of Luke and only once in the Gospel of John. If the dominant message of Matthew, Mark, and Luke is spiritual salvation, one would think that there would be many more occurrences of the family of terms related to *sōtēria*. It is also necessary to understand that this family of words does not always refer to spiritual salvation. It can also refer to physical deliverance as it does in Luke 1:72, i.e., "that we should be saved from our enemies and from the hand of all who hate us."

In Chapter Two of this book, we demonstrate that spiritual salvation is not the dominant message of the Synoptic Gospel writers. Yet, translations contribute significantly to this false interpretation. It is not clear, and neither is there a scholarly consensus, in regards to when during the historical development of the New Testament church the saints began to use *to evangelion* as a technical term for the DBRJC. We firmly believe that the *terminus a quo* should be post-Easter Sunday.

Except for the New Living Translation,[9] all modern New Testament translations render 1 Corinthians 15:1 as "the gospel," which Paul preached. Notice Paul writes in 1 Corinthians 15:3-5,

For I delivered to you as of first importance what I also received: that Christ died for our sins in accordance with the Scriptures, that he was buried, that he was raised on the third

*day in accordance with the Scriptures, and that he appeared
to Cephas, then to the twelve. Then he appeared to more than
five hundred brothers at one time, most of whom are still
alive, though some have fallen asleep. Then he appeared to
James, then to all the apostles. Last of all, as to one untimely
born, he appeared also to me.*

Even if we accept the notion that from Matthew 1:1 to
Revelation 22:21 (as MacArthur does), the phrase *to
evangelion* refers to the DBRJC, a close, accurate
examination of this passage implodes the whole notion.
Many espouse 1 Corinthians 15:1–9 as the clearest
example in the New Testament of a precise definition of
the one and only Gospel of Christ, yet there are problems
with this position.

A close examination of Paul's "gospel" in 1 Corinthians
15 reveals four components:

that Christ died for our sins in accordance with the Scriptures;

that he was buried;

*that he was raised on the third day in accordance with the
Scriptures;*

that he appeared to Cephas, then to the Twelve.

Most New Testament scholars agree that verses 3–5 are
a unit. There is debate about how verses 6–9 connect to
verses 3–5. However, even if we ignore verses 6–9, the
problem remains. Paul's definition of "the gospel" is a
package with four components: death, burial, resurrection,
and appearances. Based on the grammatical structure of 1
Corinthians 15:3–5, one cannot remove "that he appeared

to Cephas, then to the Twelve" as a component of Paul's "gospel" without severely damaging the text's integrity.

Of the four elements of Paul's "gospel," what must a person believe to be declared righteous in God's sight? Must a person believe that Jesus appeared to Cephas to receive salvation? Must a person believe that Old Testament Scripture explicitly predicts the resurrection of Jesus on the third day? If so, what Old Testament Scriptures expressly make this claim?

Paul's list makes it clear that 1 Corinthians 15:1 should not be treated as a definitive statement of what constitutes "the Gospel" as we understand it today. Instead, Paul lists vital elements of his "good news" regarding the many works of Jesus Christ. As "good news," any list can include all or any of Paul's components and still be considered *to evangelion*, the good news.

We have already shown that the death, burial, and resurrection of Jesus motif does not become part of the public discourse until the very last chapters of Matthew, Mark, and Luke, which focus on the time between our Lord's resurrection and ascension back to heaven. Thus, to make this motif the dominant message of the entirety of these books does not stand the test of critical examination. With the lone exception of John the Baptist, there is no evidence that anyone at that time understood the connection between Jesus, his death, and the removal of sin as we now understand it (John 1:19).

IT'S ALL ABOUT CONTEXT

The central issue concerns the phrase *to evangelion*. The decision to make it a technical word for the DBRJC was not the result of the language itself. In any given passage, it is the context that differentiates whether this "good news" is the Gospel or another set of good news altogether. As we see below, there are ten different genitival phrases in the NT referring to 10 different aspects of "good news."

New Testament Good News Chart

to evangelion	
	Of the kingdom
	Of Jesus Christ
	Of God
	Of the grace of God
	Of his Son
	Of Christ
	Of your salvation
	Of peace
	Of our Lord Jesus
	Of the glory of the blessed God

While our conditioning over time has taught us that there is only one "gospel" (the one and only death, burial, and resurrection of Jesus Christ for the remission of sin), English readers must resist the temptation to assume this. To assume that every occurrence of *to evangelion* refers to the Gospel of Christ is a poor exegetical methodology. Hence our insistence that modern translations abandon the translation of this phrase in the New Testament as "the gospel" and utilize "the good news" in all occurrences instead. This would help reduce the prejudicial tendencies of the reader and force the dependence on the context for accuracy.

THE ONE AND ONLY GOSPEL?

What about the articular singular noun τό εὐαγγέλιον? Does this not refer to the singular "one and only" Gospel of Christ? *Τό εὐαγγέλιον* occurs in the Gospel of Matthew (4:23, 9:35, 24:14, 26:13). It also appears in the Gospel of

Mark (1:1, 14, 8:35, 20:29, 13:10, 14:9, and 16:15). It occurs twice in the Book of Acts: once in the mouth of Peter (Acts 15:7) and once in the mouth of Paul (Acts 20:24). All the other occurrences are in the writings of Paul and 1 Peter.[10] The term does not occur in Luke's Gospel, John's letters, or in the Letter of James at all.

The Gospel of John is, without a doubt, the most salvific-focused book in the New Testament. If *to evangelion* does, in fact, refer to the DBRJC, the fact that it does not occur in any of John's writings is surprising. If this is the critical term in the New Testament for "the Gospel," and the Gospel of John is about *the* Gospel of Christ, then why did John not use it?

Probably a significant number of NT readers do not know that John 1:1–11:54 covers the first three-and-one-half years of the ministry of the Lord Jesus. This section predominates with signs and witnesses that Jesus is the Christ, the Son of God. John 11:55–20:23 covers the last nine days of our Lord's earthly ministry. Both Matthew and Mark use the term *to evangelion* twice during the final week. We realize that any argument from silence is weak, but the fact that John does not use the term, even after committing nine chapters to the last six days of the Lord's ministry, is worthy of contemplation. We have argued that a possible reason for this is that, at the time, *to evangelion* was not yet being used to represent the DBRJC. Perhaps this best explains why John does not use it. Potentially, it is only twenty-plus years after our Lord's ministry that this term came to be a summary term for his ministry related to the forgiveness of sin.

In chapter two of this book, we showed that in the gospels of Matthew, Mark, and Luke, *to evangelion* is never shorthand for the death, burial, and resurrection motif of Jesus Christ. Instead, it refers to "the gospel of the kingdom of God."

THE BEGINNING MESSAGE OF JESUS CHRIST

Mark 1:14–15 reports,

Now after that John was put in prison, Jesus came into Galilee, preaching the gospel of the kingdom of God, and saying, The time is fulfilled, and the kingdom of God is at hand: repent ye, and believe the gospel. [KJV]

Regarding these two verses and their importance, we agree with Chamblin when he writes,

The importance of Mark 1:14–15 can hardly be overstated. Here, for the first time, Mark records words of Jesus. These verses stand as a rubric over the whole of the ensuing Galilean ministry. Mark here presents a reader's digest of the gospel which Jesus declared throughout that period.[11]

Please notice that final sentence again. "Mark here presents a reader's digest of the gospel which Jesus declared throughout that period." Indeed, we extend Chamblin's assertion until Jesus dies on the cross and his final 40 days on earth before his ascension to heaven. The fact that scholars have missed this point and its significance has fed MacArthur's debate, and this author is convinced that it is the reason many believers hold to an Arminian view of salvation.

Jesus came proclaiming "God's good news." We commend the New Living Translation for consistently translating the *euang* word group "good news." May their tribe increase! The reason we draw this conclusion is because by utilizing the phrase, "the good news" rather than the phrase, "the gospel," the reader is forced to use context to determine the intended meaning of the text and thus stands a better chance of recognizing the contextual difference between references to the GKG and GC.

What is the good news from God? Is it the same as the "good news about Jesus Christ"? MacArthur and many other New Testament scholars assume that the answer is yes. Thus, they wrestle with passages that, at face value, seem to teach works-based salvation. Since works-based salvation is unacceptable to MacArthur, he is forced to interpret difficult passages in a way that harmonizes his theological convictions. Doing this leads to errors, errors, and more errors.

Again, New Testament translations would be much more helpful if they would translate *to evangelion* as "the good news." This would allow the reader to discern whether this is "the good news from God," the gospel about Christ (the Gospel), or some other "good news" based on the context. For example, Luke 1:19 records a conversation between the angel Gabriel and Zechariah, the father of John the Baptist. Gabriel tells Zechariah, "I stand in the presence of God, and I was sent to speak to you and to bring you this good news." What "good news" is Gabriel talking about here? It is the birth and ministry of John the Baptist. The context forces translators to reflect the correct nuance because there is no direct focus on Jesus Christ. At this point, there is no hint of the death, burial, and resurrection motif of Jesus. John the Baptist *is* the good news.

The same Greek verb, *euangelizō*, is used in Luke 2:10, which states, "Fear not, for behold, I bring you good news of great joy." Here, "great joy" describes the good news. The great joy spoken of is the birth of "a Savior, who is Christ the Lord." At this point, there is no hint of death connected with this child. The specific acts of the child who will save the people are the unraveling story of Mathew, Mark, Luke, and John. It will be only after our

Lord's resurrection that the Jews understand how the child saves his people.

In Luke 4:43, we learn that Jesus is preaching "the good news of the kingdom of God" (ESV). Luke states that our Lord said, "I must preach the good news of the kingdom of God to the other towns as well; for I was sent for this purpose." The phrase "as well" indicates that this is the message Jesus preached to all the cities of Galilee.

Here in Luke's account, we have three distinct messages labeled as good news: (1) the birth and ministry of John the Baptist; (2) the birth of Jesus; and (3) the kingdom of God. Therefore, "to proclaim the good news" is the better translation of the verb, which allows the context to define what that good news is. To violate this hermeneutical method is to invite error.

Mark 1:14 reports, "Now after John was arrested, Jesus came into Galilee, proclaiming the good news from God" (author's translation). Matthew 4:17 adds additional insight regarding the beginning message of the Lord Jesus. He states, "From that time Jesus began to preach, saying, 'Repent, for the kingdom of heaven is at hand.'" "From that time" is a Matthean temporal indicator. It marks a dividing line between what went before and what goes after. In essence, the Jews did not hear Jesus announce the kingdom or call for repentance before the beginning of his public ministry. This is the dominant message of Jesus' first sermon!

Luke 4:43 adds, "I must preach the good news of the kingdom of God to the other towns as well; for I was sent for this purpose." The Greek literally and emphatically says, "Because for this I was sent." Proclaiming the royal rule of God is the first dominating reason Jesus came to this earth. While there are many consequences of the Lord's first coming, it is here and in John 18:37 that it is the most precisely articulated—to announce the beginning of the reign of King Jesus over creation. While the descriptions differ, Mark, Matthew, and Luke indicate that is what Jesus teaches in his message: the good news is that, in himself, God's permanent physical manifestation of sovereign rule has arrived.[12]

Matthew informs us that this was the same summary message with which John the Baptist began his ministry: "Repent, for the kingdom of heaven is at hand" (Matt. 3:2). From the start of his ministry, Jesus continues the message of John the Baptist. According to Matthew's record, John and Jesus began their ministries preaching the exact same thing, the Gospel of God. Luke puts this same message in the mouth of the Twelve, as well (Luke 8:1; 9:2, 60; 16:16; and Acts 8:12). Finally, Luke closes the book of Acts by indicating that the apostle Paul also preached this message:

> When they [the local leaders of the Jews] had appointed a day for him [Paul], they came to him at his lodging in greater numbers. From morning till evening he expounded to them, testifying to the kingdom of God and trying to convince them about Jesus both from the Law of Moses and from the Prophets . . . . He [Paul] lived there two whole years at his own expense, and welcomed all who came to him, proclaiming the kingdom of God and teaching about the Lord Jesus Christ with all boldness and without hindrance. (Acts 28:23, 30–31)

Paul had a two-point sermon: (1) the kingdom of God and (2) Jesus, i.e., the king and his kingdom (sovereign administration). Rather than maintaining this vital distinction, most New Testament readers have dissolved any separation in the content of these messages and blended them to such a degree that the dominant message of the Synoptic Gospels is wholly lost. Jesus physically manifested the royal rule of God on earth ("the Gospel of God") and left an open invitation for his disciples to join him on his coming leadership council during his (what we now know to be a) thousand-year reign on earth.[13]

THE CHRONOLOGY OF JESUS' MINISTRY AND ITS IMPORTANCE

The chronology of the initial events of our Lord's ministry can be a bit confusing given the differences in the accounts of the four Gospel writers. Those who attempt a harmony of the Gospels agree that, for the most part, Jesus began his public ministry "after John was arrested." The importance of John's ministry to that of Jesus is critical. Luke 16:16 states,

> *Until John the Baptist, the law of Moses and the messages of the prophets were your guides. But now the Good News of the Kingdom of God is preached, and everyone is eager to get in. (NLT)*

There is debate about where to draw the line regarding John's inclusion or exclusion from the age of "the good news of the kingdom of God is preached." Perhaps, Luke 7:28 is helpful. It asserts that "among those born of women none is greater than John. Yet the one who is least in the kingdom of God is greater than he." Thus, the age of Law and Prophets ended with John, a prophet in the tradition of Elijah. Bock concludes,

> *The fundamental point here is that the kingdom period, one that followed the ministry of John, is so great that the least who share in it are greater than the greatest prophet of the older era. One gets the clear impression from this text that the*

period of the kingdom of God begins with Jesus' ministry and message.[14]

Therefore, with the ministries of John the Baptist and Jesus, two eras transitioned. Since Matthew summarizes the message of John the Baptist and the Lord Jesus Christ as "Repent, for the kingdom of heaven is at hand" (John = Matt. 3:2 and Jesus = Matt. 4:17), a comparison is easy to make. Matthew's assertion that John and Jesus preached the same message allows us to look for the defining traits of this message.

Both Matthew 3:1–12 and Luke 3:1–20 give the most extended descriptions of the ministry and message of John the Baptist. Matthew begins his account with the simple explanation that "John the Baptist came preaching in the wilderness of Judea." Having skipped John's miraculous conception, Zechariah's discipline, and John's earliest excitement at being in the presence of our Lord while he was in the womb of his mother (which Luke details), Matthew states the essence of John's message: "Repent, for the kingdom of heaven is at hand."

Whatever else "to repent" might come to mean in the New Testament era, at this early juncture, it had nothing to do with what would come to be known as "the Gospel." The average reader generally sees this New Testament concept of repentance as unbelievers turning from their past sins and accepting Jesus Christ as Lord and Savior. In the Gospels, most see this as a necessary step to "get" saved so they can go to heaven. However, making repentance a soteriological step from the initiation of the Lord's public ministry is an illegitimate identity transfer, i.e., reading a modern concept back into the biblical period.

WHAT IS THE "GOOD NEWS OF GOD"?

Matthew states the heart of our Lord's message. Mark 1:14–15 defines the essential components of this message as follows: (1) the time is fulfilled; (2) the kingdom of God is at hand; (3) repent; and (4) believe in the gospel (of the kingdom). This, according to Mark, is "the good news from God." The KJV reflects manuscript evidence supporting the longer phrase "the good news of the kingdom of God" here. While this evidence favors the shorter reading, the more extended reading does appear in the Gospel of Luke (4:43; 8:1; and 16:16).

While there is some debate about the origination of Matthew's use of the clause "the good news from God," there is no confusion regarding its origination in Luke.[15] Since both passages refer to the same message, we can take Luke's version, "proclaiming the good news of the kingdom of God," as the fullest expression of the content of the Lord's original message.

Now, for fear that the reader misunderstands the message, we need only to continue reading. Mark 1:15 says the content of the Lord's statement: "The time is fulfilled, and the kingdom of God is at hand; repent and believe in the gospel." Mark 1:15 begins with the Greek: καὶ λέγων ὅτι (*kai legōn hoti* = "and saying that"). At the time of the writing of the New Testament, writers did not employ quotation marks. To indicate direct speech (what the person said instead of a paraphrase) the Greek conjunction "Ὅτι = that" is used. Students of New Testament Greek will recognize this usage as an example of *recitative hoti*. The *Exegetical Dictionary of the New Testament* states,

The recitative ὅτι functions much like quotation marks to introduce direct speech (Matt 7:23; Mark 1:37; John 10:36; 2 Thess 3:10, etc.). Scripture quotations are also introduced in this way (Matt 21:16; Mark 12:19; Luke 2:23; John 10:34, etc.). [16]

Summarizing the grammatical significance of the phrase "and saying" with *recitative hoti*, R.A. Guelich, comments, "The epexegetic use of καὶ λέγων and the ὅτι-recitative leads to the specific message setting forth the 'gospel from God.'" [17]

Thus, we know the content of "the good news from God." Most scholars generally agree upon the basic structure of verse 15. Some focus on the grammatical components: two declarations ("the time is fulfilled" and "the kingdom of God is at hand") and two commands ("repent" and "believe in the good news"). [18] Guelich adds, "The message itself consists of two pairs of statements, each constructed in synthetic parallelism . . . ." [19]

James L. Mays draws a similar conclusion. He writes:

The quotation is composed of two movements. First there is an announcement: a pair of parallel declarations about the time and what is happening in it. The declarations give the content of the gospel of God. Then follow two imperatives urging the claims of the gospel. [20]

The term here for "announcement" is κηρύσσω (kēryssō), which means essentially "to shout out loud." One does not make such an announcement quietly. It is shouted out loud—in our Lord's case, often to several thousand people at once. Thus, we translate this verse as Jesus "shouted out loud the good news from God": that the time had come for his appearance and the physical manifestation of God's sovereign administration had begun on earth. It should be at once apparent that this message did not implicitly or explicitly suggest that Jesus would die on the cross for the forgiveness of sin. Because MacArthur misunderstood the fundamental difference between the good news *from* God and the good news *about Jesus Christ*, he manufactured another "gospel," which created far more confusion than an understanding of the New Testament.

A CLOSER LOOK AT THE GOSPEL OF GOD

The phrase "the Gospel of God" occurs seven times in the New Testament. One variation occurs in 2 Corinthians 11:7.[21] Only Mark 1:14–15 explicitly defines "the gospel from God." Sadly, New Testament scholarship consistently sees any use of the term "the gospel," regardless of the presence of a genitival modifier, as a reference to the DBRJC. This is not the case in Mark 1:14, but it is consistently interpreted as such by the overwhelming majority of New Testament scholars. Dunn's comment is typical: "Εὐαγγέλιον, "gospel," is already clearly a t[echnical] t[erm] in Christian vocabulary as *the* Gospel (1:16; 10:16; 11:28; 1 Cor 4:15; etc.)[22]

In this view, every occurrence of the term "gospel" in the New Testament references the DBRJC. Dunn could not be more wrong. Dunn, MacArthur, and many other New Testament scholars read later developments back into our Lord's words and subsequently draw erroneous conclusions. These erroneous conclusions are then fostered by modern translations. Besides Paul, the apostle Peter uses the phrase "the gospel of God" in 1 Peter 4:17–19:

For it is time for judgment to begin at the household of God; and if it begins with us, what will be the outcome for those who do not obey the gospel of God? And if the righteous is scarcely saved, what will become of the ungodly and the sinner?

Just as John the Baptist's message (the good news from God) was a message of impending judgment for which only the righteous (in actions) will escape, we find the same elements in 1 Peter 4. Peter reminds his audience (those who are elect exiles in the Dispersion) that "the end of all things is at hand" (1 Pet. 4:7). He then gives a list of behaviors that will meet with God's approval: (1) self-control; (2) being sober-minded; (3) loving one another; (4) showing hospitality; and (5) using spiritual gifts to serve one another (1 Pet. 4:7b–11). The essence of Peter's list easily matches that of John the Baptist (Luke 3:10–14), i.e., correct behavior turns away God's wrath. The chapter concludes with exhortations to suffer for doing good things and not bad ones (1 Pet. 4:12–19). The phrase "the gospel of God" occurs in this final section.

Just as in the preaching of John the Baptist, "the gospel of God" is a warning message to change behavior from evil to righteous to avoid the coming judgment. As is consistent from Adam to Abraham to David to the Twelve to us, faith in the promise of God brings righteousness from God.

It is a choice to be in a state of repentance or unrepentance. "Those who do not obey" are those who are unrepentant. It would be a significant error to conclude that Peter draws a line between believers and unbelievers here. He puts the line between those who repent and those who do not. Thus, the people of God can be among the unrepentant! To be sure, what will happen to each group is not the same, but there will be negative consequences.

Paul uses the phrase "the gospel of God" (Rom. 1:1) to summarize God's extraordinary work in Jesus that entails far more than just the DBRJC. He uses it to refer to both spiritual salvation and physical salvation and the privilege of ruling with Christ during his coming thousand-year-reign. Because Paul's "good news" includes both, it would be better to utilize "the good news" as the translation in Romans 1:1 to ensure that the phrase is contextually determined and not automatically assumed.

Paul lists several defining traits of "the gospel of God" in the opening verses of Romans 1. First, it was "promised beforehand through his prophets in the holy Scriptures." Second, it concerns the God-Man, Jesus Christ, our Lord. Third, it calls for the obedience of all of the nations. Compliance is necessary to turn away the wrath of God, which Paul details in the rest of the book of Romans.

THE "GOSPEL" PREACHED IN ROME

Recognizing the gospel of God as more than the announcement of the benefits of the death, burial, and resurrection of Jesus Christ for the forgiveness of sin explains why Paul could write in Romans 1:8–15:

First, I thank my [Father] God through [the Son of God] Jesus Christ for all of you, because your faith is proclaimed in all the world. For [the Father] God is my witness, whom I serve with my spirit in the Good News of his Son [Jesus Christ], that without ceasing I mention you always in my prayers, asking that somehow by [the Father] God's will I may now at last succeed in coming to you. For I long to see you, that I may impart to you some spiritual gift to strengthen you—that is, that we may be mutually encouraged by each other's faith, both yours and mine. I do not want you to be unaware, brothers, that I have often intended to come to you (but thus far have been prevented), in order that I may reap some harvest among you as well as among the rest of the Gentiles. I am under obligation both to Greeks and to barbarians, both to the wise and to the foolish. So I am eager to preach the good news [of God] to you also who are in Rome. (translation and emphasis mine)

After lauding the Romans for their faith being "proclaimed in all the world," and hoping that "we may be mutually encouraged by each other's faith," Paul expresses his eagerness "to preach the gospel [of God] to you also who are in Rome." Paul has restated his intent to visit the believers in Rome, given "that I [Paul] have often intended to come to you [the church in Rome] that I may reap some harvest among you as well as among the rest of the Gentiles."

Clearly, Paul had not preached to the Romans in person, but others had, and the converts had a worldwide reputation. Yet in Romans 15:20, Paul states that he makes it his ambition "to preach the gospel [about Jesus], not where Christ has already been named, lest I build on someone else's foundation." If Paul did not want to preach the Gospel in locations where it had already been preached, then why was he anxious to preach it in Rome? Scholars recognize the apparent contradiction but share no consensus as to how to resolve it. Schreiner wrestles with the situation as he writes,

A vexing question relates to what Paul wanted to accomplish with his visit to Rome. He expresses a desire to strengthen

them with a spiritual gift (v. 11), to encourage them through the faith that is in him (v. 12), to win fruit in Rome as he had among other Gentiles (v. 13), and to preach the gospel in Rome (v. 15). The goals stated here seem clear enough on first glance. They become more difficult when compared with what Paul says in chapter 15. Why did Paul want to preach the gospel in Rome (1:13, 15) if his ambition was to preach the gospel where Christ had not been previously named (15:20–21)? Paul appears to be contradicting his principle of planting churches where there were none.[23]

To get around the apparent contradiction, Dunn offers that, "The final word ("to preach the gospel") is slightly surprising, but only if we confine the sense to preaching the gospel for the first time."[24] This is an excellent example of the type of gymnastics often required by New Testament scholars who fail to understand the essential difference between the GC and GG.

Dunn misses the very point Paul intends. This is Paul's first opportunity to speak with the believers in Rome. What then is to be his message if he does not intend to "build on someone else's foundation"? Whatever else Paul might have intended; evangelism has already been expressed as one of his goals (v. 13).

Morris expresses the opinion that Paul "writes to his readers as Romans rather than as Christians... In Rome, as elsewhere, it is to nonbelievers that he would bring the gospel.[25] In essence, Paul writes to the citizens of Rome among whom are some Christians, but he hopes that he will get a chance to preach to any unbelievers left there when he arrives. After all, Paul emphasizes in 1:13 a desire to "reap some harvest among you [Romans], as well as among the rest of the Gentiles," Morris would reason.

Of the many who attempt to explain 1:15, Schreiner alone comes closest to correctly understanding Paul and his "gospels." Schreiner writes,

> One of the difficulties with Paul longing to preach the gospel in Rome is resolved when we realize that preaching the gospel for Paul involved more than initial conversion .... His goal as an apostle was to bring about the obedience of faith among the Gentiles (Rom. 1:5; 16:26). The obedience of faith, which as 1:1–7 shows is part and parcel of the gospel [from God], cannot be limited to the initial decision to join the Christian community. Paul often insists that perseverance to the end is necessary for salvation (e.g., Rom. 8:13; 1 Cor. 6:9–11; 15:1–2; Gal. 5:21; 6:8–9; Col. 1:21–23). He did not believe that his work as an apostle was accomplished unless the churches were established and persevered.

However, like MacArthur and many others, Schreiner fails to understand the difference between GC and GG. The "gospel" Paul longed to preach was not the "gospel about Christ" relating to spiritual salvation. Paul longed to preach the gospel *of God*, which warns men of the coming judgment and the coming kingdom, in which Paul wants to be included as part of the leadership. Salvation by grace through the atoning sacrifice of Jesus on the cross is an essential first step, but the gospel of God is more comprehensive. As John the Baptist had warned the people to "flee from the wrath to come," Paul warns the Romans that the wrath of God is already evident on those who do not obey the GG (Rom. 1:18–32).

The failure to appreciate this difference guarantees confusion and frustration in many texts. The merger of these two completely different messages results in twisting, squeezing, and forcing passages to conform to a false presupposition. Translations that cause both the articular noun *to evangelion* and the infinitive *euangelizesthai* to mean "the Gospel," i.e., the DBRJC for the forgiveness of sin, exacerbate the problem. Thus, attaching a need to preserve in belief because passages call for perseverance in sanctification is the mother of both lordship salvation and Arminianism.

Again, this is precisely why we advocate the translation "the good news" at every turn and that the immediate context be used to define its content. It is "the good news about Jesus Christ," which provides the basis for God's impartation of righteousness to a sinner, but "the good news from God," that promises inclusion in the leadership of the coming physical manifestation of the royal rule of God on earth.

Understanding the two different sets of "good news" is particularly critical when a New Testament author uses *to evangelion* without a genitival qualifier. Paul begins the book of Romans with an explicit declaration that he was "set apart for the gospel from God." Schreiner is correct that Paul's "good news" "cannot be limited to the initial decision to join the Christian community." "The good news from God" insists that perseverance to the end is necessary for "deliverance." Perseverance is a demand of "the good news from God" and not "the good news about Christ."

Just as John the Baptist came preaching the need to repent to the people of God, Paul came preaching "the good news from God" to the Roman believers. Belief in the death, burial, and resurrection of Jesus Christ for the forgiveness of sin will keep one out of the coming lake of fire, but it will not guarantee one's inclusion in the royal rule of God, which started with the ministry of Jesus Christ on earth and will culminate at the initialization of his thousand-year earthly reign. [26]

Paul uses the phrase "the gospel of God" again in Romans 15:16. He exalts being "a minister of Christ Jesus to the Gentiles in the priestly service of the gospel of God." He celebrates "what Christ has accomplished through me to bring the Gentiles to obedience." Notice that the fulfillment of "the ministry of the gospel about Christ" makes Paul successful in bringing "the Gentiles to obedience."

The phrase "the gospel of God" occurs three times in 1 Thessalonians 2. In the face of persecution by the Jews, Paul reminds the Thessalonians that "the gospel of God" produced results—their obedience. In proclaiming "the gospel of God," Paul and his team did not violate God's commands with wrong motives, i.e., flattery to make money or to seek the honor of men. To not infringe upon the call of "the gospel from God," Paul was committed to giving rather than receiving. Paul concludes 1 Thessalonians 2:1–16 with the sobering reality: "But wrath has come upon them at last."

Paul is speaking of those:

> who killed both the Lord Jesus and the prophets; drove us out, and displease God and oppose all mankind by hindering us from speaking to the Gentiles that they might be saved—so as always to fill up the measure of their sins.

God will punish bad behavior with his wrath. Again, we see that a discussion of "the gospel of God" occurs in a context in which behavior should be designed in light of the eschatological coming of the wrath of God. "The gospel of God" warns humankind (both believer and unbeliever alike) that living a penitent life will ensure safety from the imminent wrath of God. Unbelievers must be penitent. Believers must be repentant.

Mark 1:15 defines the good news of the kingdom of God as consisting of three primary pillars: (1) the time is fulfilled; (2) the kingdom of God is near; and (3) repent and believe the gospel [of the kingdom of God]. We shall explore each pillar separately in the next three chapters.

Notes

[1] Remember that this phrase does not occur in either the Gospel of Luke or the Gospel of John.

[2] Myers, "The Gospel Is More than 'Faith Alone in Christ Alone,'", 35.

[3] Soteriology is the "theological word commonly used to describe a biblical writer's teaching and belief about the subject of salvation based on the Greek word for salvation, *sōtēria*." Roy B. Zuck, *A Biblical Theology of the New Testament*, electronic ed. (Chicago: Moody Press, 1994), 266.

[4] The inauguration of the sovereign administration of the physical rule of God on earth began at the birth of Jesus and will conclude with his exaltation record in Revelation 11:15, which states, "The kingdom of the world has become the kingdom of our Lord and of his Christ and he shall reign forever and ever." The period from Christ's birth until his earthly exaltation is an open invitation to all saints to gain administrative privileges for the coming rule of God.

[5] James W. Sheets, Jr., *The Kingdom of God: The Missing Gospel within the Gospels* (Sacramento, CA: Adonai International Christian University, 2017), 5-6.

[6] In this context, the "gospel" can refer to simply "good news"; the "good news of God" (the arrival of God's royal rule on Earth); and the Gospel of the death, burial, and resurrection for the remission of sin.

[7] Steven R. Service, "The Lost and Forgotten Gospel of the Kingdom: A First Century Hebraic Perspective," 2nd Edition (CreateSpace Independent Publishing Platform, 2016), 5.

[8] Ibid., p. 11.

[9] The paraphrase *The Message* does not.

[10] See Romans 1:15, 16; 2:16, 10:15, 11:28, 15:16, 19; 16:25; 1 Corinthians 4:15, 9:12, 14, 18, 23; 15:1; 2 Corinthians 2:12, 4:3, 4; 8:18, 9:13, 10:14. 11:7; Galatians 1:7, 11; 2:2, 5, 7, 14); Ephesians 1:13, 3:6, 6:15, 19; Philippians 1:5, 7, 12, 16, 27; 2:22, 4:13, 5; Colossians 1:5, 23; 1 Thessalonians 1:5, 2:2, 4, 8, 9; 3:2; 2 Thessalonians 1:8, 2:14; 1 Timothy 1:10, 11; 2 Timothy 1:8, 2:8; and Philemon 13; 1 Peter 4:17.

[11] Chamblin, K. (1997). "*Euangelion* in Mark: Willi Marxsen Revisited." *Westminster Theological Journal*, 59(1), 34.

[12] Gustavo Gutiérrez, "Mark 1:14-15," *Review and Expositor*, 88 (1991), 428.

[13] This is the core message of Chapter 5.

[14] Kaiser, Walter C., Blaising, Craig A. *Dispensationalism, Israel and the Church: The Search for Definition* (Grand Rapids: Zondervan Publishing House, 1992), 39.

[15] The grammatical formulation is different in Luke from Matthew and Mark. Luke prefers the verb εὐαγγελίζω (*euangelizō*) "to proclaim," while Matthew and Mark prefer the verb κηρύσσω (*kēryssō*) "to proclaim."

[16] Balz, H. R., & Schneider, G. (1990–). In *Exegetical Dictionary of the New Testament* (Grand Rapids: Eerdmans), vol. 2, 539.

[17] R. A. Guelich, "Mark 1–8:26," Vol. 34a, *Word Biblical Commentary* (Dallas: Word, Incorporated, 1988), 43.

[18] John D. Grassmick, "Mark," in *The Bible Knowledge Commentary: An Exposition of the Scriptures*, ed. J. F. Walvoord and R. B. Zuck, vol. 2 (Wheaton, IL: Victor Books, 1985), 107.

[19] Robert A. Guelich, "Mark 1–8:26," vol. 34A, *Word Biblical Commentary* (Dallas: Word, Incorporated, 1989), 41.

[20] James L. Mays, "Jesus Came Preaching," *Int* 26 (1972), 31-32.

[21] Mark 1:14; Romans 1:1, 15:16; 1 Thessalonians 2:2, 8, 9; and 1 Peter 4:17.

[22] James D. G. Dunn, "Romans 1–8," vol. 38a, *Word Biblical Commentary* (Dallas: Word, Incorporated, 1988), 10.

[23] Thomas R. Schreiner, Romans, vol. 6, Baker *Exegetical Commentary on the New Testament* (Grand Rapids: Baker Books, 1998), 52.

[24] James D. G. Dunn, Romans 1–8, vol. 38a, *Word Biblical Commentary* (Dallas: Word, Incorporated, 1988), 36.

[25] Leon Morris, "The Epistle to the Romans," *The Pillar New Testament Commentary* (Grand Rapids: Leicester, England: W.B. Eerdmans; Inter-Varsity Press, 1988), 65.

[26] This point I shall prove beyond a shadow of doubt in Chapter 5.

CHAPTER 4

What Time Is It?

It may be a challenge for many people to accept that Jesus' references to "the kingdom of God" do not refer to the Gospel of Christ. It's become so widely accepted and ingrained in the thinking of so many in the church, but there is no scriptural basis for it. It's not just the language of the New Testament that tells us this. It's also its place in the chronological timeline of the Synoptic Gospels where we find support for our conclusion.

In Mark 1:15, the clearest and most precise definition of the good news (gospel) from God occurs. Mark records that Jesus' first sermon listed three essential tenets of the GG. The first pillar concerns the unique age that began with the birth of the Messiah—Jesus, the Son of God and Son of Man. Jesus stated, "The time is fulfilled" (Mark 1:15a). The Gospel of Mark, alone, restates the declarative statement of Jesus, but without any illuminating commentary. What time is Jesus referring to here? When did it begin? Did those who heard Jesus speak immediately understand the referent? Is this period of time strictly Jewish?

To find answers, we must consult both Matthew's and Luke's accounts because both writers expand and highlight the significance of our Lord's original statement in different but insightful ways. It is in the Gospel of Luke in which we are given the most theologically developed understanding of what Jesus initially meant by this new age or period of time. Luke will do it in a way that is unique and theologically sophisticated.

It is the permanent physical manifestation of God on the earth that marks the new age. To better help the reader understand the uniqueness of this age, Luke re-purposes the Nazareth rejection narrative[1] of Jesus because it contains the most explicit self-identification by Jesus that he is the long-promised Jewish Messiah. Jesus makes this identification by quoting Isaiah 61:1–2a. What is so special about Luke's account is not just *where* Luke places it in the chronological timeline of our Lord's forty-two-month-ministry but also the purposeful rearrangement of the Isaianic passage, which make two critical points: (1) the four attributes of the messianic age for mankind and (2) the dawning of the age of God's favor.

A JOURNEY BACK THROUGH HISTORY

The temporal timeline of Israel's Old Testament history concludes with the book of Nehemiah. This conclusion is a gloomy one. For their disobedience, the tribes of Israel would be enveloped by a shroud of darkness. That shroud would last more than 400 years. Yet, the tribes were not left without hope. The prophet Malachi recorded that this darkness would be broken by the re-appearance of "Elijah the prophet," who would come at a time to inspire family reconciliation to turn away the wrath of God.

Malachi 4:5–6 states,

> "Behold, I will send you Elijah the prophet before the great and awesome day of the LORD comes. And he will turn the hearts of fathers to their children and the hearts of children to their fathers, lest I come and strike the land with a decree of utter destruction."

The tribes were likely looking for a quick fulfillment of this promise, yet this was not to be. The promise would go unfulfilled for 400 years. Then, suddenly and without warning, the silence would be broken by an angelic visit telling of the imminent birth of a Davidite. The delivery and early life of this child—the Lord Jesus—receive little attention in the biblical record. It is with Jesus' public ministry that his biographies are focused.

The Synoptics situate the beginning of Jesus' ministry as fulfilling Old Testament prophecy. Matthew and Mark agree that the public ministry of Jesus begins "after John the Baptist was arrested."[2] We might then describe this transition from the preaching of John to the teaching of Jesus as a ministerial "handing off of the baton." The difference is that John's ministry pointed to Jesus, and Jesus' ministry pointed to himself. Each Gospel writer describes Jesus' "breaking into history" in a unique way. All insert Jesus as God's solution for Israel's problem (silence), but each does it differently and not to the same degree.

BREAKING OF SILENCE IN MATTHEW

Matthew describes the beginning of the Lord Jesus' ministry as follows:

> *Now when he [Jesus] heard that John had been arrested, he withdrew into Galilee. And leaving Nazareth he went and lived in Capernaum by the sea, in the territory of Zebulun and Naphtali, so that what was spoken by the prophet Isaiah might be fulfilled. (Matt. 4:12–16)*

In his account, Matthew frames up Jesus' in-breaking of the prophetic silence with a prophecy from Isaiah. He references Isaiah 9:1–2, which describes a time of gloom and darkness for Zebulun and Naphtali (two northern tribes on the east side of the Jordan River).
Isaiah describes this time as follows:

> *But there will be no gloom for her who was in anguish. In the former time he brought into contempt the land of Zebulun and the land of Naphtali, but in the latter time he has made glorious the way of the sea, the land beyond the Jordan, Galilee of the nations. The people who walked in darkness have seen a great light; those who dwelt in a land of deep darkness, on them has light shone. (Isa. 9:1–2)*

Isaiah depicts conditions that resulted from the exile of the people. He also predicts the future coming of light by a son. Both predictions unite in the message of the Lord Jesus, the good news (gospel) from God. For Matthew, the time has come for the light to shine on the people of Galilee.

BREAKING OF SILENCE IN MARK

What Matthew details, Mark will significantly abbreviate:

> *Now after John was arrested, Jesus came into Galilee, proclaiming the gospel of God, and saying, "The time is*

fulfilled, and the kingdom of God is at hand; repent and believe in the gospel." (Mark 1:14–15)

In verse 15, the verb πληρόω ("to fulfill") is our clue as to how Mark 1:15 makes the connection between exile and the new era of "freedom." If "brevity is the soul of wit," then Mark wins. With one sentence, he addresses the issue of timing. This is well summarized by D.S. McComiskey in his article, "Exile and Restoration from Exile in the Scriptural Quotations and Allusions of Jesus." McComiskey writes,

> *Delitzsch demonstrates that, with the Hebrew wording (כעת הראשון), "The prophet intentionally indicates the time of disgrace . . . would extend over a lengthened period." Accordingly, since in the N.T. πληρόω always refers to completion of a period of time when it refers to time, Jesus, in Mark's estimation, must mean that some commonly known period of time is completed, and that time is most likely the aspect of the exile described in Isa 9:1. Therefore, Jesus considered the inception of the kingdom of God at the beginning of his ministry to coincide in some sense with the close of the exile.[3]*

For Mark, four hundred years of silence ended with our Lord's proclamation of the good news from God. In Mark 1:2–3, Mark first situates the method, ministry, and message of John the Baptist as prophetic fulfillment by combining three separate Old Testament passages. Mark writes:

> *As it is written in Isaiah, the prophet, ["Behold, I send my messenger before your face,] {who will prepare your way,} (the voice of one crying in the wilderness: 'Prepare the way of the Lord, make his paths straight')."*

In this passage, we see Mark combining three separate Old Testament passages:

"Behold, I send an angel before you to guard you on the way and to bring you to the place that I have prepared." (Ex. 23:20)

"Behold, I send my messenger, and he will prepare the way before me. And the Lord whom you seek will suddenly come to his temple; and the messenger of the covenant in whom you delight, behold, he is coming," says the LORD of hosts. (Mal. 3:1)

A voice cries: "In the wilderness prepare the way of the LORD; make straight in the desert a highway for our God." (Isa. 4:3)

With slight modifications, Mark, guided by the Holy Spirit, fashions these three verses to bring three essential concepts together.[4]

God ordained both the ministries of John the Baptist and Jesus. As reflected in the Gospel of Mark, four verses summarize the entirety of John's ministry. With the statement, "The time is fulfilled," the Lord Jesus draws a decisive line in the sand of time. The term for "time" (καιρός)[5] occurs in Mark 1:15. Unlike the Greek term *chronos*, which typically limits the reference to a measurable, quantitative aspect of time, *kairos* refers not so much to an hour or a date but to a particular moment or historic occasion. Guelich is correct in our estimation when he writes, "Instead of announcing a period of time reaching its conclusion, Jesus announces the coming to pass of a decisive moment in time."[6]

The days of darkness must give way to a season of light. Matthew's account focuses on the spiritual restoration of Zebulun and Naphtali, and indirectly of all Israel, from their era of darkness. Those who believe the message of the Lord Jesus will no longer walk in ignorance (darkness) of God's plans.

BREAKING OF SILENCE IN LUKE

While Matthew and Mark both position Jesus as the fulfillment of Old Testament prophecy, Luke takes this a step further. He frames up the Lord's earthly ministry as inaugurating a decisive turning point in human history. The event only hinted at in Mark 1:15a receives a remarkable exposition by Luke. In Mark, we learn that this is an important time. In Luke, we learn what time it is!

This remarkable exposition revolves around Luke's use of Isaiah 9:1. Matthew utilizes Isaiah 9:1 to focus on the time for light to dispel the darkness for God's people that began during their exile. Luke is more ingenious. He defines "the time is fulfilled" with theological precision. To build his case, Luke utilizes Isaiah as well. He takes an event from the life of Christ as the basis for his assertion: when Jesus reads Isaiah 61:1–2a in the synagogue at Nazareth and proclaims that the hearers are witnessing its prophetic fulfillment. This event (called "the rejection event" by scholars) likely occurred near the midpoint of Jesus' ministry. However, unlike Matthew and Mark who record this event in chronological order, Luke chooses to record it earlier, on the front end of his account.

THE POINT OF THE REJECTION NARRATIVE

The Synoptics record that Jesus walked into the synagogue of Nazareth, opened the scroll, and read aloud Isaiah 61:1–2a, which describes the essential components of the prophesied Messiah's ministry. Jesus then puts down the scroll. He sits down, looks at his audience, and says, "Today this Scripture has been fulfilled in your hearing." His audience was stunned. There was no mistaking what he was saying. Jesus had just announced that the benefits of the long-awaited Messiah were to be fulfilled in him. He, himself, was ushering in the temporal royal rule of God (and, by extension, the eschatological Jubilee) foretold by the ancient prophets. These were long-awaited events that brought the promise of God's kingdom on earth and freedom for God's people. They were also temporal events that were separate and distinct from the spiritual salvation that would come as a result of Jesus' sacrifice at Calvary.

While the average modern reader might not fully appreciate the impact of Jesus' announcement, it would not have been lost on Jesus' hearers. The nation of Israel had been waiting for thousands of years to see the fulfillment of Old Testament prophecy. The Jews in Nazareth did not reject Jesus because they had a problem with Scripture being fulfilled. They rejected Jesus because they had a problem with him being the one to do it. It did not help that Jesus confronted his hometown crowd with their unbelief. When Jesus announced that these prophecies were "fulfilled in your hearing," it set the Jews of Nazareth's teeth on edge.

Nothing about the rejection narrative suggests that the people of Nazareth understood that the death of Jesus would benefit mankind for spiritual salvation. They wanted to kill Jesus for their reasons. Let's see exactly why this is true.

Let's start with Luke's decision to move the rejection account to the beginning of his narrative account of the ministry of Jesus. This decision is distinct from Matthew and Mark who decided to place it in the correct chronological sequence. Luke's decision reflects the significance he places upon Jesus' announcement in his development of the storyline of the Lord's ministry. By doing so, Luke uses the narrative to frame up the rest of his Gospel.

Anderson summarizes:

> *Whereas in Mark's record the Rejection episode is placed just before the Galilean ministry draws to its close (Mark 6:1–6), and whereas Matthew presents it as the climax of the Galilean ministry (Matt. 13:53–58), in Luke's Gospel it appears to stand as a preface to the public ministry.*[7]

Luke sees the fact that the Lord Jesus defined his ministry in light of Isaiah 61:1–2a as so significant that he places this pericope out of historical chronological sequence. Among NT scholars, there is much debate about why Luke rearranges the sequence to put this sermon at the beginning of his account. Our view is that, whereas Matthew and Mark tell us what the Lord preached, Luke additionally tells us *why* he preached.

Luke 4:16–19 indicate that Jesus' ministry on earth would be a prophetic fulfillment of Isaiah 61:1–2a. Luke alone records,

> *And the scroll of the prophet Isaiah was given to him. He unrolled the scroll and found the place where it was written, "The Spirit of the Lord is upon me, because he has anointed me to proclaim good news to the poor. He has sent me to proclaim liberty to the captives and recovering of sight to the blind, to set at liberty those who are oppressed, to proclaim the year of the Lord's favor."*

Whether Jesus asked for the scroll or whether Isaiah was the book to be read on this particular day, Luke does not say. What is clear is that our Lord "unrolled the

scroll and found the place where it was written ...."
Given what the Lord says about the passage, we can
safely conclude that Jesus' choice in reading that
passage was intentional.

It is a majority view of New Testament scholarship
that Luke 4:18–19 = Isaiah 61:1–2a reflects the Septuagint,
the Greek translation of the Old Testament rather than
the Hebrew Masoretic text.[8] One basis for this claim is
"that 24 out of 26 words in the quotation are identical
with the LXX."[9] What is even more significant is the
LXX's utilization of the verb *euangelizesthai* ("to
proclaim good news") to translate the Hebrew verb בשׂר,
which means "to bear tidings."

In this passage, Jesus quoted Isaiah 61:1–2a and
announced, "Today this Scripture has been fulfilled in
your hearing." Many New Testament scholars see this
section in Luke as a summary of his ministry and
message during his time on earth.[10] One author writes,
"Luke 4:16–30, because of its placement at the
beginning of Jesus' public ministry, functions in a
programmatic way for the whole of Luke.[11] By
"programmatic," scholars are suggesting summarization.
In other words, everything Luke records—the entire
summation of Jesus' ministry in his eyes—is wrapped up
in this one statement: "Today this Scripture [the
physical manifestation of God on earth] has been
fulfilled in your hearing."

Hagner writes,

> This key pericope is virtually a programmatic or summarizing
> statement for the importance of living according to the
> righteousness of the newly arrived kingdom.[12]

Joel B. Green sets forth five supporting features of Luke 4:14–30 that form the basis for his claim that this pericope is programmatic for the whole of Luke's Gospel. He argues that

> *(1) [I]t is a specific illustration of the summary statement in Luke 4:14–15; (2) it is the first account of Jesus' public ministry in Luke's gospel; (3) it is the only place where Luke describes the substance of Jesus' synagogue teaching and is therefore representative for all of Jesus' synagogue teaching; (4) it is linked with both previous and subsequent emphases on the Spirit and the Sonship of Jesus; [and] (5) it is mentioned elsewhere in Luke–Acts (Luke 7:21–22; Acts 10:38).[13]*

David Hill also supports the programmatic thrust of Luke 4:16–30. He writes, "The position of the pericope is due to its character as an 'advance' notice of the essential message of Luke's theology . . . ."[14] If this is true, we should find throughout the rest of Luke's writings a constant reference to "the gospel of God" and the crucial time (the time of the royal rule of God) in which we live. Indeed, we do. Luke's account focuses heavily on the essence of this temporal period—the arrival of Messiah Jesus and the evidence of such, including his ministry and all of the accompanying miracles. Luke allows our Lord's reading of Isaiah 61:1–2a to define the time.

A closer examination of Luke 4:18–19 reveals several peculiarities. Notice,

> *"The Spirit of the Lord is upon me, because he has anointed me to proclaim good news to the poor. He has sent me to proclaim liberty to the captives and recovering of sight to the blind, to set at liberty those who are oppressed, to proclaim the year of the Lord's favor."*

Now notice how the verses read from Isaiah 61:1–2:

The Spirit of the Lord GOD is upon me, because the LORD has anointed me to bring good news to the poor; he has sent me to bind up the brokenhearted, to proclaim liberty to the captives, and the opening of the prison to those who are bound; to proclaim the year of the LORD's favor, and the day of vengeance of our God; to comfort all who mourn. (emphasis mine)

The first peculiarity concerns what is left out of the quote of Isaiah 61:1–2: the clause "he has sent me to bind up the brokenhearted." Second is the fact that the latter half of verse two drops off as well: "and the day of vengeance of our God; to comfort all who mourn." Additionally, a clause from Isaiah 58:6 is added: "to proclaim good news to the poor." What is the significance of these details? We just do not have enough information to determine whether the Lord Jesus introduced the clause from Isaiah 58:6 into his sermon or whether Luke introduced it to explain his original intent. Either way, it is safe to conclude that its inclusion helps Luke's readers to fully comprehend the Lord's intent by reading from the Isaianic text.

What we do know is that a comparison of the resultant text in Luke 4:18–19 reveals a clear intent of the Author/author to emphasize "the ministry of release" begun by Jesus.

Notice:

"The Spirit of the Lord is upon me, because he has anointed me to proclaim good news to the poor. He has sent me to proclaim liberty to the captives and recovering of sight to the

blind, to set at liberty those who are oppressed, to proclaim
the year of the Lord's favor."

JESUS THE ESCHATOLOGICAL JUBILEE

By the addition of Isaiah 58:6, Luke emphasizes that the Lord Jesus was sent by God "to proclaim *liberty* to the captives" and "to set at *liberty* those who are oppressed." Our English term "liberty" captures the Greek term ἄφεσις (*aphesis* = "release," "liberty"). This term is used more often by Luke than by any other NT writer.

More importantly, the Greek term ἄφεσις translates the Hebrew term דְּרוֹר (*děrôr*), (meaning "release" or "emancipation"), which occurs in Isaiah 61:1, and יוֹבֵל (*yôbēl*) (meaning literally "ram's horn," "trumpet," or transliterated "jubilee"), which occurs in Leviticus 25:10. Thus, with the ministry of Jesus, a new era begins.

While Matthew and Mark make a general reference to the rejection of our Lord in Nazareth (Matt. 13:53–58, Mark 6:1–6), it is Luke who both references the event and details the content of his message. Analysis reveals the core message of the Lord as he went from synagogue to synagogue, teaching.

Luke picks up on the Lord's reference to Isaiah 61 because of the significant theme Isaiah developed there. We agree with Bergsma, who states, "Isaiah 61 stands as the text that represents the most widely recognized biblical allusion to the jubilee outside of the Pentateuch."[15]

Luke alone develops this aspect of the Lord's ministry. The modern reader of Scripture typically does not appreciate the importance of the Jubilee doctrine developed in Leviticus 25, which outlines God's plan to give rest to the land and freedom for his people. Every 50 years was to be a year of jubilee in which the land was to be left fallow, slaves were to be set free, and land and property sold due to financial hardship were to be returned. The Jubilee had temporal significance, and it had spiritual significance, as well, reflecting God's sovereignty over his creation and his character as one who redeems and restores.

The Jubilee is central to God's character—so central, in fact, that God's decision to allow the enslavement of Judah to the Babylonians for 70 years is directly attributed to Judah's disregard for keeping it. 2 Chronicles 36:17–21 sketches the consequences of this failure. It records,

> Therefore, he brought up against them the king of the Chaldeans, who killed their young men with the sword in the house of their sanctuary and had no compassion on young man or virgin, old man or aged. He gave them all into his hand. And all the vessels of the house of God, great and small, and the treasures of the house of the LORD, and the treasures of the king and of his princes, all these he brought to Babylon. And they burned the house of God and broke down the wall of Jerusalem and burned all its palaces with fire and destroyed all its precious vessels. He took into exile in Babylon those who had escaped from the sword, and they became servants to him and to his sons until the establishment of the kingdom of Persia, to fulfill the word of the LORD by the mouth of Jeremiah, until the land had enjoyed its Sabbaths. All the days that it lay desolate it kept Sabbath, to fulfill seventy years.

God enslaved his people for 70 years in order to reclaim the land's right to have a sabbath rest.[16] Clearly, Judah did not learn the lesson. There is no report of the people celebrating or honoring a Sabbath-year rest after returning from Babylon.

Daniel 9:2 confirms that Judah's freedom came exactly 70 years later. Daniel 9:2 records, "In the first year of his reign, I, Daniel, perceived in the books the number of years that, according to the word of the Lord to Jeremiah the prophet, must pass before the end of the desolations of Jerusalem, namely, seventy years."

By referencing Isaiah 61:1–2a, once again Jesus brings to the forefront God's value of the Jubilee. What our Lord references briefly, Luke develops extensively. Having set the basis for his theological assertion by quoting both Isaiah 61:1–2a and 58:6, both of which emphasize "release," Luke develops this theme throughout the rest of both his Gospel and the book of Acts. By quoting two passages with this same idea in Isaiah, Luke establishes the controlling theme of our Lord's message. He came to establish God's eschatological "release" (or jubilee) of his people.

The most explicit NT reference to the Jubilee is found in Luke 4, where Jesus applies the Jubilee proclamation of Isaiah 61 to himself.[17] Thus, Jesus is God's Jubilee for his people. The Isaiah quote ends with our Lord's assertion that liberty (ἄφεσις) has come in the year of God's favor. Jesus, God's anointed one, brings "good news" of ἄφεσις (liberty, release) to the poor, blind, captives, and oppressed. Through his ministry, Jesus proves that both physical and spiritual realities are present in his proclamation.

What Jesus alludes to in brief, Luke expands significantly. The noun ἄφεσις occurs 17 times in the New Testament. Ten of these occurrences are divided equally between Luke's Gospel and Acts. With the exception of Luke 4:18, which quotes Isaiah 58 and 61 and emphasizes the consequence of sin's enslavement of mankind, the rest of the occurrences of the noun in these two books accompany the noun ἁμαρτία (*hamartia* = sin). Jesus proclaims man's release or liberty from sin. In every occurrence, the term ἁμαρτία is plural. Thus, the ministry of Jesus announces that both the enslavement to sin and the punishment associated with that enslavement are ended. Those who believe in both the message and the messenger of God are free, liberated, and released to live as God intended. This is not just a release from sin, but also a much larger package of liberties that includes bondage, oppression, physical sickness, demonic possession, and poverty. Jesus released the power of God in his people and his community in a way that his listeners had never seen before.

That the ministry and message of Jesus Christ is the inauguration of a new era for God's people—the year of God's favor—is explicitly stated by Luke in his Gospel. One very explicit declaration of this fact is found in Luke 16:16:

> *The Law and the Prophets were until John; since then the good news of the kingdom of God is preached, and everyone forces his way into it.*
>
> *This verse makes three assertions:*
>
> 1. *The Law and the Prophets until John;*
>
> 2. *From then on, the good news of the kingdom of God is preached;*
>
> 3. *Everyone should make every effort to find their way into it.*

The first assertion literally says, "the Law and the Prophets until John." There is no verb in the clause in the original Greek sentence. Which verb one adds depends on the interpreter's understanding of the Lord's assertion. So how do we know which verb to use?

The phrase "the Law and the Prophets," with several other variations, occurs more than ten times in the New Testament.[18] Most New Testament scholars agree that this phrase is a reference to the entirety of the Old Testament.[19] In order to determine the verb for the first assertion, the NASB and the NIV base it on the verse's second assertion, "From then the good news of the kingdom of God is preached." By using the second assertion as the basis for the first, they translate it, "The Law and the Prophets *were proclaimed* until John." However, we believe it is wiser to more deeply understand the significance of the second assertion before we commit to a verbal insert for the first. Indeed, after this analysis, we will offer our own (more accurate) translation of this verse.

The second assertion begins with the temporal marker ἀπὸ τότε (*apo tote* = "from then"), which indicates "a time from which some event has occurred."[20] Bock offers this conclusion regarding the significance of ἀπὸ τότε, i.e., that it is a key phrase used by Luke to denote a significant turning point in the sequence of events.[21] In essence, from the time John [was handed over to prison], "the [the good news of the] kingdom of God has been shouted out loud" (ἡ βασιλεία τοῦ θεοῦ εὐαγγελίζεται). A definition of "the kingdom of God" does not occur in this verse. Luke frequently uses the verb εὐαγγελίζεται.[22] The verbal aspect allows for the conclusion that this message was ongoing, as Luke 4:43 makes clear. In other words, Jesus had a one-point sermon during the first three years of his ministry— the good news of the kingdom of God.[23]

What is "the good news of the kingdom of God"? As the reader will discover in the following chapter, "the kingdom of God" is a technical term that refers to the permanent physical manifestation of God's sovereign or royal rule on the earth in sovereign power. Just as heaven has a permanent physical representation of God's sovereign administration (God rules in person through both divine and angelic leadership), earth's transition has begun to achieve a similar reality. In heaven, God's sovereign administration is carried out by angels with various levels of authority in concert with their assigned duties. On earth, it will be carried out with Messiah Jesus (and, ultimately, King Jesus) and his administrators (the disciples, ultimately, those who prove themselves worthy of this honor).

Jesus not only announced this new reality but demonstrated it through his works and the works of those invited to participate in his sovereign administration. The evidence of this includes healing, exorcisms, justice, provisions for the poor, and the ability to set aside natural law, i.e., walk on water and multiply physical resources.

Thus, we can conclude that the commonality between "the Law and the Prophets" and "the kingdom of God" is the revelation and execution of God's will. The instruments of God's revelation on earth were the Law of Moses and the prophets, which ended with John the Baptist (Matt. 11:13) as God's executors. The disclosure and execution of God's will now work through the God-Man and his disciples.

"EVERYONE FORCES HIS WAY"

The third and final assertion of Luke 16:16 is notoriously tricky to understand.[24] The ESV suggests, "And everyone forces his way into it." The NET Bible says, "And everyone is urged to enter it." Perhaps a better way to discover Luke's intended meaning is to begin with those aspects of the clause generally agreed upon by most scholars.

There is much debate regarding the verb βιάζεται (*biazetai*) as to its intended meaning in the clause. There is little debate about the coordinating conjunction καί ("and") and its indication of a sequence of closely related events.[25] The adjective πᾶς (*pas*) is highlighted explicitly in the *Greek-English Lexicon of the New Testament and Other Early Christian Literature* concerning Luke 16:16 to mean "Everyone without exception."[26] This is an important detail because it can mean one of two things: (1) Every man, woman, and child desires to enter the kingdom of God; or since we know that this is not true (2) All are commanded, encouraged, or motivated to do so.[27] In other words, whatever the object of concern, every man, woman, boy, and girl of the specific category must be capable of doing it.

It is the verb βιάζεται (*biazetai*) that is the *crux interpretum*. Cortés and Gatti offer an excellent overview and scholarly conclusions regarding the meaning of Luke 16:16. They conclude that the verb *biazetai*:

Basically means "to force." It is frequently used in the middle voice, "everyone makes use of force," either in a positive sense— "tries hard to enter"—or in a negative, hostile sense— "uses force against it." . . . . However, it is not limited to physical force. The verb is used very often in the sense of moral force or insistence, that is, "of the genteel constraint imposed on a reluctant guest," or a friend or relative ....[28]

Bock offers an excellent summation of what the term potentially means in Luke 16:16:

Option 1:
The term is negative and in the middle voice: "all act violently against it"; the kingdom is subject to universal opposition.

Option 2:

The term is harmful and should be translated as "everyone forces his way into it"; people try to bring the kingdom to earth violently.

Option 3:

The term is positive and in the middle voice: "Everyone tries to force his way into it [the kingdom]."

Option 4:

The verb has a softened force and is passive: "All are urged insistently to come in."[29]

Both Bock and Cortés/Gatti come to similar conclusions. Cortés and Gatti's findings are worth stating in full:

> *We conclude, therefore, that this interpretation is grammatically, linguistically, and syntactically correct. In addition to making perfect sense, it seems to be the most acceptable, in the context of the entire gospel as well as in the immediate context. The preaching of the good news of the kingdom has as a corollary the invitation to all listeners to belong to such a kingdom. We have seen that, according to the five strata of tradition, it is not accurate that all were rushing to accept the good news or that all were rejecting it. The appeal, however, to receive such good news is made to all, opponents and nonopponents, pious and sinners, rich and poor alike. "The law and the prophets were in effect up until John [the Baptist]; from that time on the good news of the reign of God is being announced, and every person [without exception] is expressly invited to belong to it."[30]*

In summary, we see Luke 16:16 as another way of saying the same thing as Mark 1:14–15. The Lord Jesus consistently shouted out loud the good news of God. Just as does Mark 1:14–15, so does Luke 16:16, evidence of a significant temporal divide, the subject matter of the kingdom, and man's need to respond appropriately. My translation of Luke 16:16 follows:

> *The Law and the Prophets ruled until John; from then, the good news of the sovereign administration of God is shouted out loud, and everyone is expressly invited to participate.*

The royal rule of God is open to all disciples who take up their cross and follow our Lord's example. All disciples should strive as their primary goal to join the Lord Christ on his throne, ruling over all creation for one thousand years!

Notes

[1] Scholars typically label the account that describes Jesus' explicit self-identification as the Messiah by pointing to the fulfillment of Isaiah 61:1-2a and the response of the people of Nazareth by revolting and attempting to kill him "the rejection" account.
[2] Matthew 4:12 and Mark 1:14.
[3] McComiskey, D. S. (2010). "Exile and Restoration from Exile in the Scriptural Quotations and Allusions of Jesus," *Journal of the Evangelical Theological Society*, 53(4), 677.
[4] Notice, Exodus 23:20 and Malachi 3:1 = "As it is written in Isaiah the prophet, 'Behold, I [God] the Father] send my messenger [John the Baptist] before your [Jesus'] face, who will prepare your [Jesus'] way'"; Isaiah 40:3 = "The voice of one [John the Baptist] crying in the wilderness: 'Prepare the way of the Lord [Jesus], make his [Jesus'] paths straight.'"

[5] Louw and Nida conclude that καιρός generally has the meaning "an indefinite period of time, but probably with the implication of the relation of a period to a particular state of affairs— 'age, era.'" Louw, J. P., & Nida, E. A. (1996). In *Greek-English Lexicon of the New Testament: Based on Semantic Domains* (electronic ed. of the 2nd edition., vol. 1, 647). United Bible Societies.

[6] Robert A. Guelich, "Mark 1–8:26," vol. 34A, Word Biblical Commentary (Dallas: Word, Incorporated, 1989), 43.

[7] Anderson, Hugh. "Broadening Horizons: The Rejection at Nazareth Pericope of Luke 4:16-30 in Light of Recent Critical Trends," *Interpretation* 18 (1964): 260.

[8] Choosing the Septuagint gave Luke the grammatical basis to employ the verb "to announce good news," which is used in Isaiah 61:1. That verb becomes the dominant one throughout his Gospel. There is no evidence that writers were using that verb extensively at that time. There is research that shows Luke uses the Septuagint because it allows him to tie the ministry of Jesus to Isaiah and therefore to extend it beyond Isaiah into the other prophecies that relate to the Messiah. The tie between Luke and Isaiah is that Jesus believed that he fulfilled these prophecies and Luke *shows* that he fulfilled them. This allows Luke to expand on this notion of Jesus as the fulfiller of those prophecies. (The Hebrew word *basar* used in Isaiah has the same significance but is not as overt.)

[9] Combrink, H. J. B. (1973). "The Structure and Significance of Luke 4:16–30," *Neotestamentica*, 7, 34.

[10] Walt Russell concludes:

> The number of Lukan scholars who see Luke 4:16–39 in a paradigmatic or programmatic light is legion. Most significantly see Bruce Chilton, "Announcement in Nazara: An Analysis of Luke 4:16–21, " in Gospel Perspectives, Vol. 2 ed. (R. T. France and David Wenham; Sheffield: JSOT, 1981) 147–72; ed. H. Conzelman, The Theology of Luke (New York: Harper, ET 1960); H. Anderson, "Broadening Horizons," Int 18 (1964) 259-75; L. C. Crockett, "The Old Testament in the Gospel of Luke" (unpublished dissertation; Brown Univ., 1966); idem, "Luke 4:25–27 and Jewish-Gentile Relations in Luke-Acts, "JBL 88(1969) 177-183; David Hill, "The Rejection of Jesus at Nazareth," NovT 13 (1971) 161-180; and R. C. Tannehill, "The Mission of Jesus according m Luke 4:16–30, " in Jesus in Nazareth (Berlin: de Gruyter, 1972), 51-75.

Walt Russell, "The Anointing with The Holy Spirit In Luke-Acts" (1986). *Trinity Journal*, 7, 48; footnote 2.

[11] Siker, J. S. (1992). "'First to the Gentiles': A Literary Analysis of Luke 4:16–30," *Journal of Biblical Literature*, vol. 111, 75.

[12] Donald A. Hagner, "Matthew 1–13," vol. 33A, *Word Biblical Commentary* (Dallas: Word, Inc., 1993), 101.

[13] Joel B. Green, *The Gospel of Luke* [*NICNT*] (Grand Rapids: Eerdmans, 1997), 207.

[14] David Hill, "The Rejection of Jesus at Nazareth," *NovT* 13 (1971), 178.

[15] Bergsma, John Sietze. "The Jubilee from Leviticus to Qumran: A History of Interpretation" (Netherlands: Brill, 2007), 198.

[16] The reason Judah spent seventy years in captivity in Babylon was her refusal to celebrate the year of Jubilee during her first 490 years in the land of promise.

[17] Christopher R. Bruno, "Jesus is Our Jubilee . . . But How?" *JETS* 53/1 (March 2010), 95.

[18] "The Law and the Prophets" (Matt. 7:12, 22:40, Luke 16:16, John 1:34, Acts 13:15, 24:14, Rom. 3:21); "the Law or Prophets" (Matt 5:17), "all the Prophets and the Law" (Matt 11:13); "the Law of Moses and the Prophets" (Luke 24:44, Acts 28:23).

[19] Donald A. Hagner, Matthew 1–13, vol. 33A, *Word Biblical Commentary* (Dallas: Word, Inc., 1993), 105. Leon Morris, "The Gospel According to Matthew," *The Pillar New Testament Commentary* (Grand Rapids, MI; Leicester, England: W.B. Eerdmans; Inter-Varsity Press, 1992), 107. J. Reiling and J. L. Swellengrebel, *A Handbook on the Gospel of Luke*, UBS Handbook Series (New York: United Bible Societies, 1993), 567–568.

[20] Stanley E. Porter, *Idioms of the Greek New Testament* (Sheffield: JSOT, 1999), 147.

[21] Darrell L. Bock, Luke: 9:51–24:53, vol. 2, *Baker Exegetical Commentary on the New Testament* (Grand Rapids, MI: Baker Academic, 1996), 1351.

[22] Bammel, E. "Is Luke 16,16-18 of Baptist's Provenience?" *The Harvard Theological Review* 51, no. 2 (1958): 101–6. http://www.jstor.org/stable/1508933.

[23] See a defense of this ascertain in Chapter 2 of this book.

[24] Cortés and Gatti writes,

> I. H. Marshall wrote not long ago: "Few sayings in the Gospels are so uncertain in interpretation as this one." Other authors would agree with E. Moore's statement: "Most students of the Gospels would concur with Etienne Trocmé in placing this saying high on the list of 'obscure and sometimes totally incomprehensible dominical sayings' "; or with E. F. Scott: "Not a few commentators have confessed themselves utterly baffled by it"; C. Spicq: "Ces versets sont parmi le plus énigmatiques de N.T., et toute interprétation qu'on en propose ne peut être qu'une hypothèse." C. Stuhlmueller writes more specifically: "The last part of v. 16 is very difficult." Cortés, J. B., S. J., & Gatti, F. M. (1987). "On the Meaning of Luke 16:16," *Journal of Biblical Literature*, 106, 247.

[25] Johannes P. Louw and Eugene Albert Nida, *Greek-English Lexicon of the New Testament: Based on Semantic Domains* (New York: United Bible Societies, 1996), 788.

[26] William Arndt et al., *A Greek-English Lexicon of the New Testament and Other Early Christian Literature* (Chicago: University of Chicago Press, 2000), 783.

[27] The prepositional phrase εἰς αὐτὴν (*eis autan* = "into it") has little, if any, exegetical debate.

[28] Juan B. Cortés S.J. and Florence M. Gatti, "On the Meaning of Luke 16:16," *Journal of Biblical Literature* 106 (1987): 249–250, 252.

[29] Darrell L. Bock, Luke: 9:51–24:53, vol. 2, *Baker Exegetical Commentary on the New Testament* (Grand Rapids, MI: Baker Academic, 1996), 1352-1353.

[30] Juan B. Cortés S.J. and Florence M. Gatti, "On the Meaning of Luke 16:16," *Journal of Biblical Literature* 106 (1987): 258–259.

CHAPTER 5

What Is the Kingdom of God?

Mark 1:14–15

Now after John was handed over (to prison), Jesus came into Galilee, shouting out loud the good news (about the sovereign administration of) God, by saying, "The time is fulfilled, and the sovereign administration of God is at hand; repent and believe in the good news (about the sovereign administration of God)." (author's translation, emphasis added)

Our Lord's message of the good news primarily concerns two things: timing ("the time is fulfilled") and rule ("the sovereign administration of God").

In the previous chapter, we discovered that our Lord's definition of "the good news from God" involved a decisive temporal turning point—that is, a demarcation between the age of the Law and Prophets and the kingdom of God.

We now focus on the second declarative statement: "The kingdom of God is at hand" (ESV).

George E. Ladd concludes: "[T]he Kingdom of God was the central message of our Lord's ministry."[1] Yet, for those who believe in the priority of Mark's Gospel, the first occurrence of the phrase comes without a definition or an explicit Old Testament history.[2] As his ministry progressed, Jesus made several explanatory comments about the nature of the kingdom of God. Of particular importance is Luke 17:20–21, which records a dialogue between Jesus and the Pharisees regarding the nature of this kingdom. Luke reports,

> *Being asked by the Pharisees when the sovereign administration of God would come, he [Jesus] answered them, "The sovereign administration of God is not coming in ways that can be observed, nor will they say, 'Look, here it is!' or 'There!' for behold, the sovereign administration of God is in the midst of you." (author's translation)*

This passage has been greatly misunderstood by both liberal and conservative scholars alike. Confusion about the nature of the kingdom of God naturally leads to confusion about what the Lord Jesus meant when he talked about it. Clearly, the Pharisees' misunderstanding did not end with their generation. We see the same in the Church Fathers and modern scholarship. Yet, Gerald F. Hawthorne argues that "Luke 17:20–21 contains the clearest enunciation of the *essential* nature of the Kingdom anywhere recorded in the words of Christ.[3]

Regarding the Pharisee's question, Hawthorne reasons,

> *The Pharisees' question . . . showed exactly what their concept of the nature of the Kingdom was, and what it was they were*

emphasizing. For to the Pharisees the Kingdom of God was primarily something that could be comprehended in a space-time concept: "When shall the Kingdom come?" To them it was "a world-embracing order, into which men may 'enter,' or from which they may be excluded" . . . political, national, especially involving them as God's chosen people; physical, primarily of this world.[4]

The Jews saw the coming rule of God over Israel as the center of the earth. To them, breaking off the yoke of Rome would have been the best evidence that the kingdom had arrived, and that is precisely what they were expecting. We continue to see this expectation even in the disciples' question just minutes before our Lord ascended to heaven a few days before Pentecost. They asked, "Lord, will you at this time restore the kingdom to Israel?" (Acts 1:6).

But the Lord Jesus made clear to his audience that the sovereign administration of God would not first evidence itself by overturning earthly governments. In fact, the rule of God has been on earth since before creation itself. Just because God has limited the overt manifestation of his sovereign rule does not mean that he is not in control. What was in question was the degree to which man is involved in God's rule on earth and the evidence thereof. How much of God's authority does man have and what are the overt manifestations that we can see?

Our Lord's declarative assertion is that "the sovereign administration of God is already among you [ἐντὸς ὑμῶν]." Scholars have wrestled with the final clause of verse 21. Modern translations offer several possible ways to translate the original Greek, including "within you" (ESV); "among you" (NLT); and "in your midst" (NET). Because the sovereign administration of God involves jobs that men and women must earn,[5] we agree with Colin H. Roberts' conclusion regarding the meaning of ἐντὸς ὑμῶν as "with you, in your possession, if you want it, now."[6] Roberts, an Oxford papyrologist, suggested that the expression means "within your reach."[7] G.R. Beasley-Murray cites Roberts with approval regarding this translation.[8] Bock also makes room for this sense.[9] Professor H. J. Cadbury, writing for the *Christian Century,* also endorses Roberts' thesis, saying that so understood "the sentence means . . . the availability, the accessibility, the opportunity, of the kingdom."[10]

Our Lord's essential points were that the sovereign administration of God cannot come where it already exists and that participation in the rule of God remains open to men and women, i.e., leadership positions remain to be filled. This is the critical stage where disciples must make every effort "to participate in the sovereign administration of God."

Sadly, our English translations do not help much when a particular nuance of a term is required. For example, our English term "kingdom" is pretty much limited to geography. When the average English speaker hears the term, he or she immediately thinks of a physical location. This is how the term is generally used in everyday conversation.

The Exegetical Dictionary of the New Testament suggests "kingdom" or "reign" as the correct translation of the Greek noun βασιλεία (*basileia*/kingdom).[11] It concludes:

> *In secular Greek the meaning of the word alternates between a functional sense—royal sovereignty, monarchy, royal dignity, royal office—and the geographical sense of kingdom or realm .... Both meanings are also represented in the NT: sometimes the reference is to kingdom or realm (e.g., Matt 4:8; Mark 6:23; 13:8; Rev 16:10), and sometimes to royal sovereignty (e.g., Luke 19:12, 15; Rev 1:6; 17:12). At times*

which it represents cannot be determined (e.g., Matt 12:25f.). This poses difficulties for translation, since kingdom ... does not include the functional meaning, and the use of sovereignty ... to represent the geographical sense is obsolete today.[12]

A Greek-English Lexicon of the New Testament and Other Early Christian Literature also agrees with this basic assessment.[13] In their lexicon, Louw and Nida draw a similar conclusion.[14] Therefore, lexically speaking, *basileia* (βασιλεία) can have either a functional or a geographical sense. How a particular author uses the term in a particular passage must be discerned from the immediate context.

In reference to God, one will need to pay close attention to the context. A majority of New Testament scholars agree that in the NT, when coupled with God, βασιλεία (kingdom) "is essentially an abstract noun referring to the 'rule' or 'kingship' of God."[15] I. Howard Marshall would add,

[T]here is a growing agreement that the phrase KG should be taken to refer primarily to God's sovereignty rather than to the realm over which he is sovereign.[16]

As far back as 1902, Dalman wraps both the Old Testament (*malkut* = kingdom) and the New Testament (βασιλεία = kingdom) in this conclusion when he writes,

[T]hat in the OT, Jewish literature, and in Jesus' teaching, "malkut, when applied to God, means always the 'kingly rule,' never the kingdom,' as if it were meant to suggest the territory governed by him."[17]

In 1988, Joel Marcus published an excellent article entitled, "Entering into the Kingly Power of God," in which he concludes,

> *Relying especially upon exegesis of Jewish parallels and of the first category of Jesus' sayings, many twentieth century interpreters have claimed that the predominant meaning of malkûtā'/basileia in Jesus' teaching is "reign," "rule," "sovereignty," "dominion," "kingly power" rather than "realm."*[18]

Even more insightful is Marcus' assertion that the New Testament emphasis is not so much on the fact of God's reign, but the exercising impact of this reign on his creation, something he calls "a 'dynamic' interpretation of *basileia*." He writes,

> *In speaking of a "dynamic" interpretation of basileia, I depart somewhat from Dalman, whose favorite translations of malkut/basileia are "sovereignty," "kingly rule," and even "theocracy." These translations are not explosive enough; they portray God's basileia as the abstract fact that he rules, rather than the force of his personal self-assertion that manifests his kingship by overpowering the resistance to it in the earthly sphere. . . Camponovo . . . points out that in the targum malkûtā' is never used to translate stative references to God's kingship ("God is king"), but rather is always used dynamically ("God has displayed his kingly power").*[19]

A BETTER TRANSLATION

While Dalman's favorite translation is "sovereignty" and Marcus prefers "kingly power," we prefer "sovereign administration." By using "the sovereign administration of God," we emphasize the active role God is now playing in the day-to-day running of this world through his Son Jesus, the God-Man, and those whom the Father gives to him. The phrase "the sovereign administration" focuses on the rulers of the coming physical manifestation of God on earth. When God manifests his physical presence, it will no longer be through burning bushes, storm clouds, fire on mountaintops, or other inanimate objects. Instead, it will be through the God-Man and those whose extreme faithfulness is rewarded with this honor. The sovereign administration of God refers to Jesus' administration or government.[20] All disciples are greatly encouraged to pursue participation in the leadership of the coming kingly rule.

Perhaps nothing has contributed more to the confusion regarding the meaning of the phrase "the kingdom of God" than the New Testament use of the verb "to enter." Matthew (19:24), Mark (9:47, 10:23, 24, 25), Luke (18:24, 25), John (3.5), and Paul (Acts 14:22) all employ a Greek infinitive with a preposition to express this idea. The clause εἰσελθεῖν εἰς τὴν βασιλείαν τοῦ θεοῦ = "to enter the sovereign administration of God" occurs nine times in the New Testament.[21] As English speakers, we use the verb with several different nuances. For example, we say that a person enters a building, room, or car. When we do, we understand intuitively that the person moved from one physical location to another. We also used the verb "to enter" in a non-local sense. We have all probably at one time or another been approached about "entering" a raffle to win a prize. In this sense, we pay a fee, write our information on a form, or are given a ticket with a matching number as the other part is dropped into a basket. Without any need for explanation, we understand that, by doing so, we have "entered" the contest. Yet, we do not personally get inside the basket! We could have just as easily said that we agreed "to participate" in the contest.

This latter sense is found in the New Testament. As the second possible nuance of the Greek verbal εἰσελθεῖν εἰς, Arndt, Danker, Bauer, and Gingrich in their lexicon suggest that New Testament usage supports the sense "to enter into an event or state, of pers[on] come into someth[ing] = share in someth[ing], come to enjoy someth[ing]."[22] Louw and Nida suggest a similar sense: "[t]o begin to experience an event or state—'to begin to experience, to come into an experience, to attain.'"[23]

In the New Testament, we see this usage as the best way to explain how one enters into a state or condition in specific contexts. Matthew 25:21 promises the faithful a reward. That reward is defined as "entering into the joy" of their master. The joy of one's master is a state of being. One can share, experience, or participate in another's joy.

Therefore, we offer the following translation of Luke 17:20–21:

Being asked by the Pharisees when the sovereign administration of God would come, he answered them, "The sovereign administration from God is not coming in ways that can be observed, nor will they say, 'Look, here it is!' or 'There!' for behold, the sovereign administration is available to you now."

GOD'S FOUR-STEP PLAN

God the Father has assigned the God-Man several responsibilities to carry out in order to manifest a physically sustained appearance on the earth.

Phase 1 was the physical manifestation of himself through Jesus to combine the rule of heaven (God) and earth (Man) under the God-Man. This phase was accomplished through the life, death, and resurrection of Jesus Christ, which is reflected in John 10:30, 33–38. Phase 2 was to reward with the kingship of the earth the faithful God-Man whose completion is evidenced by his seat at the right hand of the throne of God (Heb. 12:2). Phase 3 is the building of a kingdom leadership team, first from his first-century disciples, then from the larger class of disciples called the church. Only the most faithful will receive an invitation to be included in the ruling class of the God-Man's rule on earth during the Millennium. Inclusion in this leadership team is not automatic. One must earn it by faithfulness. Phase 4, the final phase of the Father's plan, culminates with the God-Man delivering all authority back to the Father for all eternity-future (1 Cor. 15:24).

Seeing the intended meaning of the phrase "the kingdom of God" as the sovereign administration of God through the physical manifestation of his authority on the earth is critical. This alone explains the multiple conditionalities expressed in the New Testament for how a disciple attains elite status in the court of the ruling class with Jesus Christ. Understanding the nature of the sovereign administration of God will protect the intent of the New Testament and prevent false doctrine. Otherwise, one will have to believe in works salvation. There is no other way to harmonize the good news from God and the good news about Jesus Christ.

To acquire elite status in the ruling class is a matter of sanctification and not salvation. The recognition of this one fact would have prevented the whole lordship salvation debate from arising in the first place (and robbing many of their confidence in the good news of salvation by faith alone). Participation in the sovereign administration of God is a reward gained by faithfulness. If one proves unfaithful, he or she will not participate in it. In essence, he or she will not rule with Christ.

SUFFERING: A CONDITION TO RULE

That this is true is easily proven. Luke writes that the apostle Paul exhorted his Asian converts to suffer so they could "participate in the sovereign administration of God." Notice in Acts 14:21–22, Luke writes,

> *When they had preached the gospel to that city and had made many disciples, they returned to Lystra and to Iconium and to Antioch, strengthening the souls of the disciples, encouraging them to continue in the faith, and saying that through many tribulations we must earn participation in the sovereign administration of God. (author's translation)*

Acts 14:22b should remove any doubt in the readers' mind that the prerequisite of suffering "to participate in the sovereign administration of God" makes the attainment of salvation (the forgiveness of sin) outside the intent of this passage. Scripture nowhere teaches that a person must suffer to be saved from his or her sin.

Paul had already preached to these converts, and they had expressed faith in Jesus Christ prior to Paul's final exhortation. The disciples in Lystra, Iconium, and Antioch were already faithful believers. Yet Paul calls for suffering to "to participate in the sovereign administration of God."

Whatever else the clause "to participate in the sovereign administration of God" might mean, it cannot be the attainment of personal salvation from sin. To receive the righteousness of God, one must believe in the Lord Jesus Christ, period. There is no other conditionality. One does not have to suffer to be saved from his or her sins. One may suffer because he or she is saved, but no one obtains salvation by personal suffering. Otherwise, one would need to determine how much suffering one would need to experience to be saved. Could one know if he or she has suffered enough to be saved before death? The questions are endless!

We understand that there are those who believe that salvation is obtained through works. While the phrase "once saved always saved" is overly simplistic, we unashamedly adhere to the belief that just as Abraham believed the promise of God and obtained justification, we, too must do the same.

In no less than six separate passages in the New Testament, the clause "enter the kingdom of God" occurs. Mark 9:47 has the clause once. Mark 10:23–25 has it three times (with parallels in Matthew 19:23–24 [twice] and Luke 18:24–25 [twice]). John 3:5 and Acts 14:22 both have the clause once. In each case, there is a conditional prerequisite beyond simple faith.

As we shall see, one is able to participate in God's coming rule on the earth, but not as a member of the elite ruling class. This conclusion makes room for the possibility that one's faithfulness will determine rewards and that unfaithful believers will not share in kingdom leadership or a host of other blessings associated with the Lord Jesus and his earthly rule.

FAITHFULNESS: A CONDITION TO RULE

Matthew 21:43 makes it crystal clear that one's participation in the sovereign administration of God can be lost due to unfaithfulness. The text states,

"Therefore, I tell you, the sovereign administration of God will be taken away from you and it will be given to a people producing its fruits." (author's translation)

In context, the Lord Jesus is addressing "the chief priests and the elders of the people," who were questioning him about his authority (Matt. 21:23). In response, Jesus asks a question: "The baptism of John, from where did it come? From heaven or from man?" Because the Pharisees and elders were unwilling to answer the Lord's question, he did not answer theirs.[24]

Please notice that this was not the end of the matter. The unwillingness of the Pharisees and elders to believe "the baptism of John" was from heaven (and therefore, required that their submission and repentance) had tremendous ramifications. In response to their heart-heartedness, the Lord rebuked them (Matt. 21:31b–32) and pronounced that their participation in "the sovereign administration of God" would be taken away and given to a people producing its fruit. That participation in this sovereign administration can be taken away should settle the debate regarding what it is not. It is not spiritual salvation. Salvation—i.e., forgiving one's sin—cannot be taken away from one person and given to another. Participation in royal leadership of the coming rule of God is what the Jewish leaders lost.

In our Lord's denunciation of the Jewish leaders, he states, "Truly, I say to you, the tax collectors and the prostitutes go into the kingdom of God before you." Instead of the usual verb εἰσελθεῖν, the text has προάγω, which means to "go before, lead the way, lead forward."[25] Literally, Matthew 21:31b says, "Truly, I say to you all, "The tax collectors and the prostitutes are going ahead of you all into the sovereign administration of God."

If the phrase "the kingdom of God" means "the sovereign administration of God" as we suggest, then how can the tax collectors and prostitutes go ahead of the Jewish leaders? The road to reigning with Jesus begins with repentance (Matt. 3:2). Man must reverse his behaviors to come into compliance with the rules of heaven. He or she commits to living under the manifested authority of God. He or she obeys the good news from God. Repentance makes all men equal in the eyes of God. Each is able to gain elite status. It all depends on one's faithfulness.

The reason repentant tax collectors and prostitutes can gain participation in the sovereign administration of God while the Pharisees and Jewish leaders are losing it is because of the difference in their states of repentance. The self-righteous religious leaders see no need for repentance, while the humble sinners gladly receive the grace of God and live in light of it. One repents, and the other does not. It is that simple. This is precisely what John the Baptist was teaching, too!

PIETY: A CONDITION TO RULE

Mark 10:23-25 indicates that the rich will have great difficulty participating in the sovereign administration of God. Notice,

> *Jesus looked around and said to his disciples, "How difficult it will be for those who have wealth to participate in the sovereign administration of God!" And the disciples were amazed at his words. But Jesus said to them again, "Children, how difficult it is to participate in the sovereign administration of God! It is easier for a camel to go through the eye of a needle than for a rich person to participate in the sovereign administration of God." (author's translation)*

These comments of the Lord Jesus follow a question-and-answer session with a rich young ruler, who asks,

"What must I do to inherit eternal life?" This question could potentially have been asked out of ignorance. Perhaps the young man did not know that righteousness comes by believing the promise of God as Abraham had done. Perhaps by "inheriting eternal life" the young man was asking how to get his sins forgiven so he could go to heaven when he dies. However, if he asked the wrong question because he did not understand the issues correctly, it seems incumbent on the Lord Jesus to have set him straight. Thus, the Lord Jesus might have said, "Your question is incorrectly phrased. If you want to know how to get your sins forgiven so you can go to heaven, then you must believe in the Gospel." Plain and simple, right?

Yet, this is not what Jesus did. First, he told the rich young ruler to work hard by keeping all of the commandments. Then after the young man reported that he had kept all the commands from his youth, the Lord Jesus doubled down on the work ethic. He told the young man to go work even harder by giving all his wealth to the poor and come follow him, presumably to death. Even if the young man had been capable of keeping the law perfectly, it still would not have resulted in his salvation. Even if the young man had sold all that he had and given the proceeds to the poor, it still would not have resulted in his sins being forgiven. So why did the Lord Jesus give this young man what appears to be incomplete information? If you bring a modern and limited understanding of what the "gospel" is, you will conclude the wrong thing.

To "inherit eternal life" does not mean to believe in Jesus for the forgiveness of sin. Notice that the Lord equated his question with "participating in the sovereign administration of God." What the young man was asking Jesus is this: "How can I ensure that I will be a ruler in the coming sovereign administration of God?" Jesus informed him that by rejecting worldly pleasure in this life, he could have wealth in the next. Building great treasures in heaven now ensures that one will be included in the coming sovereign administration from heaven.

Sadly, the young man walked away. The level of commitment necessary to receive great rewards in heaven was more than he was prepared to do. Thus, he will have no position of authority in the coming sovereign administration of God. This rich young ruler is the poster child for the third soil in Jesus' parable of the sower.[26] The deceitfulness of riches choked the Word.

SPIRITUAL SALVATION: A CONDITION TO RULE

John 3:3, 5 says that one must be born of the water and the Spirit to see/enter the kingdom of God. In what are the only occurrences of the phrase "the sovereign administration of God" in the complete corpse of Johannine literature, John 3:3, 5 is unique. Please pay close attention to Jesus' remarks that John repeats in this passage. In a dialogue with Nicodemus about the need for a second birth, Jesus educates him about the *spiritual* birth. The reader must understand that Nicodemus not only believes in the existence of God, but he also believes in the promises of God. He understands the basics and can dialogue with Jesus as long as the conversation utilizes language he understands. However, just like many modern readers, once the language changes from what he is accustomed to, there is a bit of confusion. So the Lord changed the reference point.

First, the Lord states, "Unless one is born again, he cannot see the sovereign administration of God." In the second statement, he says, "Unless one is born of water and the Spirit, he cannot participate in the sovereign administration of God." Taken at face value, one would think that the two verses mean the same thing. Seen in parallel:

Unless one is born	again	he cannot see the kingdom of God
Unless one is born	of water/the Spirit	he cannot enter the kingdom of God

It would appear that verse five defines verse three. To be born of water and the Spirit explains how one is born again. To be born of water is repentance as evidenced by the ministry of John the Baptist, which the Pharisees and the elders refused to do because of their self-righteousness. To be born of the Spirit is to receive righteousness by faith in the promise of God. We know what "to participate in the sovereign administration of God" means. Is it the same as "to see the kingdom of God?"

The verb ὁράω (horaō = to see), which literally means to see with the eyes, appears more than 400 times in the New Testament, with a human doing the seeing. Of the seven different nuances listed by Louw and Nida, "to experience" is among them, specifically "to experience an event or state, normally in negative expressions indicating what one will not experience— 'to experience, to undergo.'"[27] According to Louw and Nida, John 3:36 should reflect this nuance in the translation. Instead of the ESV's translation, "Whoever believes in the Son has eternal life; whoever does not obey the Son shall not see life," a better reflection of the intended meaning is, "Whoever does not obey the Son shall not experience life." John 8:51 and Hebrews 11:5 also have this nuance. Remember, this is one of the same nuances for "to enter" that is our basis for the conclusion that "to participate" or "share in" is the intended meaning of the phrase "enter the kingdom of God." Without the new birth, one cannot participate or share in the sovereign administration of God.

Perhaps some might argue that John is unnecessarily pleonastic at this point. The Jews had among them those who believed that their Jewishness ensured their inclusion in the coming Davidic kingdom. Nicodemus, like everyone else we meet in the stories about Jesus, is ignorant about the exact nature of the kingdom of God and in need of instruction about how it comes and who will participate in it. Thus, if the new birth is necessary to participate in the sovereign administration of God, then it certainly cannot be *equal to* the sovereign administration of God. It is the difference between sanctification and salvation.

Paul writes in 1 Corinthians 6:9–10 that only faithful believers will inherit the kingdom of God. He writes,

Or do you not know that the unrighteous will not inherit the kingdom of God? Do not be deceived: neither the sexually immoral, nor idolaters, nor adulterers, nor men who practice homosexuality, nor thieves, nor the greedy, nor drunkards, nor revilers, nor swindlers will inherit the kingdom of God.

Sadly, in order to maintain their theological systems, some New Testament teachers must maintain that Paul is here speaking of unbelievers. Their belief system does not allow for unfaithful believers to suffer adverse consequences at the Bema Seat judgment. Thus, all conditional passages in the NT either speak of people who were once saved but are subsequently lost again, or they were never saved and were simply masquerading as believers.

LOSING RULING STATUS

Perhaps no church in the New Testament was as gifted as the church in Corinth. It had all the gifts of the Spirit. They had the best Bible teachers in church history: the apostle Paul, Peter, Apollos, Aquila, and Priscilla. Yet, they had more problems than many other churches combined. A study of 1 and 2 Corinthians reveals various issues emanating from the wicked culture of the city of Corinth. Just as today, Christians were living with one foot in the world and one foot in the church. Thus, they were being called out by the apostle Paul. Some were acting in ignorance. Others were acting in willful disobedience. All were in serious need of repentance.

The use of "unrighteous" (*adikos* = adjective) in 1 Corinthians 6:9 follows the verb "to do wrong" (*adikeō* = to do wrong) in 1 Corinthians 6:8. It is members of the Corinthian church who are doing wrong and whom Paul is rebuking. There is no indication that Paul considers the man in 1 Corinthians 5 who is cohabitating with his stepmother to be an unbeliever. Instead, Paul treats him as a brother in Christ. In fact, Paul says in 1 Corinthian 5:9–11:

> *I wrote to you in my letter not to associate with sexually immoral people—not at all meaning the sexually immoral of this world, or the greedy and swindlers, or idolaters, since then you would need to go out of the world. But now I am writing to you not to associate with anyone who bears the name of brother if he is guilty of sexual immorality or greed, or is an idolater, reviler, drunkard, or swindler—not even to eat with such a one.*

The issue does not seem to be who is saved or not, but who is living a repented life or not. Paul's laundry list of sinful behaviors renders one unable to "inherit the kingdom of God." Some quickly conclude that to "inherit the kingdom of God" means the same thing as "to be saved so he or she can go to heaven." Those who believe this view see these individuals as disinherited or having lost their salvation due to their sinful behavior.

Yet Paul states in 2 Timothy 2:19, "Let everyone who names the name of the Lord abstain from wrongdoing." The question is not whether Christians can commit these sins. (We all know they can.) The question is what the consequences will be for those who lived sinfully. Robertson and Plummer are correct when they say,

> The word ['wicked' in v. 9] is suggested by the previous, adikeō ['you cheat and do wrong,' v. 8], and not with the adikoi, ['the wicked,' of v. 1]."[28]

Therefore, we are confident that Paul is speaking of true believers in Corinth whose lifestyle will deny them an inheritance in the sovereign administration of God. Louw and Nida indicate that the verb "to inherit" in the New Testament means to receive something of considerable value that has not been earned,[29] which is true in a technical sense. However, when used to refer to spiritual matters, we are convinced that the meaning refers to rewards that must be earned.

It is also easily demonstrable that sons received their inheritance if and only if they remained faithful to their benefactor. Two Old Testament illustrations make this point. Rueben, the oldest son of Jacob dishonored his father by sleeping with one of Jacob's concubines. In punishment, God gave his birthright to the sons of Joseph (see 1 Chronicles 5:1). Likewise, Esau lost his inheritance due to his frivolous disdain for family tradition (see Genesis 25:31). Thus, in a sense, inheritance was earned.

Consistent throughout both the Old and New Testaments is the notion of possession. Once an inheritance was taken, one could exercise all the rights and privileges of ownership. Thus, for a believer to have no rights or privileges indicates the loss of rewards and not legal status.

Finally, Paul encourages the Thessalonians about their worthiness to participate in the sovereign administration of God because they were suffering. He encourages them by saying,

> This is evidence of the righteous judgment of God, that you may be considered worthy of the sovereign administration of God, for which you are also suffering—since indeed God considers it just to repay with affliction those who afflict you, and to grant relief to you who are afflicted as well as to us, when the Lord Jesus is revealed from heaven with his mighty angels in flaming fire, inflicting vengeance on those who do not know God and on those who do not obey the good news of our Lord Jesus. (author's translation)

Acts 14:22 indicates that Paul admonished new churches to accept suffering as their ticket to participation in the sovereign administration of God. The Thessalonians received Paul's instructions and were commended for their suffering. Through suffering, the Thessalonians become *worthy* of this honor. Balz and Schneider list as the definition "consider worthy" for the verb *kataxioō* used in 2 Thessalonians 1:5.[30] That suffering for righteousness results in a gain of rewards is a fundamental truth of the New Testament (Matt. 5:10–12; Luke 22:28–30). Notice that belief in Jesus Christ alone does not make one worthy. To be worthy, one must add suffering!

These added conditionalities make it impossible to see entering the kingdom of God as being equal to obtaining salvation from sin. As we understand the nature of salvation, there is only one condition: believe on the Lord Jesus and you shall be saved. Faith in the finished work of Jesus Christ brings personal salvation. Faithfulness to Christ brings rewards, which is what the New Testament teaches of the kingdom of God, a reward for faithfulness.

When one encounters the phrase "the kingdom of God," he or she should think of "the physical manifestation of the sovereign administration of God on earth." God is not waiting to rule, but rather his rule now manifests in the person and works of Jesus Christ. God's authority over creation is physically manifested through the deeds of the God-Man and those to whom he permits to wield that authority.

ALREADY AND NOT YET

The physical manifestation of the sovereign administration of God on earth has already begun. It began with the life and ministry of Jesus Christ. Some New Testament scholars recognize this "already/not yet" aspect of this time.

David Nah explains,

"Already/not yet" is the view that the kingdom of God has already been inaugurated in the person and ministry of Jesus Christ but will not reach consummation until his return in glory.[31]

Dr. Darrell Bock has argued to our satisfaction the validity of the "already/not yet" understanding of our Lord's ministry. In his book *Progressive Dispensationalism*, Bock writes,

> *The biblical characteristic of viewing events from a variety of perspectives shows us that one can make points from "both-and" perspectives without denying either side of the present-future relationship. It is possible to get fulfillment "now" in some texts, while noting that "not yet" fulfillment exists in other passages. In fact, in some texts, fulfillment can be initial or partial, as opposed to being final and total. As a result, one can speak of inaugurated eschatology without denying either what the Old Testament indicates about a future, earthly kingdom or what the New Testament asserts about the arrival of the kingdom as part of fulfillment in the first coming of Jesus. To call such eschatology inaugurated is only to say the process of fulfillment has commenced; there is more—even much more—to come . . . . "Already-not yet" teaching links the plan of God into a unified whole. It allows one to see both continuity and discontinuity in the outworking of God's promises.*[32]

Bock's argument for seeing an "already/not yet" perspective in the writings of Luke/Acts is detailed in his article "The Reign of the Lord Christ" in the book *Dispensationalism, Israel, and the Church: The Search for Definition.*[33]

In one of his responses to the religious leaders challenging his authority, Jesus said,

> *"But if it is by the finger of God that I cast out demons, then the kingdom of God has come upon you. When a strong man, fully armed, guards his own palace, his goods are safe; but when one stronger than he attacks him and overcomes him,*

he takes away his armor in which he trusted and divides his
spoil." (Luke 11:20–22)

Jesus' ability to drive out demons and to give that authority to whomever he desires is evidence that the sovereign administration of God has come to earth. Satan's kingdom is being systematically ruined by the more muscular man Jesus, who takes his spoils by making believers from the kingdom of darkness. Also, evidence of the works of the "strong man Jesus" includes raising the dead, healing the sick, and setting aside natural law, i.e., walking on water. The works of Jesus are still possible in the lives of his converts, which continue the evidence of the ever-present reality of the physical manifestation of God's sovereign earthly rule.

This is why we speak of the traditional phrase "kingdom of God" as the "physical manifestation of the sovereign administration of God on earth." It better reflects our understanding of the New Testament's use of the word "kingdom." This is critical for the reader to understand.

The good news from God involves the announcement that the physical manifestation of the sovereign administration of God has come near. The age of this administration has physically manifested on earth in the ministry of Jesus Christ. The God-Man rules actively and is building his administration.

The active rule of God on earth manifested with the conclusion of the age of Law and Prophets and the beginning of the ministry of the Son of God on earth. In Jesus Christ, God physically manifested himself on earth by exercising sovereign authority.

BRINGING SOVEREIGN RULE TO EARTH

Since God has ruled all creation from heaven since before creation itself, in what sense has the sovereign administration of God come to earth? How is God's manifest earthly rule different from God's sovereign rule from heaven? During the age of the Law and Prophets, God largely worked the miraculously supernatural from heaven. The only exceptions were the prophets who, through God, exercised supernatural power on earth. As reflected in the Old Testament, not a single man or woman exercised sovereign power on earth who was not a prophet or prophetess, with the lone exception of a few judges.[34] Outside of the prophets Moses, Elijah, Elisha, and Samuel, there were no other miracle workers during the age of Law and Prophets.

However, Jesus came preaching that the physical manifestation of the sovereign administration of God had come near. He announced that the lordship of God over his creation was no longer being exercised from heaven exclusively by God or his messengers. It was now being exercised on earth through anyone who believes in God, including his Son.

Jesus made clear that the evidence of the physical manifestation of God's sovereign administration on earth is the ability of his disciples to set aside natural law. Luke 9:1 and 2 report,

And he called the twelve together and gave them power and authority over all demons and to cure diseases, and he sent them out to proclaim the sovereign administration of God and to heal. (author's translation)

Subsequently, Luke10:1–2a and 9 also report,

> *After this the Lord appointed seventy-two others and sent them on ahead of him, two by two, into every town and place where he himself was about to go. And he said to them . . . "Heal the sick . . . . and say to them, 'The sovereign administration of God has come near to you." (author's translation)*

Luke 10:17 reports, "The seventy-two returned with joy, saying, 'Lord, even the demons are subject to us in your name!'" The evidence of God's active sovereign rule on the earth is the ability of a disciple of Christ to exercise power over all demons and to heal all diseases. A disciple can be a man, a woman, a boy, or a girl. This is the age of the physical manifestation of the sovereign rule of God on earth.

Sadly, New Testament scholarship for the most part has failed to understand the intended meaning of our Lord's proclamation in Luke 10:9. Primarily, the majority focus has been on the meaning of ἤγγικεν, which is often translated as "to come near" or "approach."

Dr. Bock is correct when he writes,

> *There is currently a large debate about the meaning of the term ἤγγικεν. Does the perfect tense here of the verb "to draw near" mean "to approach," or does it mean "to arrive"?*

Louw and Nida suggest "come near"[35] as the basic meaning of the term. Thus, scholars debate the influence of the stative aspect on the meaning. As with so many theologically significant truths in the Bible, scholars often create more problems than they solve. The stative aspect (perfect tense) conceives of the action by the language user as reflecting a given state of affairs.[36] The resultant state is primary in the mind of the speaker. The sovereign administration of God has come near and remains as such until a change is announced, which Jesus did not do.

On several occasions, ἤγγικεν has contextual qualifying details that help establish our Lord's intent. The question of whether the sovereign administration of God has "approached" or "arrived" is scholarship debating peripherals. We are inclined to follow Guelich's conclusion:

> Thus the Kingdom of God has "come into history," the appointed time "has been fulfilled," even though the full appearance is yet to come. [37]

This interpretation supports the "already/not yet" aspect of the sovereign administration of God. The sovereign rule of God has come to earth, and men and women can now participate in it. [38]

Notes

[1] George Eldon Ladd, The Gospel of the Kingdom (Grand Rapids: Eerdmans, 1959), 7. This conclusion is also supported by G.R. Beasley-Murray, Jesus and the Kingdom of God (Grand Rapids: Exeter, 1986), x; B. Chilton (ed.), The Kingdom of God (London/Philadelphia 1984), 1.

[2] The phrase "the kingdom of God" does not appear in the Old Testament at all. See Mark 1:15.

[3] Gerald F. Hawthorne, "The Essential Nature of the Kingdom of God," Westminster Theological Journal 25, no. 1 (1962): 35.

[4] Ibid., 35-36.

[5] This conclusion we shall defend later in this chapter.

[6] Colin H. Roberts: "The Kingdom of Heaven (Lk. XVII.21)," *Harvard Theological Review*, XLI, 1, Jan. 1948, 8.

[7] C. H. Roberts, "The Kingdom of Heaven" (Lk XVII.21)," HTR 41 (1948), 1-8.

[8] G. R. Beasley-Murray, "The Kingdom of God in the Teaching of Jesus," *Journal of the Evangelical Theological Society* 35, no. 1 (1992): 23.

[9] Darrell L. Bock, "The Son of David and the Saints' Task: The Hermeneutics of Initial Fulfillment," *Bibliotheca Sacra* 150 (1993): 450.

[10] H.J. Cadbury, "The Kingdom of God and Ourselves," *Christian Century* 67 (1950), 172-173.

[11] Horst Robert Balz and Gerhard Schneider, *Exegetical Dictionary of the New Testament* (Grand Rapids, Mich.: Eerdmans, 1990–), 201.

[12] Ibid.

[13] Arndt, W., Danker, F. W., Bauer, W., & Gingrich, F. W. (2000). In *A Greek-English Lexicon of the New Testament and Other Early Christian Literature* (3rd ed.). University of Chicago Press, 168-169.

[14] Louw, J. P., & Nida, E. A. (1996). In *Greek-English Lexicon of the New Testament: Based on Semantic Domains* (electronic ed. of the 2nd ed., vol. 2), 44

[15] France, R. T. (2002). *The Gospel of Mark: A Commentary on the Greek Text* (W.B. Eerdmans: Paternoster Press), 93.

[16] I. Howard Marshall, "The Hope of a New Age: The Kingdom of God in the New Testament," *Themelios* 11, no. 1 (1985): 6.

[17] G. Dalman, *The Words of Jesus, Considered in the Light of Post-Biblical Writings and the Aramaic Language* (Edinburgh, 1902), 91-147.

[18] Joel Marcus, "Entering into the Kingly Power of God," *Journal of Biblical Literature*, vol. 107, No. 4 (Dec, 1988), 663-664.

[19] Ibid, footnote 9.

[20] In the United States, it has become common to speak of a president's "administration" as shorthand for the president, his cabinet, and the policies that characterize his running of the country.

[21] Matthew 19:24 is parallel to Mark 10:25 and Luke 18:25. Mark 10:23 is parallel to Luke 18:24.

[22] William Arndt, Frederick W. Danker, et al., *A Greek-English Lexicon of the New Testament and Other Early Christian Literature* (Chicago: University of Chicago Press, 2000), 294.

[23] Johannes P. Louw and Eugene Albert Nida, *Greek-English Lexicon of the New Testament: Based on Semantic Domains* (New York: United Bible Societies, 1996), vol. 1, 806–807.

[24] Matthew 22 does answer the Pharisees and elders' question about the source of the Lord's authority. It comes from his Father. The parable of the wedding feast is especially insightful (Matt. 22:1–14) in this regard.

[25] Balz & Schneider, 1990–vol. 3, 150.

[26] The traditional interpretation of the parables of the four soils is consistently misinterpreted and applied because most do not understand the difference between the good news of God and the good news of Jesus Christ.

[27] Johannes P. Louw and Eugene Albert Nida, *Greek-English Lexicon of the New Testament: Based on Semantic Domains* (New York: United Bible Societies, 1996), 807–808.

[28] A.T. Robertson and Alfred Plummer, *A Critical and Exegetical Commentary on the First Epistle of Paul to the Corinthians*, (Edinburgh: T & T Clark, 1914), 118.

[29] Johannes P. Louw and Eugene Albert Nida, *Greek-English Lexicon of the New Testament: Based on Semantic Domains* (New York: United Bible Societies, 1996), 572.

[30] Horst Robert Balz and Gerhard Schneider, *Exegetical Dictionary of the New Testament* (Grand Rapids: Eerdmans, 1990–), 265.

[31] David Nah, "The Already and the Not Yet," in Lexham Survey of Theology, ed. Mark Ward et al. (Bellingham, WA: Lexham Press, 2018).

[32] Craig A. Blaising and Darrell L. Bock, *Progressive Dispensationalism* (Wheaton: Victor, 1993), 97-98.

[33] Darrell L. Bock, "The Reign of the Lord Christ," *Dispensationalism, Israel, and the Church: The Search for Definition*, ed. by Craig A. Blaising and Darrell L. Bock (Grand Rapids: Zondervan, 1992), 37-67.

[34] Joshua, Gideon, and Samson.

[35] Balz & Schneider, 1990–vol. 1, 370.

[36] Stanley E. Porter, *Idioms of the Greek New Testament* (Sheffield: JSOT, 1999), 21, 22.

[37] R.A. Guelich, "Mark 1–8:26," vol. 34A, 44.

[38] The meaning of the phrase "to enter the kingdom of God" will be discussed in Chapter 7 of this book.

CHAPTER 6

Repent and Believe in the Good News

Now after John was handed over (to be imprisoned), Jesus came into Galilee, shouting out loud the good news from God by saying, "The time is fulfilled, and the sovereign administration of God is at hand; change your behavior and believe in the good news from God." (Mark 1:14–15, author's translation)

The final component of the good news about the sovereign administration of God is a two-part command. Literally, the clause reads, "You all change your behavior, and believe in the good news from God" (author's translation). Just as John the Baptist (whose message is synonymous with our Lord's message), repentance is the primary responsibility of the people of God and should result from belief in God's good news.

As with so many other soteriological truths, the verb "to repent" has taken on a life of its own that often bears no relationship to a specific text. Just as the term "gospel" suffers from illegitimate totality transfer, "repentance" is no longer contextually defined either. It is given a generic meaning in every place it occurs in the New Testament. Regardless of translation, there is no distinction offered between what the term meant during the ministry of Jesus and what it came to mean during the ministry of Paul and the apostles or our modern age.

The following paragraph, taken from *The Bible Knowledge Commentary* published by the faculty of Dallas Theological Seminary, is typical. It says,

> *Repentance and faith (belief) are bound together in one piece (not temporally successive acts).[1] To "repent" (metanoeō; cf. Mark 1:4) is to turn away from an existing object of trust (e.g., oneself). To "believe" (pisteuō, here pisteuete en, the only NT appearance of this combination) is to commit oneself wholeheartedly to an object of faith. Thus, to believe in the good news meant to believe in Jesus Himself as the Messiah, the Son of God. He is the "content" of the good news (cf. v. 1). Only by this means can one enter into or receive (as a gift) the kingdom of God (cf. 10:15).[2]*

John D. Grassmick makes the same mistakes as most New Testament conservative scholars. First, in their attempt to protect the doctrine of salvation by faith alone, "repentance" and "belief" are equated. Second, they insist that "to repent" means to turn away from an object of trust. Third, they instruct that to "believe in the gospel" means to believe that Jesus is the Messiah, the Son of God, and that this meaning occurs from the very first day of our Lord's ministry. Fourth, they teach that Jesus is the "content" of the gospel in Mark 1:15. Lastly, they posit that one is guaranteed "entrance" into the kingdom of God by believing in Jesus. None of these conclusions is true.

Adopting Grassmick's conclusion leads to many contradictions in the writings of Paul, Peter, and John. To reach this conclusion, the command "to repent and believe" is assigned a non-contextual meaning. In order to maintain the false teaching that every occurrence of the term must refer to the death, burial, and resurrection of Jesus Christ for the forgiveness of sin, the language of the text must be made to say that which one would not normally conclude. Similarly, "to repent" must be made to mean changing one's mind about Jesus Christ, which results in personal salvation from sin. Contextual meaning is ignored to foster this prejudiced notion.

Grassmick states that only by repentance and belief in Jesus "can one enter into or receive (as a gift) the kingdom of God." As is so typical, he insists that "repentance" and "faith" are opposite sides of single coin. Yet, it must have clearly escaped Grassmick that Jesus told the chief priests and the Pharisees, "The kingdom of God will be taken away from you and given to a people producing its fruits" (Matt. 21:43). If the kingdom of God can be taken away, then in no sense can it be equated with personal salvation. Unless, that is, one is willing to conclude that God can take away personal salvation for unfaithfulness, which is precisely what one must conclude if he or she follows Grassmick's logic.

Students of Scripture must never conclude what a particular word or phrase means in a particular passage until he or she has studied it in its proper historical context. Repentance in the New Testament has suffered from this error. Many assume incorrectly that any talk of repentance automatically refers to personal salvation from sin by believing in Jesus Christ. But does it? From the opening pages of the New Testament, repentance is commanded—first by John the Baptist, then by Jesus

Christ. In both cases, contextual clues are given regarding the intended meaning. If John or Jesus intended something different than what the religious leaders would have understood, given their knowledge of Israel's past history, nothing in the text signals that this is the case.

HISTORICAL EVALUATION OF THE TERM: REPENTANCE

The very first recorded occurrence of the verb "to repent" as a translation of the Greek verb μετανοέω (*metanoeō*) falls from the lips of John the Baptist in Matthew's Gospel. Did the people instantly understand what John meant? The answer is an emphatic *no*. Luke 3:10 makes that abundantly clear. We know this because the people asked him, "What then shall we do?" One would naturally think that such a direct question warrants a very direct answer. If the modern definition of repentance is accurate, why did John not simply respond, "Believe in Jesus, the Christ, and be saved"?

We describe John the Baptist's call for repentance in Luke 3:10–14 as a reformation of behavior. Certain behaviors were to stop and other behaviors were to start. The new behavior would put one in a proper relationship with God at his coming wrathful judgment. John's call to "repentance" is aimed at the children of God (not a bunch of unbelievers in the modern sense of the word). With this in mind, perhaps we should abandon the term "repentance," given that it has acquired a meaning not intended by its first usage in the New Testament. No one, certainly not John the Baptist, attached the meaning "the death, burial, and resurrection of Jesus Christ" to this word. This would be a later development that must not be read back into the synoptic record.

Consistent with Old Testament usage, a call to change one's behavior in order to turn away the wrath of God was never the first command to "unsaved folk." It is a command to the people of God. Even our English term "repent," with its prefix "re," inherently acknowledges that to re-pent, the person must have previously been penitent.

What is clear from a study of the Old Testament is this: There was no clear prescription that everyone followed when called to turn to God. It was not a twelve-step program. What one did depended on what one needed to avoid.

COMMANDS TO GOD'S PEOPLE IN THE OLD TESTAMENT: *SHUV (TURN)*

The term most consistently used throughout the Old Testament to describe the commanded behavior of God's people when they had abandoned righteous living is the Hebrew verb שׁוּב (*shúv*). Regarding this verb, David A. Lambert summarizes that none of the other Old Testament terms for the concept had

> the number of attestations or the suggestiveness to stand as the appointed articulation of "repentance" in the Hebrew Bible. That honor has been reserved for a peculiar phrase, "return [shuv] to YHWH," whose range proves far more impressive, from the early, eighth-century prophets, to Jeremiah, to the deuteronomistic writings, and on to a variety of postexilic texts.[3]

Lambert additionally, adds,

> Whereas shuv lends the sense of a particular kind of turn, it is the prepositions with which shuv is paired that determine whether the emphasis in the verse is placed on what the agent turns toward or what he or she turns away from. Turning "away" (min) and turning "toward" ('el) can be, ultimately, the same physical motion of reversal.[4]

Mark J. Boda, in his book, *Return to Me*, an in-depth theological study of the doctrine of repentance in both the Old and New Testaments, draws similar conclusions to Lambert regarding the meaning of the verb *shúv*. He writes,

> *Within Hebrew the most common word associated with repentance is the verb šûb (qal; 'turn', 'return').[7] One can 'turn' (šûb) to God or righteousness,[8] as well as 'turn away' (šûb) from evil.[9] This root is employed in the hiphil [Hebrew verb where the subject causes the action] to refer to turning away from evil[10] as well as to the action of one to prompt repentance in another.[11] The noun šûbâ refers to repentance in Isaiah 30:15.[12]* [5]

One must pay close attention to Boda's footnote comments in this section. He demonstrates that, in the Old Testament text, the idea of turning "from" or "to" something or someone is the function of the preposition attached to the Hebrew verb. The verb שׁוּב (*shúv*), itself, simply means "to turn."

More than one verb or noun is used in both the Old and New Testaments to express the idea of "turning." There is also the recognition that repentance is expressed through images, forms, and concepts. Regardless, one is called to either make an internal shift or a change in external behavior, or both. Neither the Hebrew nor the Greek term is used to refer to an unbeliever who becomes a converted member of the children of the Jewish God.

As Boda recognized in his insightful work, Zechariah 1:1–6 may be considered a good commentary on the Old Testament concept of repentance.[6] Zechariah 1:1–6 records,

In the eighth month, in the second year of Darius, the word of the LORD came to the prophet Zechariah, the son of Berechiah, son of Iddo, saying, "The LORD was very angry with your fathers. Therefore say to them, Thus declares the LORD of hosts: Return [שׁוּב (šûb)] to me, says the LORD of hosts, and I will return [שׁוּב (šûb)] to you, says the LORD of hosts. Do not be like your fathers, to whom the former prophets cried out, 'Thus says the LORD of hosts, Return [שׁוּב (šûb)] from your evil ways and from your evil deeds.' But they did not hear or pay attention to me, declares the LORD. Your fathers, where are they? And the prophets, do they live forever? But my words and my statutes, which I commanded my servants the prophets, did they not overtake your fathers? So they repented [שׁוּב (šûb)] and said, 'As the LORD of hosts purposed to deal with us for our ways and deeds, so has he dealt with us.'"

The Hebrew verb שׁוּב (*shúv*) is used in this passage to describe both the actions of the Jewish people and God, the Almighty. No notion of coming to faith in a salvific sense is intended here. The text does not describe a call to unbelievers to become believers in God in a salvific sense. The people of God are called upon to change their behavior (to stop sinning), which will cause God to change his behavior (to start blessing them again).

THE NEW TESTAMENT USAGE OF SHÚV

Boda highlights a similar passage in the New Testament, Acts 26:16–20. Here interpreters must force themselves not to rush to judgment. While it is typical of New Testament students to label Paul's Damascus Road experience as his conversion, one must not frontload the meaning of the term "conversion." If by "conversion" one means spiritual salvation by faith in Jesus Christ, a very serious error results.

If we believe that Abraham was made righteous by faith in the promise of God, and we very well should because it is true (Gen. 15:6, Rom. 4:3), then Paul certainly believed in the God of Abraham and operated his life on the basis of belief in the promises God made to Abraham, Isaac, Jacob, and King David. Paul's conduct prior to his encounter with Jesus Christ on the Damascus Road is consistent with Old Testament saints. His ignorance about who Jesus Christ was should not be interpreted to mean that Saul (eventually changed to Paul) was unsaved in the later New Testament sense. To do so is to commit an illegitimate totality transfer.

In Acts 26:12–18, the apostle Paul rehearses for the last time his Damascus Road experience. After Saul asks a question about the identity of the one who appeared to him, the Lord Jesus states,

> "I am Jesus whom you are persecuting. But rise and stand upon your feet, for I have appeared to you for this purpose, to appoint you as a servant and witness to the things in which you have seen me and to those in which I will appear to you, delivering you from your people [the Jews—genitive masculine singular] and from the Gentiles [genitive plural]— to whom [masculine plural] I am sending you to open their [masculine plural] eyes, so that they may turn [epistrepho—to turn-infinitive] from darkness to light and from the power of Satan to God, that they may receive forgiveness of sins and a place among those who are sanctified by faith in me.' "Therefore, O King Agrippa, I was not disobedient to the heavenly vision, but declared first to those in Damascus, then in Jerusalem and throughout all the region of Judea, and also

to the Gentiles, that they should repent and turn to God,
performing deeds in keeping with their repentance."

That Paul was ignorant of Jesus Christ's identity does not mean that Paul was unsaved. In his case, his "repentance" involved a change in his understanding and behavior toward Jesus. He came to believe in Jesus Christ as the fulfillment of all Old Testament promises, which required his repentance regarding his previous unbelief. However, "to repent" does not mean that one changes his or her mind about Jesus Christ in all cases. Nor does it mean "to get saved" automatically. Rather, accurately understanding the call to repent and turn to God requires careful attention to the audience that receives the command. For the children of God (Israel), repentance is very different than for the Gentiles, who did not know God for generations. The call for repentance by Jesus in connection with the "gospel" of God in Mark 1:15 must not include the post-Easter call to repentance for the Gentiles. Rather, the good news from God commands repentance by the Jews in light of their rebellious living.

THE "AT HAND" NATURE OF THE KINGDOM OF HEAVEN

Why does the "at hand" nature of the kingdom of heaven require repentance = a call to return to God? Both John the Baptist and Jesus preached the same message. The message of Matthew 3:2, 4:17, and Luke 3:18 is summarized by saying, "He [John] preached good news to the people." Matthew 3:6 indicates that the people "were baptized by him [John the Baptist] in the river Jordan, confessing their sins." The reader must understand that neither the Lord Jesus nor John the Baptist called people to repent of their sins and believe in the Lord Jesus so they could go to heaven. Rather, John declared that in association with the physical manifestation of God on earth would be the manifestation of God's wrath that could be avoided only by living a righteous life.

John the Baptist told the people that one coming after him "will baptize you with the Holy Spirit and fire" (Matt. 3:9). Who or what John meant is not made clear in the text, and certainly not a one, if any, of his listeners fully understood when and how the fulfillment would come.

This fact is borne out in the Book of Acts. In Acts 19:1–7, the apostle Paul encounters disciples of John the Baptist more than 25 years after they received the baptism of John. These disciples were completely ignorant of the good news about Jesus Christ or that the baptism of the Spirit had come. Yet these devotees to John's teaching were serious people. Notice,

> And it happened that while Apollos was at Corinth, Paul passed through the inland country and came to Ephesus. There he found some disciples. And he said to them, "Did you receive the Holy Spirit when you believed?" And they said, "No, we have not even heard that there is a Holy Spirit." And he said, "Into what then were you baptized?" They said, "Into John's baptism." And Paul said, "John baptized with the baptism of repentance, telling the people to believe in the one who was to come after him, that is, Jesus." On hearing this, they were baptized in the name of the Lord Jesus. And when Paul had laid his hands on them, the Holy Spirit came on them, and they began speaking in tongues and prophesying. There were about twelve men in all.

Paul's encounter with these disciples of John the Baptist is insightful. His question, "Did you receive the Holy Spirit when you believed?" is rather surprising. One would think Paul's first question would have been an inquiry about their faith in Jesus Christ. Did their response to John's message bring their salvation? The text is not clear regarding what Paul expected them to have believed.

Their response, "No, we have not even heard that there is a Holy Spirit," is even more interesting. First, in Matthew 3:11, John is reported to have promised, "I baptize you with water for repentance, but he who is coming after me is mightier than I, whose sandals I am not worthy to carry. He will baptize you with the Holy Spirit and fire." Now, we were not privy to every sermon John preached. We don't know whether John said the same thing every single day or whether what we read in Matthew and Luke are summary conclusions.

What exactly these twelve men heard from either John the Baptist or the disciples of John the Baptist (see John 1:35; Mark 2:18) is not certain. However, if we take their words at face value, it seems very odd that they would not have heard John's promise of a coming baptizer with the Holy Spirit. Equally, the text does not identify the men as Jewish (and thus knowledgeable of the Old Testament Scriptures), but as disciples of John. Thus, the idea that they had never heard of the "Holy Spirit" seems incredible.

Perhaps Acts 19:2 does not correctly express the original intent of the Greek text as reflected in the ESV. The way Luke expresses the men's response to Paul is not easy to understand. Some have suggested the verse should read, "We did not so much as hear whether the Holy Spirit is given." In this reading, the men are not expressing ignorance of the Holy Spirit, but ignorance regarding his coming.

We agree with H.A.W. Meyer, who asserts,

> *The existence of the Holy Spirit at all cannot have been unknown to the men, because they were disciples of John and John's baptism of water had its essential correlate and intelligible explanation in the very baptism of the Spirit—even apart from the O.T. training of these men, according to which they must at least have been aware that the Holy Spirit was something existing—ἔστιν (to be so accented) must necessarily be taken as …. No, we have not even heard whether the Holy Spirit is there (already present on the earth). Accordingly, they still remained ignorant whether that which John had announced, namely, that Jesus would baptize with the Holy Spirit, had already taken place, and thus the πνεῦμα ἅγιον had become present.*

Thus, what the men were ignorant of was not the existence of the Holy Spirit, but the fulfillment of John's promise that "He will baptize you with the Holy Spirit and fire." It is a little under 2,500 miles from Jerusalem to Ephesus. In our modern way of thinking, we expect news to travel fast. Yet, this was not the case in ancient times. Israel was a small nation with very little international importance. Not much would have made the front-page news coming out of Israel for the rest of the world during Jesus' day.

Luke organizes the book of Acts around the four different groups who received the baptism of the Holy Spirit with the evidence of speaking in tongues to show God's inclusion of all peoples in his new work: the disciples of Jesus (Acts 2:4), the Samaritans (Acts 8:14–17); Gentiles (Acts 10:44–46); and the disciples of John the Baptist (Acts 19:6). In each case, the Holy Spirit came to a group that had not experienced the promise of John the Baptist.

In Acts 19:1–7, we see men who were very serious about living their daily lives in light of the promise resulting from John's baptism. John's message was not a call to start believing in God, but a message to start living as God demands. It was a call for the people to live their daily lives in such a way as to avoid a negative judgment by God.

John the Baptist declares that the soon-coming judgment of God made repentance necessary so that people could avoid the negative consequences of the coming great separation. Sadly, by translating every occurrence of τὸ εὐαγγέλιον (*to euaggelion*) "the gospel," modern translations prejudice the reader in favor of "the gospel of Christ," instead of "the gospel from God," which was John the Baptist's focus.

"The Gospel" in the modern sense was not known or taught by the followers of Jesus Christ until after his death, burial, and resurrection. The essence of John the Baptist's message is not to believe in the death, burial, and resurrection of Jesus Christ for the forgiveness of sins so one can go to heaven. Neither Jesus nor John the Baptist taught such a thing explicitly during the entirety of their ministries.

Surely, some of John's Jewish audience members would have included those who believed in God and his promises but who needed revival due to God's silence for more than 400 years. It is an assumption on the part of many that John the Baptist was drawing a distinction between saved and lost people, i.e., believers and unbelievers, disciples and non-disciples. The assumption is that John calls unbelieving Jews to faith in God for salvation from sin and that one of the steps required is repentance. This assumption is false.

THE OBJECT OF JOHN'S MESSAGE

Both Matthew and Luke indicate that John had a harsh tone of judgment to his message. Matthew 3:7 says that John's tone pointed at the Pharisees and Sadducees. Luke begins by saying that John spoke "to the crowds that came out to be baptized by him." There is no basis to limit the audience to Jews only. Neither is there any reason to limit it to nonbelievers. In fact, Matthew 3:5–6 asserts, "Then Jerusalem and all Judea and all the region about the Jordan were going to him, and they were baptized by him."

Upon closer examination of John's message, we discover two metaphors of judgment that signal the need to repent immediately. The soon-coming judgment is an expression of God's wrath: "Who warned you to flee from the wrath to come?" The word "wrath" (ὀργή, *orgē*) speaks of God's indignation/anger against sin. Louw and Nida add, "Though the focal semantic element in ὀργή is punishment, at the same time, there is an implication of God's anger because of evil."

When told of the imminent outburst of God's wrath on the earth, Luke 3:8–14 reports that members of the crowds asked, "What then shall we do?" Again, as we alluded to earlier, if the issue is the lostness of their souls, we naturally expect an answer detailing our Lord's role in salvation. However, John the Baptist points, not to a lack of salvation, but to a lack of good fruit. Again, if the modern Gospel were in focus, one would think John would have pointed out the problem of a lack of faith in Jesus. Rather, the type of repentance John is calling for is a behavioral change.

Told not to depend on their Abrahamic lineage to escape the coming wrath, John describes the kind of actions that can avert God's wrath. He exhorts the crowds:

"Whoever has two tunics is to share with him who has none, and whoever has food is to do likewise." Tax collectors also came to be baptized and said to him, "Teacher, what shall we do?" And he said to them, "Collect no more than you are authorized to do." Soldiers also asked him, "And we, what shall we do?" And he said to them, "Do not extort money from anyone by threats or by false accusation, and be content with your wages."

John's answers ought to remove any possibility that he is preaching about Christ's provision of his life for man's sin. There is nothing, either explicit or implicit, here about needing faith in Jesus to have your sins forgiven. Rather, John the Baptist focuses on behavior. The good news from God calls upon men to bring their behavior in line with living under God's rule.

If John had been talking about provision for man's sin, we would have expected him to outline the plan of salvation in a post-Easter sense. Rather, just as with Abraham, he called on the people to believe God's promise: "repentance for the forgiveness of sins." Belief in this promise is evidenced in their behavior. Salvation came to Abraham, the Jews in Jesus' day, and to us in the exact same way: belief in the promise of God. Clearly, the content of the promise from man's perspective changes.

There does not seem to be any confusion on the part of the people about John's message or their necessary response. Equally, there is no basis for anyone to claim that the general masses thought Jesus was God or able to forgive sins. The reader must remember that, at the time, Jesus had just begun his public ministry with a message he labeled "the good news from God." Repentance must be seen in the light of this message.

The call to repent is found in both the Old and New Testaments. On one occasion, Jesus remarked, "The men of Nineveh will rise up in the judgment with this generation and condemn it because they repented at the preaching of Jonah, and indeed a greater than Jonah is here" (Matt. 12:41). On two separate occasions, our Lord will speak of Assyrian cities that either did or would have responded to the call for repentance: Nineveh (Matt. 12:31) and Tyre and Sidon (Luke 10:13).

Who were the Assyrian people? Why did God demand repentance or destruction of the great city of Nineveh? Were the Ninevites once a people of God? Does national repentance imply a previous relationship between God and those called "to turn back to God"?

If these questions had as their primary subject the children of Israel, then the answer to these questions would be an emphatic yes! However, no less emphatic is the fact that all nations owe their existence to the God of the Bible. Psalm 86:9 declares, "All the nations you have made shall come and worship before you, O Lord." In the same way that all the nations shall be blessed through Abraham (Gen. 12:3), all the nations will draw his wrath for their wicked rebellion (Psalm 2:1–3) against his law (Gen. 9:1–7). There is going to be an eschatological punishment of all the nations of the world, but for now, God extends grace. Nineveh is one such recipient of this grace.

Looking back at the ministry to the Ninevites, Jonah came preaching, "Yet forty days, and Nineveh shall be overthrown" (Jonah 3:4). Jonah then informs the reader, "The people of Nineveh believed God" (Jonah 3:5). In Ninevah's case, the threat of God's wrath is met with repentance. Notice,

The word reached the king of Nineveh, and he arose from his throne, removed his robe, covered himself with sackcloth, and sat in ashes. And he issued a proclamation and published through Nineveh, "By the decree of the king and his nobles: Let neither man nor beast, herd nor flock, taste anything. Let them not feed or drink water, but let man and beast be covered with sackcloth, and let them call out mightily to God. Let everyone turn from his evil way and from the violence that is in his hands. Who knows? God may turn and relent and turn from his fierce anger, so that we may not perish." When God saw what they did, how they turned from their evil way, God relented of the disaster that he had said he would do to them, and he did not do it. (Jonah 3:6–10)

Jonah's account is an excellent example of biblical repentance. The threat of God's wrath requires man "to turn from his evil way." Man, for his part, attempts to convince God of the seriousness of his decision to turn away from his rebellion by demonstrating physical, mental, spiritual, and psychological suffering. For the king and the citizens of Nineveh, "repentance" did not involve coming to faith in God. It involved a change in their behavior to turn away God's wrath. For the people of Nineveh, repentance was not coming to faith in Jesus, but a decision to heed God's warning. Robert N. Wilkin's summary is essentially correct when he states,

The repentance of the Ninevites was not faith in Christ and it was not a necessary precursor to faith in Christ. They decided to turn from their sins because they hoped to escape the destruction of their city and the widespread loss of lives that Jonah had proclaimed ("Who can tell if God will turn and relent, and turn away His fierce anger, so that we may not perish?"—Jonah 3:9)

That the call to repent is not always a step to gain eternal life or synonymous with "coming to faith" should not require proof beyond the context of the passage: "When God saw what they did . . . they turned from their evil way." The people of Nineveh changed their behavior to turn away God's wrath.

THE CENTRAL MESSAGE OF JOHN THE BAPTIST

If, as we suggest, the good news from God highlights the coming physical manifestation of God's wrath on earth, which portends judgment of the wicked, then there is no surprise that the message of John the Baptist warned of God's impending judgment. John used two metaphors of judgment in his message recorded in both Matthew and Luke. Both project a harvest separation with a fiery destiny for those who fail to repent. The first metaphor involves the tree fallen by an axe. John declares, "Even now, the axe is laid on the root of the trees. Every tree, therefore, that does not bear good fruit is cut down and thrown into the fire" (Matt. 3:10–12). The description of judgment as the "felling of trees with an axe" occurs several times in the Old Testament. Isaiah, Ezekiel, and Daniel all make use of this metaphor. Importantly, John clarifies that once the felling of trees starts, there will be no opportunity to change the nature of the trees. Repentance must be done now.

The second metaphor of judgment involves the harvest of wheat, symbolized by the winnowing fork. John states,

"His winnowing fork is in his hand, and he will clear his threshing floor and gather his wheat into the barn, but the chaff he will burn with unquenchable fire." (Matt. 3:12)

David J. MacLeod summaries the significance of John's second metaphor of judgment in this way:

With this figure of speech, John makes four points: First, the judgment is imminent. The "winnowing fork" is in the hands of the Messiah. Second, a separation is near at hand. "He will thoroughly clear His threshing floor." Third, those who have repented will enter Messiah's kingdom. Messiah, says John, "will gather His wheat into the barn." Finally, those who have not repented of their sins— "the chaff"—will be punished. They will be burned "with unquenchable fire."

With this final metaphor, Matthew ends his account of the ministry and message of John the Baptist. Thus, having begun with a summary of John's message, "Repent, for the kingdom of heaven is at hand," we see the defining traits of John's full message in summary fashion here.

Notice:

1. *The judgment is imminent.*
2. *The separation of peoples is near at hand.*
3. *The repentant will enter the Messiah's kingdom.*
4. *The unrepentant will be burned "with unquenchable fire."*

Only by bringing one's behavior in line with God's commands can anyone hope to escape his coming judgment. Luke adds one additional note of importance relative to John's ministry. He states, "So with many other exhortations he [John the Baptist] preached good news to the people."

In typical Lukan fashion, Luke uses the verb εὐαγγελίζω to express John's message. In Luke 4:43; 8:1; and 16:16, "the kingdom of God" defines what good news is preached. Essentially, John the Baptist preached the good news of the kingdom, which Jesus also preached (Matt. 4:23).

The Gospel of John has a very narrow focus on John the Baptist's ministry and message. All four Gospel accounts refer to his prophetic announcement, "After me comes he who is mightier than I, the strap of whose sandal I am not worthy to untie. I have baptized you with water, but he will baptize you with the Holy Spirit."

The Gospel of John is unique from the other Gospels in that the writer records John the Baptist specifically identifying the Lord Jesus as the Lamb of God who takes away the sin of the world (1:29) and as "the Son of God" (1:34). Many conclude based on John 1:36 that the apostle John is one of the disciples of John the Baptist who became a disciple of the Lord Jesus.

The Gospel of John focuses on only two days of the life of John the Baptist. The writer's focus is clearly on John the Baptist's Spirit-inspired prophetic utterances during those two days. None of the Gospel accounts indicates how long John's ministry lasted or how long he was in prison. However, John's certainty about Jesus' identity dwindled after his imprisonment by Herod. Matthew 11 reports that he sent two of his disciples to question Jesus, "Are you the one who is to come, or shall we look for another?"

THE IMPORTANCE OF GALILEE

A second critically important point in connection with the beginning of our Lord's ministry and message is that Jesus began his public ministry in Galilee. Mark 1:9 affirms, "In those days Jesus came from Nazareth of Galilee and was baptized by John in the Jordan." John's call was to right living so one would be worthy of the coming kingdom of God. Thus, Jesus would need to do the same thing every other man would, live a holy life.

After his baptism by John, the Lord's three temptations by Satan occurred in the wilderness. After this, the Lord returned to Bethany, after which he journeyed to Capernaum (John 2:12). Jesus attended Passover in Jerusalem, then spent time baptizing with some of his disciples in the Judean countryside (John 3:22). Report of his ministry (John 4:1–3) caused the Lord to move back to Galilee. It is at this point that we pick up the story in Mark's account.

As Jesus returned to Galilee and headed to his home in Nazareth, he began his proclamation. (One would think that Jesus would have begun his public ministry in Jerusalem. Yet, it is Galilee of the Gentiles that had this honor. Jerusalem will play the central role at the end of the Lord's ministry.) Thus, as Jesus began his ministry, he called for repentance in response to his announcement of "the good news of the sovereign administration of God" (Mark 1:14–15). The third chapter of the Gospel of John records that "Jesus and his disciples went into the Judean countryside, and he remained there with them and was baptizing." Later in chapter four, John clarifies that "Jesus himself did not baptize, but only his disciples."

There is no explicit or implied basis to claim that the disciples of Jesus were baptizing people into Christ in a salvific sense. The Pharisees do not seem to associate our Lord's baptism with the baptism of John. Rather, the issue seems to be the relative merits of John's baptism because Jesus surpasses John in the number of individuals submitting to his baptism. John explains to his disciples that because of who Jesus is, it is only natural that he should see more success. John clarifies at the beginning of chapter four that once Jesus learned that the Pharisees heard that he was "making and baptizing more disciples than John ... he left Judea and departed again for Galilee."

That Jesus would stop baptizing and return to Galilee ought to make plain that there was no salvific significance to his baptism. In fact, John the Baptist is recorded to have said, "Whoever believes in the Son has eternal life" (John 3:36). The opposite is also true. No Son, no life. Such a one will experience the wrath of God. That the only use of the term "wrath" in John's Gospel falls from the lips of John the Baptist signals that "the good news of the kingdom" is his focus. One is under God's wrath now. Repentance removes it.

In light of the good news of the sovereign administration of God, repentance should be every man's first priority. The urgency of repentance is directly tied to one's belief about our Lord's proclamation. Thus, the Lord calls for "repentance and belief in the good news."

The verb πιστεύω (pisteuō = believe, have faith) occurs in the Gospel of Mark sixteen times. In Mark 1:15, this term, in combination with the preposition ἐν (en = in), occurs nowhere else in the New Testament. Stanley Porter lists five overarching uses of the preposition ἐν in the New Testament:

(1) Locative
(2) Distributional

(3) Spherical

(4) Temporal

(5) Instrumental (manner, accompaniment, cause).[7]

For the spherical usage, Porter adds:

Something or someone may be located within the sphere of influence, control or domain of another or larger group ('in'), in the same way that one object or person may be within the confines of another.[8]

Both A.T. Robinson and J. H. Moulton quote A. Deissmann with approval that the spherical sense is best for the intended meaning of Mark 1:15.[9] Robertson, in fact, states,

It is rather remarkable that ἐν occurs only once (Mk. 1:15, πιστεύετε ἐν τῷ εὐαγγελίῳ) explained by Deissmann[3] as meaning 'in the sphere of,' to which Moulton agrees.

Daniel B. Wallace takes a different understanding of the usage in Mark 1:15 when he states,

When a verb of motion is used with a stative preposition, again the verb is usually dominant: The entire construction indicates motion. For example, πιστεύω + ἐν is the equivalent of πιστεύω + εἰς (cf. Mark 1:15; John 3:15) .... The idea is "put one's faith into" even though ἐν is used .... What is the value of this discussion for exegesis? It is simply that too often prepositions are analyzed simplistically, etymologically, and without due consideration for the verb to which they are connected. Prepositions are often treated in isolation, as though their ontological meaning were still completely intact.

By using this unique clause, Mark captured the intent of the Lord Jesus' call for men and women to entrust themselves to the good news of the sovereign administration of God. It is not a call merely to give intellectual ascent to an idea. Rather, disciples—both then and today—are called upon to abandon themselves completely to the mission.

As we have asserted several times before, modern translations prejudice most readers by translating τῷ εὐαγγελίῳ (tō euangeliō) as "the gospel." Given that Matthew, Mark, and Luke never refer to the death-burial-resurrection motif of the Lord Jesus with the term "the gospel" (as a technical term or otherwise) unnecessary errors of interpretation abound when translations fail to recognize this fact.

Contextually, Jesus did not refer to his death, burial, and resurrection as "the gospel" or the correct translation "the good news" anywhere in Matthew, Mark, Luke, or John's Gospels. The closest reference to Mark 1:15 of good news" is Mark 1:14—the good news from God.

The good news from God is not the good news of the death, burial, and resurrection of Christ for the forgiveness of sins. In Mark 1:15, the call to believe in the good news of God by our Lord is a call to prepare to live under the physical manifestation of the sovereign administration of God on earth. In the ministry and message of Jesus and his disciples, we see the rule of heaven has come to earth.

Guelich summaries it best when he says,

> [T]he broader context of 1:14–15 and the immediate setting of the call to repentance in 1:15 indicates that Jesus, who fulfills the promise of Isa 52:7; 61:1 by proclaiming the good news of the fulfillment of time and the coming of God's rule into history, summons one to "believe the good news" (1:15),

which is the "good news from God" (1:14). Thus one "repents," turns in total surrender to God, as one "believes the gospel" about God's rule.[10]

It is a good hermeneutical principle to define terms, ideas, or concepts by the reference closest to the term, idea, or concept in question. In this case, the good news of Mark 1:15 finds a definition in Mark 1:14's "the good news of God."

Notes

[1] In the paragraph quoted from John D. Grassmick, there are no less than five aggreges statements that are patently false.

[2] John D. Grassmick, "Mark," in *The Bible Knowledge Commentary: An Exposition of the Scriptures*, ed. J. F. Walvoord and R. B. Zuck, vol. 2 (Wheaton, IL: Victor Books, 1985), 107.

[3] David A. Lambert, *How Repentance Became Biblical: Judaism, Christianity, and the Interpretation of Scripture* (Oxford University Press, 2016) (Kindle Edition), 71.

[4] Ibid., 73-74.

[5] Mark J. Boda, *'Return To Me': A Biblical Theology of Repentance*, Vol. 35, (*New Studies in Biblical Theology*, InterVarsity Press 2015, Kindle Edition), 25-26.

[6] Ibid., 30.

[7] Stanley E. Porter, *Idioms of the Greek New Testament*, 156–159.

[8] Ibid, 157.

[9] A.T. Robertson, *A Grammar of the Greek New Testament in the Light of Historical Research* (Logos Bible Software, 2006), 540. Moulton, J. H. (2006). *A Grammar of New Testament Greek*, Volume 1: Prolegomena. Vol. 1: 2d ed., with corrections and additions. (67). Edinburgh: T. & T. Clark.

[10] R. A. Guelich, *Mark 1–8:26* (vol. 34A), 45.

CHAPTER 7

The Parable of the Soils: The Secret of the Kingdom of God

Mark 1:14–15

Now after John [the Baptist] had been handed over to the prison, Jesus came into Galilee, shouting out loud the good news from God consisting of "The time is fulfilled, and the sovereign administration of God is at hand; repent and believe in the good news [from God]." (author's translation)

Mark 1:14–15 is the key to understanding the Gospel of Mark. G. R. Beasley-Murray is not the only scholar of reputation who has captured the significance of this passage. His summary reflects exactly what we believe:

This passage, set by Mark as the climax to his prologue to the ministry of Jesus ... is intended to supply a summary of the gospel preached by Jesus, of which the teaching of Jesus in the body of the gospel can be viewed as exposition.[1]

Sadly, though Mark tells the reader exactly the essence of our Lord's message, many New Testament students ignore Mark's explicit claim and conclude that the Lord's pre-Easter message is the same as the church's post-Easter message. This conclusion ensures faulty interpretations of our Lord's mission, message, and ministry. One such area that suffers abuse as a result is his kingdom parables.

Many of the kingdom parables are explicitly identified as presenting some aspect of the kingdom of God. (Hence why they are called "kingdom parables.") A key to interpreting this parable (and all parables) is that their meaning is not universal. The meaning of a parable is defined by the intent of the person giving it. In the Synoptics, the speaker is the Lord Jesus. If the mission, message, and ministry of Jesus are framed up in Mark 1:14–15, then the focus of his ministry—and, by extension, his parables—is that the long-promised physical manifestation of God's rule on earth has come. This is the "good news from God."

Jude reminds us that this "good news" looks back to Enoch. But in Enoch, the focus doesn't seem like such good news from a human perspective. Notice:

> Enoch, who lived in the seventh generation after Adam, prophesied about these people. He said, "Listen! The Lord is coming with countless thousands of his holy ones to execute judgment on the people of the world. He will convict every person of all the ungodly things they have done and for all the insults that ungodly sinners have spoken against him." (Jude 14–15, NLT).

The emphasis in this passage is on the judgment of man for his behavior. The wrath of God will come physically to earth, evidenced by the judgment of the living. Enoch's message is also the core message of John the Baptist, the Lord Jesus, and his apostles and subsequent disciples.

This judgment is what the Jews had been waiting for. But they were expecting it to fall on their enemies. They were expecting the "good news from God" to manifest itself in the coming of Messiah who would throw off the yoke of Rome. This expectation existed even in the minds of the apostles, who even after Jesus' resurrection, asked, "Lord, are you at this time going to restore the kingdom to Israel?" (Acts 1:6).

A JOURNEY TOO FAR

Thus, in bringing "the good news from God," Jesus had a lot of misconceptions to correct. As he begins to unfold the broad mysteries of God's plan, we finally begin to understand what God has been planning and executing from the fall of creation. As the Son of God, Jesus Christ fulfilled the promise of the physical manifestation of God on earth. He faithfully accomplished all that the Father assigned him to do; in return, his reward is to reign over all the earth for one thousand years (Revelation 20, Heb. 12:2). But not all of the details of God's plan were revealed in the Old Testament. Among them is how long the preparation stage for the kingdom would take. That this restoration would not occur immediately with the revelation of the Messiah was not something that the Jews were expecting. When the Messiah's coming did not happen as they expected, they turned on him. If Jesus did not overthrow the yoke of Rome as they expected the Messiah to do, then in their minds, he must not be the Messiah at all. (See Luke 24:13–21 for this perspective.)

This was not the only aspect of the coming of the "good news from God" that made its message difficult for them to hear. Another aspect was that the Messiah would come in the form of a God-Man—one hundred percent God and one hundred percent man, inseparably united yet without mixture. Today, this concept is accepted by many Christians, but it was not so in Jesus' day. What many now take for granted, the Jews of Jesus' day struggled with greatly.[2]

For many Jews living two thousand years ago, the idea that God would become a man by being born of a woman was beyond fantastic. Remember, every good Jewish person was taught from early childhood to recite the Shema twice daily: "Hear O Israel, the Lord is our God, the Lord is One." This saying—etched into the heart and soul of the Jewish people—affirms Judaism and declares the monotheistic unified wholeness of God. Israel had one God! That he existed as three distinct persons equal in every way, yet with individual distinctions, was incomprehensible to many Jews. Now add to that the idea that God became or added humanity to the Godhood, is it any wonder the Jews had great difficulty with Jesus and what he said?

The Jews of Jesus' day had long been awaiting God's reign on earth. For fourteen hundred years, they had not only been waiting but formulating expectations about what this kingdom would look like. Thus, into fourteen hundred years of conditioning walked a man who spoke and acted differently than anyone had ever seen. At no time did Jesus have to convince the people of God's existence or his promises to the Jewish people. What he would have to convince the multitudes was that he was not only the Messiah but also a Messiah as they had never seen nor conceived—fully God and fully man. Also difficult for the Jews to comprehend was that with the revelation of the God-Man, the mysteries of God's plan would now be open to *all* men and women of faith, both Jew and Gentile. For many Jews, it would be a journey too far.

THE HOSTILITY OF THE CROWD GROWS

Thus, our Lord's ministry and message had a profound and winnowing impact on those who saw and heard him. One was either moved to belief or hardness of heart. For many of the religious leaders, it was the latter (Mark 3:5). Mark concludes, "The Pharisees went out and immediately held counsel with the Herodians against him, how to destroy him." The verb "to destroy" comes from the Greek verb ἀπόλλυμι (*apollymi*), which means to "destroy; lose; die; be lost."[3]

Balz and Schneider add,

The basic negative meaning of the entire word group, frequently with a violent tendency, aims to express loss, destruction, and annihilation (e.g., of wealth) in a very general sense which can extend to the final destruction of the human being in death (Homer, Herodotus, Plato, Xenophon).[4]

It is not that the religious leaders merely wanted to stop Jesus' ministry and message, but their aim was to see him dead without any hope of God's redemption. Members of Jesus' family began to say, "He is out of his mind" (Mark 3:21). The religious leaders from Jerusalem ascribed his ministry to Beelzebub (Mark 3:22).

Having already alluded to the size of the crowds pressing against the Lord (Mark 3:9), the fourth chapter of Mark opens with the report that the boat he previously ordered (Mark 3:9) was ready. It is obvious that not everyone in the crowd was a friend. Our Lord's enemies were growing and looking to trap him with his own words in order to seize him and put him to death. Thus, two groups were ever-present: insiders and outsiders. Insiders bore no ill will for Jesus. Outsiders did!

Unlike the parable-filled chapter of Matthew 13, which contains eight parables,[5] Mark 4 contains only three explicit parables: (1) the parable of the sower (Mark 4:3–9, 13–20); (2) the parable of the earth bearing fruit by itself (Mark 4:26–29); and (3) the parable of the mustard seed (Mark 4:30–32).[6] Mark limited his utilization of parables to only three, each dealing with seeds, growth, and production. This is a clue about the intent of Mark's account in this chapter.

To appreciate the fourth chapter of Mark, we need to have a good understanding of what both precedes and follows it. What precedes it is our Lord's appointment of the Twelve "so that they might be with him and he might send them out to preach and have authority to cast out demons" (Mark 3:13–19). What follows is his sending out of the Twelve to do exactly that (Mark 6:7–13). Between the appointment and the sending are instructions. Mark 6:12 makes clear that their preaching consisted of "the good news of the sovereign administration of God," in light of which men and women should repent and believe the good news. Also in this "between section" are the parables.

Why are these instructions necessary? Just as with the Lord Jesus, the message and ministry of God's good news will not see national and international success to the degree one might expect. This lack of success is not the fault of the message, ministry, or methods of Jesus or his workers. Rather, Jesus explains that the problem is in the hearts of the hearers. The majority will reject the message. The parabolic section of Mark 4:1–34 explains why this is the case as follows:

Mark 4:1–2 – Mark's Introduction to the Parabolic Section

Mark 4:3–9 – Jesus Gives the Soil Parable

Mark 4:10–12 – Jesus Explains the Utilization of Parables

Mark 4:13–20 – Jesus Explains the Soil Parable

Mark 4:21–25 – Jesus Explains the Intent of Parabolic Truth

Mark 4:26–29 – Jesus States the Parable of Earth Bearing Fruit

Mark 4:30–32 – Jesus States the Parable of the Mustard Seed

Mark 4:33–34 – Mark's Editorial Comments on Parabolic Teachings

If one completely removes from his or her thinking the good news about Jesus Christ (the death, burial, and resurrection of Jesus for the forgiveness of sins), then the correct interpretation of Mark 4 is possible. Nowhere is this more essential than in the interpretation of the kingdom parables. The gospel of Christ is not the focus nor goal of Jesus' teaching in Mark 4.

Having set the stage by explaining the constituent groups among the crowds pressing against the Lord, Mark 4 explains Jesus' attempt to separate himself both physically and spiritually from the masses. Thus, Jesus divides the people into two groups: insiders and outsiders. Mark 4:1–2 begins,

Again, he [Jesus] started to teach along the seashore. For a very large crowd gathered before him so much so that he had to step onto a boat and set himself on the sea as the whole crowd faced him from the shore. Now he began ongoing instructions to them by means of parables. (author's translation).

If we follow A.T. Robertson's chronology of the Gospels, the events detailed in Mark 4 occur at most 18 months before Jesus' crucifixion.[7] Perhaps this gives more insight as to why he needed to continue his ministry in stealth. There is much more our Lord will need to teach his disciples, but he will also need to limit his critics' cases against him by limiting the understood truths he speaks in their presence. At his eventual trial, their case will be built with false accusations because he gave them so little truth that they could understand.

For the first time, Mark informs his readers that Jesus began his stealth campaign by masking truths of the kingdom with simple stories. Our English term "parable" is a transliteration of the Greek term παραβολή = *parabolē*. Mark does not begin with a definition or explanation of what a parable is or does. Rather, he gives an example first.

Mark 4:2b–9

Now in his teaching, he said to them: "Listen! Behold, a sower went out to sow. And as he sowed, a seed fell along the path, and the birds came and devoured it. Another seed fell on rocky ground, where it did not have much soil, and immediately it sprang up since it had no depth of soil. And when the sun rose, it was scorched, and since it had no root, it withered away. Another seed fell among thorns, and the thorns grew up and choked it, and it yielded no grain. And other seeds fell into good soil and it kept producing grain, growing up and increasing and kept yielding thirtyfold and sixtyfold and a hundredfold." And he said, "He who has ears to hear, let him hear." (author's translation)

Since Mark gives us an illustration of what a parable is, we should limit our definition to his usage. When evaluating Matthew's account, it is best to see that our Lord gave a series of parables (Matt. 13:3) while on the boat. After he had done so, Mark informs us that "when he [Jesus] was alone, those around him with the twelve kept asking him about the parables." This indicates that the teaching from the boat is over and the Lord is debriefing the Twelve and other listeners. The imperfect aspect of the verb ἐρωτάω (erōtaō, "to ask") suggests ongoing questioning. This usage supports the idea that the insiders kept asking Jesus about each parable given during his sea-based teaching.

Mark indicates that the disciples (the Twelve and others = insiders) asked the Lord about the parables, plural. Were they asking, "Why do you speak in parables?" or were they asking, "What is the meaning of each parable?" Matthew 13:10 indicates that they were concerned with *why* he was speaking parables. Even though Mark and Luke focus on the meaning of the parables, do not miss this point: Neither the insiders nor the outsiders understood the point Jesus was making. The key difference is who requested more information.

Our Lord's answer in Mark 4:11 focuses on both usage and meaning. He states, "To you all [those around him with the Twelve = insiders] has been given [to know] the secret of the kingdom of God, but for those outside everything is in parables." Thus, the purpose of the parables is to tell stories everyone can hear (both insiders and outsiders) but to limit the real message to those who want to know more (insiders). The audience on this occasion included "those around him with the Twelve." Concerning this larger group, it is very important that we not divide them into saved and lost or disciple and non-disciple. Remember that, at this point, Judas is one of the Twelve.[8] As well, disciples are making decisions daily regarding their commitment to abide with Christ or to leave him (John 6:64,66). These are not decisions regarding salvation in our modern sense. Some come to Jesus, hear, and stay. These Jesus labels as "true disciples" (John 8:31). Others come, hear, and stay for a while. Lastly, some come, hear, and immediately leave.

To assume all are saved or all are lost is to miss the point. It would have been very difficult to find a Jewish person living during the ministry of Jesus who did not believe in the God of Abraham, Isaac, and Jacob. They believed in the promises God made to these men, and this became the basis of their lives, daily religious practice, and future expectations. One of those expectations was that God was going to act on those promises very soon and that this would ultimately result in the removal of Roman slavery. This faith (in the promises of God) is the essence of Abraham's journey to righteousness as reflected in Genesis 15:6.

The issue for many Jews was figuring out how Jesus fit into God's plans. As Jesus began to reveal that all the promises recorded in the Law, the Prophets, and the Writings found their fulfillment in him, many could not comprehend it. Modern readers take for granted many of the concepts and ideas Jesus preached two thousand years ago. However, in the first century, Jesus was a radical by any measure. Thus, a Jew could have believed in the promises of God and received God's righteousness, and still not have believed in Jesus.

Our point here is that whatever the distinction between those on the inside and those on the outside, it is not an issue of saved and lost. It also is noteworthy is that once Jesus explained the facts to the insiders, they would have been able to explain them to the outsiders.

THAT OTHER GOSPEL • 175

The last point that should inform our understanding regarding the identity of the outsiders in comparison to the insiders is the fact that the insiders did not understand the meaning of the parables either. Were it not for the explanation they received from Jesus, they would have remained just as ignorant as the outsiders of the sovereign administration of God!

The perfect aspect of the verb δίδωμι (*didōmi* = to give) suggests that once given, the information will be forever available. *The Exegetical Dictionary of the New Testament* adds that this verb

> *is the most common expression for the procedure whereby a subject deliberately transfers something to someone or something so that it becomes available to the recipient.*[9]

The point of Balz and Schnider is that our Lord is not involved in a bait and switch. His stories communicate real permanent truth for those who draw near to him for understanding. What does he intend by the phrase "the secret of the kingdom of God?" Unlike both Matthew and Luke, Mark does not include the infinitive form of the verb γινώσκω (*ginōskō* = "to know; understand"). It is our conviction that the infinitive is understood—that it must be supplied as it appears in the accounts of both writers. This is in contradiction to Étienne Trocmé, who argues,

> *Perhaps some readers will find it difficult to admit that this sentence might not be a description of a cognitive event such as the "knowledge of the mysteries of the Kingdom of Heaven" (Matthew xiii. 11). But in Mark iv. 11 we read "mystery" in the singular and there is no mention of a knowledge of this mystery.*

Given that the insiders were no more able than the outsiders to "get" the meaning of the parables without our Lord's enlightenment, additional knowledge is the big difference between the two groups. Most modern translations render the Greek μυστήριον (*mystērion*) as "secret" (singular) in Mark 4:11. The reason is well reflected in the comments of France when he writes:

> *The mention of a μυστήριον immediately sets the tone for Jesus' response, but can easily mislead English readers who naturally think of a 'mystery' as something which is inherently hard to understand, and which can be unravelled only by unusual cleverness—if it is not totally incomprehensible. But the true sense of μυστήριον is better captured by the English 'secret', which denotes not incomprehensibility but hiddenness. A secret is that which is not divulged—but once known it need not be hard to grasp. It is privileged information rather than a puzzle.[10]*

Thus, the parables of our Lord allowed information to be shared in an open area without divulging the "secret meaning" that only the speaker knew. While Matthew and Luke make clear by their use of secrets (plural), Mark is concerned with one secret: the sovereign administration of God. We believe that by "secret" (singular), Mark refers to the fundamental core value upon which all other insights about the kingdom are based. Indeed, for Mark, the parable of the sower (Matt. 13:18) is "the parable about parables."[11]

WHY KEEP IT A SECRET?

In chapter three of this book, we defined the phrase "the kingdom of God." There we concluded that "the sovereign administration of God" better reflects the intended textual meaning. The physical manifestation of God's rule has come to earth. Contrary to the belief of many of the Jews at the time, the presence of God physically on earth would not result in an immediate challenge to the political establishment. The secret of the sovereign administration of God explains why.

Given the self-evident capabilities of Jesus to set aside natural law, completely control the kingdom of darkness, and heal every kind of disease, confusion reigned among the Jews. Many were asking why Jesus wouldn't "just do it"! The reason is the secret of the sovereign administration. However, this information is withheld from those outside: "To you has been given the secret of the kingdom of God, but for those outside, everything comes in parables: in order that they may indeed look, but not perceive, and may indeed listen, but not understand" (Mark 4:11). There is much debate among scholars regarding what two groups are represented in this verse. "To you" refers to "those around him with the Twelve." "Those outside" must be defined contextually.

Because of their disgust with Jesus, Mark 3:6 reports that "the Pharisees went out and immediately held counsel with the Herodians against him, how to destroy him." The Pharisees went out from our Lord's presence, registering their unbelief (hardness of heart). Mark 3:13 highlights that Jesus "called to him those whom he desired." There is debate about the actual number of individuals called. Whether he called just twelve men or a larger group from which he chose the Twelve is not clear. However, our emphasis is on the call itself. Unlike the hard-hearted Pharisees who went out of his presence, his disciples entered his presence—they sought it.

Mark 3:21 indicates that personal family members "went out to seize him, for they were saying, 'He is out of his mind.'" Mark 3:31 also places family members "outside." Again, we see those who do not believe our Lord's report as being outside. The third chapter of Mark ends with our Lord making the declarative statement that "whoever does the will of God, he is my brother and sister and mother."

The ultimate example of obedience is to believe that Jesus was sent from God. Therefore, we see a clear delineation between "those outside" who do not do the will of God and "those inside" who do. Jesus began his ministry with a call "to repent and believe in the good news." Those who desire to come and remain in the Lord's presence receive the secrets of the sovereign administration of God. Both insiders and outsiders hear parables, but unlike those who are privy to the Lord's decoding (private interpretation), the outsiders remain unilluminated.

Mark 4:12 explains why this is the case. The meaning of Mark 4:12 has found little consensus among students of Scripture regarding the intent of the text. The text says:

> *"So that 'they may indeed see but not perceive, and may indeed hear but not understand, lest they should turn and be forgiven.'"*

Outsiders are kept in ignorance through the use of parables because, as we will discuss, only the speaker of the parables knows their intent. Since the outsiders refuse to come into Jesus' presence, this locks them out from understanding. Jesus states that the price of unbelief in the good news from God is continued ignorance of the opportunity to join in the ruling class of his coming kingdom on earth, which has begun.

Isaiah 6:9–10, which our Lord quotes, is among the most debated Old Testament passages used in the Gospel of Mark. France gives a very good summary of the reason for so much debate. As he writes so eloquently:

> *The content of these verses is apparently quite simple: a limited group, apart from the crowd, ask Jesus about parables, and he explains that while they are privileged to understand the secret of the kingdom of God, others have everything in parables, in order that they will not share that saving understanding. But few [scholars] have been content to believe that Jesus really meant to say just that, and there are sufficient ambiguities or obscurities in the wording to allow wide scope for scholarly ingenuity to discover a more acceptable intent .... In particular the condensed quotation of Is. 6:9–10 in v. 12 provides ample room for debate, both as to the original sense of the Isaiah prophecy and as to the significance of its application to Jesus' parables.* [12]

We agree with France that "the content of these verses is apparently quite simple." We also agree that "sufficient ambiguities or obscurities in the wording . . . allow wide scope for scholarly ingenuity to discover a more acceptable intent." However, we disagree that "the outsiders" are denied "saving understanding." Isaiah 6:9–10 is not about being saved or lost. It is about being faithful or unfaithful.

What "the outsiders" are being excluded from is not personal salvation. This assumption is shared by the overwhelming majority of New Testament scholars. The assumption that a "saving understanding" (how one is to be saved) is kept from the "outsiders" offends many and thus leads them to work overtime to make Mark 4:12 conform to their theological persuasion. Notice Douglas S. McComiskey's comment:

Jesus' quotation of Isa 6:9–10 in the purpose of parables passages raises the question of whether he desired some people not to be saved, which is really the central exegetical issue.[13]

McComiskey and so many others allow this false assumption to control their exegesis. This guarantees an incorrect interpretation every time. The good news of Christ is not in focus. Rather, the controlling theme of our Lord's ministry is the good news from God. This promise was made to mankind as far back as Enoch—that God would physically manifest his presence on earth to rule. The secret of the sovereign administration of God is that the God-Man rule extends to men and women. There is not going to be a single King, but many kings (Matt. 19:28, Rev. 3:21). The ultimate opportunity of inclusion in kingdom leadership is earned by faith works. Sadly, few will have sufficient fruit to earn commendation, exaltation, and "honoration". This is what we shall discover when our Lord interprets the parable of the sower.

WHAT DOES IT MEAN TO "BE SAVED"?

Isaiah 6:9–10 falls within one of the greatest (if not the greatest) chapters in the first half of the book of Isaiah. The call of Isaiah to deliver a prophetic word occurs in the context of one of the greatest theophanic manifestations of God's physical presence on earth prior to the incarnation of Christ recorded in Scripture. Isaiah 6 does not describe the conversion of Isaiah in a New Testament sense. To believe that Isaiah "got saved" in chapter six is to completely misunderstand salvation in the Old Testament. Just as with Abraham, salvation came to a man or woman by faith in the promise(s) of God. Isaiah's message to Judah is not a call to faith. It is a call to faithfulness/faithful sonship.

Isaiah 6 shows that when a person who believes in God's existence and holds to his promises is privileged to personally see the physical manifestation of God on earth (the good news from God), man's first response should be humility. It is not altogether clear whether the theophanic manifestation is of God the Father or a pre-incarnate appearance of the Lord Jesus, but it really does not matter because the point is simply God's physical manifestation on earth. Sadly, it would not be permanent. However, in Jesus, the first step to permanency occurred.

With the "otherness" of God and man's "unlikeness of God" firmly established in the mind of Isaiah, i.e. God is not like us and we are not like God, Isaiah becomes an instrument of use for God's glory. With such a glorious manifestation of God, the true anointing, and a call to deliver a message from God to Judah, Isaiah is on a roll. However, once Isaiah receives the deliverable, optimism turns to pessimism. The long-promised exile for disobedience has been set in motion. His message will confirm that repentance that turns away wrath is no longer possible—not because God no longer desires it, but because man's heart is beyond repentance. God commands Isaiah to state the facts of the peoples' prolonged history of willful rebellion against his commands. Instead of producing repentance, Isaiah's message will produce the opposite effect— hardheartedness. God declares,

"Go, and say to this people: 'Keep on hearing, but do not understand; keep on seeing, but do not perceive.' Make the heart of this people dull, and their ears heavy, and blind their

eyes; lest they see with their eyes, and hear with their ears, and understand with their hearts, and turn and be healed." (Isa. 6:9–10)

"Keep on hearing, but do not understand; keep on seeing, but do not perceive" perfectly describes the conduct of Judah for 490 years. By this time, possibly as many as four prophets had called the people to consistently live in righteousness, but the people's seesaw relationship had degenerated into continual evil. Unlike the prophets of the past who called Judah to repentance to avert exile, Isaiah tells the people that that exile is now inescapable.

By telling Judah the truth, Isaiah will only cause her to hasten to her destiny. More than one prophet was killed for telling the people the truth. Isaiah 6:9–10 describes the cause-effect behavior that occurs repeatedly throughout Judah's history. A New Testament parallel occurs in the book of Acts. When confronted with the truth, the Jews responded to Stephen exactly as Isaiah described. Stephen declared,

"You stiff-necked people, uncircumcised in heart and ears, you always resist the Holy Spirit. As your fathers did, so do you." (Acts 7:51)

Notice the Jews' reaction,

Now when they heard these things they were enraged, and they ground their teeth at him . . . they cried out with a loud voice and stopped their ears and rushed together at him. (Acts 7:54–55, 57)

"Make the heart of this people dull, and their ears heavy, and blind their eyes" describes the effect the truth will have on the people. The clause "lest they see with their eyes, and hear with their ears, and understand with their hearts, and turn and be healed" does not mean that God is responsible for the people's failure to repent. We disagree with Mccomiskey, who writes,

> According to the Hebrew wording of this passage, God simply does not want the people to repent. Isaiah's preaching empowered by God is the action that avoids the people's corporate repentance. It appears that the ultimate function of the hardening is to ensure that the exile, now ordained by God as the just punishment for Judah's sins, necessarily occurs.[14]

For 490 years God sought repentance. Dead prophets and written threats prove it. God describes to Isaiah the impact of telling Judah the truth. Just as the Jews responded to Stephen, Judah responded to Isaiah. God responds to their behavior.

In reality, our Lord's use of Isaiah 6:9–10 in Mark 4:11–12 has an opposite intent. Unlike Isaiah, who told the people the truth only to see them act as the Jews did with Stephen—rush to destruction—our Lord hides the truth to prevent the rejectors (the outsiders) from any possibility of "entering the kingdom of God."

Thus, I would rewrite France's otherwise excellent comment to say,

> The content of Mark 4:11–12 is apparently quite simple: a limited group, apart from the crowd, ask Jesus about parables, and he explains that while they are privileged to understand the secret of the kingdom of God, others have everything in parables in order that they will not share in the sovereign administration of God.

Why would the King allow rejectors of his right to rule to serve in his elite administration? Such behavior might be humanistic, but it has no place in the divine workings of the coming rule of God on earth. This is the very point of the parable of the sower.

Having defined the difference between insiders and outsiders, the Lord will now explain "the secret of the sovereign administration of God" to the insiders. In essence, who and how one earns the right to reign with Christ is completely opposite from the national expectations of the Jews. Kingdom inclusion and leadership participation is not hereditary. Nor is it limited to Jews only. It must be earned. By "right to reign," we mean to actually participate in the administration of the day-to-day affairs of state once the "not yet" aspect of our Lord's rule begins.

Mark 4:13–20 returns to the parable of the sower with a detailed explanation. While Mark lists three parables, he only records one detailed explanation for one of them. Thus, the parable of the sower holds importance for Mark's storyline. This section begins with a question our Lord asks the insiders, "Do you all not understand this parable? How then will you understand all the parables?" (Mark 4:13).

Our Lord's first question makes perfect sense here. By definition, a parable's meaning cannot be discerned by the hearer unless the author explains his intent. What a parable represents or is intended to mean is known only in the mind of the speaker. A parable without authorial intent is just another common everyday descriptor of some human action. The parable of the sower has the breadth to represent many truths. Only the author (in this case, Jesus) knows his personal intent, which he will have to explain in order for true communication to occur.

The point of our Lord's rhetorical question is to strengthen the insiders' understanding that they will need special insight that can only come from himself. Neither insiders nor outsiders can understand the Lord's parables without his explanation. Thus, it is all the more important that the insiders stay close to Jesus.

The second question, "How then will you understand all the parables?" signals the importance of the parable of the sower. In this regard, Guelich is very helpful when he states,

> The second question, "How will you understand all the parables" (πῶς πάσας τὰς παραβολὰς γνώσεσθε) indicates the significance of this parable for understanding the others. [15]

God has divinely decreed that all insiders will be given the secret of the kingdom of God. This is the essence of this parable. It is at this point in the narrative that fulfillment comes. Once explicated, insiders will have the necessary components to decipher all of the kingdom parables.

THE SEED'S IDENTITY

"The Sower sows the word." (Mark 4:14)

Neither Mark nor any of the other New Testament writers identify the sower. However, we already see in Mark's account that John the Baptist, Jesus, and his disciples are communicators of "the good news of the sovereign administration of God." Thus, there is little need to explicitly identify a single sower.

However, Matthew, Mark, and Luke offer insight regarding the seed. Mark identifies the seed as "the word"

(Mark 4:14). Matthew adds the seed as "the word about the kingdom" (Matt. 13:19). Finally, Luke adds that the seed is "the word of God" (Luke 8:11).[16] At first glance, it would seem to be an ironclad case for identifying the "seed" as the gospel of Christ, which is exactly what MacArthur and a majority of NT conclude.

The majority of New Testament teachers automatically assume that the seed is the modern Gospel message. They rush head-long to teach that the soils represent various responses to the message of our Lord's death, burial, and resurrection for the forgiveness of sin. This simply isn't true. The complete phrase that most accurately defines the seed is "the word about the sovereign administration of God," which Luke on three separate occasions explicitly identifies as the core message of Jesus Christ (Luke 4:43, 8:1, 16:16). As Jesus went about preaching throughout the land of Israel, he proclaimed God's invitation for men to earn a spot in the coming administration of God's rule on earth. How men and women respond to this message is the point of the parable of the sower.

THE FIRST SOIL'S RESPONSE

"And these are the ones along the path, where the word is sown: when they hear, Satan immediately comes and takes away the word that is sown in them." (Mark 4:15)

The description of the first response covers the first of three responses of the outsiders. Their rejection of the messenger ensures their ignorance of his message. When outsiders hear the message about the sovereign administration of God, they do not understand it. This allows the devil to easily take the message away. Matthew

13:19 describes the problem of hearing with no understanding.

It is critically important to remember that Mark 1:14–15 informs us that Jesus began his public ministry shouting out loud the good news from God. The good news from God was not given in parabolic form. For over two years, people heard, saw, and personally experienced evidence of God's physical manifestation on earth. The secret is not the sovereign administration of God itself. Rather, it is how men will respond to the message about it. The consequences of an incorrect response are not good. Notice how Luke describes it: "The devil comes and takes away the word from their hearts, so that they may not believe and be saved" (Luke 8:12).

Now most readers will automatically conclude that Luke 8:12 describes people who miss out on salvation. Balz and Schneider identify the ἵνα (hina) clause as purpose,[17] which is not significant given that Boyer identifies "the vast majority" of ἵνα clauses as true purpose clauses (97%)[18] in the New Testament. Thus, the purpose of the devil taking "the word from" the outsider's hearts is "so that they may not believe and be saved." Luke's description, perhaps more than any other detail, supports those who see personal salvation as the theological focus here. Clearly, "to not believe and be saved" refers to the rejection of the gospel of Christ in their thinking. However, at the time this parable was given, there had been no explicit declaration that our Lord's death, burial, and resurrection for the forgiveness of a person's sins had been preached or understood by the disciples or anyone else. The twelve disciples certainly did not see our Lord's death as necessary to save men and women from eternal punishment. Peter's reaction to Jesus' first explicit announcement of his imminent death was met with derision and rebuke. (See Matthew 16:21–23.)

Jesus' earliest prediction of his death occurs in a heated exchange between Jesus and the Pharisees regarding a sign to prove his authenticity. Jesus responds to their request by saying,

> *"An evil and adulterous generation seeks for a sign, but no sign will be given to it except the sign of the prophet Jonah. For just as Jonah was three days and three nights in the belly of the great fish, so will the Son of Man be three days and three nights in the heart of the earth." (Matt. 12:39–40)*

There is no evidence the Pharisees understood what Jesus meant by this statement. Equally, there is no indication that the disciples understood it either. Even if they had, they would not have understood why it would be necessary for Jesus to die. It is critical that modern readers not read subsequent theological developments back into what Jesus meant. How we understand it now is not how the original audience understood it two thousand years ago.

While there are those of certain theological persuasions who might accept the notion that the devil can stop a person from coming to faith in Jesus Christ, we are not among them. Are you among those who believe that the devil can take the Gospel from the heart of unbelievers and thereby keep them from coming to faith in Christ? If Luke 8:12 refers to salvation in the sense of having your sins forgiven by the blood of Jesus Christ through faith, then you are forced to this conclusion. If the devil were able to prevent any man from coming to faith in Jesus Christ, why would any man ever come to faith? Why would the devil allow some to hear, understand, and believe unto salvation, but not others? If he had the power to stop a person from obtaining salvation, wouldn't he want to stop the salvation of all?

For an accurate interpretation, we must understand Luke 8:12 historically. That is, at the time Jesus spoke the parable, the gospel of God was the focus, not the gospel of Christ. The Lukan phrase "to believe and be saved" in the original Greek looks like this: ἵνα μὴ πιστεύσαντες σωθῶσιν. A literal translation gives the impression that spiritual salvation is in view. However, this passage does not automatically refer to personal, spiritual salvation. Luke 8:50 says, "Do not fear; only believe, and she will be well." Literally, the Greek says, "Do not fear; only believe, and she will be saved," which is reflected in the New Revised Standard Version. Clearly, the context here indicates that "to be saved" means to be healed of physical sickness. There is no emphasis on spiritual salvation.[19]

Likewise, Luke 8:48 is in reference to the woman with the discharge of blood who believed that if she touched Jesus, she would be saved (healed). Jesus tells her, "Daughter, your faith has made you well; go in peace." Literally in Greek, it says, "Daughter, your faith has saved you." Clearly, "to be saved" does not automatically refer to spiritual salvation in every case. The devil cannot stop spiritual salvation, but he can stop progressive sanctification. One of his chief means of doing so is ignorance. By stealing the unrecognized truth from the hearts of outsiders, the devil keeps them ignorant of God's will. In this case, they continue to ignore "the good news of the sovereign administration of God." No progress is made in their lives to earn the right to sit with Christ as rulers in the coming kingdom of Christ.

Just as our Lord declared in Mark 1:14–15, the correct response of men and women to the message of the sovereign administration of God is "repent and believe the good news from God." This response delivers them from the coming wrath of God and may, with effort, earn them superior positions of honor in the coming administration of the Lord Jesus Christ.

THE SECOND SOIL'S RESPONSE

"And these are the ones sown on rocky ground: the ones who, when they hear the word [about the sovereign administration of God], immediately receive it with joy. But they have no root in themselves, thus endure for a while; then, when tribulation or persecution arises on account of the word [about the sovereign administration of God], immediately they fall away." (Mark 4:16, author's translation)

The second type of response describes a temporary acceptance until trouble changes their minds. Matthew's description of the second possible response is similar to Mark's. However, Luke adds, "They believe for a while, and in time of testing fall away." Thus, for those who advance the false narrative that spiritual salvation is in focus here, Luke's wording is additional proof for seeing the gospel of Christ in focus rather than the gospel of God. Is it any wonder Arminians feel good about their interpretation? However, only by reading modern conclusions back into the text does one find support for this position. This type of interpretation is a clear example of illegitimate totality transfer.

Believing the good news from God does not necessarily result in spiritual salvation, but this is what some believe. One should ask, "What do the hearers believe for a while?" What is the object of their belief?

The text says, "The word." What word? The word about the sovereign administration of God: "Repent, for the kingdom of God [heaven], is at hand." One who hears this message will need personal salvation to fully comply. Personal salvation may be included in the response of a hearer, but in the preaching of John the Baptist, the Lord Jesus, and his disciples, it is not exclusively the desired response as seen.

Failure to recognize this fact causes interpreters to do gymnastics with the text. Notice how the *Bible Knowledge Commentary* handles Luke 8:13:

> *The fact that they believe for a while but . . . fall away means that they only accept the facts of the Word mentally and then reject it when "the going gets rough." It does not mean they lose their salvation, for they had none to lose.*[20]

The Bible Knowledge Commentary says exactly what we would expect from those who do not see a distinction between the gospel of God and the gospel of Christ. For Calvinists, the lack of distinction is necessary to prevent the Arminian conclusion that loss of salvation is possible. This is the kind of reasoning that drives those who read modern views back into the text. Luke says they "receive [the word about the sovereign administration of God] with joy." Of the 56 times the verb *dechomai* ("to take, receive") occurs in the New Testament, there is no single example of a distinction in meaning as *The Bible Knowledge Commentary* advances.

John Nolland gets it half right. He states,

> *Luke changes Mark's verb for "they receive" to δέχονται and thus creates a phrase with the following "the word" which elsewhere regularly indicates a believing response to the*

preaching of the gospel (Acts 8:14; 11:1; 17:11; 1 Thess. 1:6; 2:13; Jas. 1:21).

Every word in Nolland's statement is correct. However, he fails to distinguish between the pre-Easter message of the Lord Jesus and the post-Easter message of the Apostles. There is no evidence of a half-hearted mental game being played here. True belief in the gospel of God occurs. Temporary belief in the good news from God is possible. The good news that God has opened up the candidacies for rulers in the leadership of his coming kingdom creates joy in the hearts of our Lord's disciples. Excitement about the offer fades when the reality of the price required becomes clearly understood. "When tribulation or persecution arises because of the word [about the sovereign administration of God]," the once excited disciples stop following Jesus. John 6:60–70 perfectly illustrates this point. The most probative question is why this word brings such tribulation or persecution. So, we ask, "Who sponsors the "time of testing?" Who ensures that "tribulation or persecution arises on account of the word" in the lives of the second soil?

Scripture on more than one occasion confirms that "troubles" will come to those who commit to living under the rule of God (Mark 8:35; 10:29–30; John 16:33; Acts 14:22). Again, we ask, "Why?"

CHALLENGING THE GOD OF THIS WORLD

The word about the sovereign administration of God directly challenges the authority of Satan, the god of this world. The message of God's rule from heaven coming to earth is met with resistance, with Satan evidencing his displeasure through those whom he can influence. All three accounts of the parable of the sower explicitly identify God's arch enemy (Mark: "Satan"; Matthew: "the evil one"; Luke: "the devil") at work against God's plan. While explicit identification is made regarding the evil one's involvement in the negative outcomes of the first soil, the lack of such an overt identification in the remaining soils should not be taken to mean that he isn't trying.

What Luke calls a "time of testing" (Luke 8:13) both Matthew and Mark call "tribulation or persecution because of the word." The noun *peirasmos* occurs a total of twenty-one times in the New Testament, with six of them occurring in Luke's Gospel. As Louw and Nida make clear, *peirasmos* has both a positive and negative nuance. They highlight the positive sense to mean:

> To try to learn the nature or character of someone or something by submitting such to thorough and extensive testing— "to test, to examine, to put to the test, examination, testing."[21]

They indicate a negative sense, as well:

> To endeavor or attempt to cause someone to sin— "to tempt, to trap, to lead into temptation, temptation."[22]

Thus, we advance the notion that God tests his people, but Satan tempts them. God allows and encourages such testing. The first occurrence of *peirasmos* in the Gospel of Luke concerns Jesus being "led by the Spirit in the wilderness for forty days, being tempted by the devil" (Luke 4:1). After three separate unsuccessful attempts, Luke reports that "when the devil had ended every temptation, he departed from him until an opportune time" (Luke 4:13). Notice the connection between "testing" and "time" on both occasions.

A significant number of scholars recognize that the accounts of the Lord's "time of testing" in both Matthew and Luke have close parallels and explicit framing with Deuteronomy 6–8, where Israel's "time of testing" is directly referenced.[23] Deuteronomy 8:2 explicitly states,

> *And you shall remember the whole way that the LORD your God has led you these forty years in the wilderness, that he might humble you, testing you to know what was in your heart, whether you would keep his commandments or not. (emphasis added)*

The expressed purpose of God's tests of Israel was to know what was in her heart, and whether she would keep his commandments or not. In comparison to Israel, the Lord Jesus is led by the Holy Spirit for the purpose of being tested by Satan. Jesus is put to three specific temptations: (1) self-sufficiency; (2) self-preservation; and (3) self-exaltation.[24] Unlike unfaithful Israel, the Son of God proved faithful to God's will in that he was willing to be fully dependent on God, i.e., being sustained in life and death if necessary.

Neither test—the one of Israel nor the one of the Lord Jesus—involved a call to personal salvation. Neither required putting faith in God. Rather, each required being faithful to God in light of his promises. The second seed responds in a positive way to the sower. A positive response about the word of the kingdom is dampened by a "time of testing," which causes some disciples to "fall away." There is a uniform belief among many New Testament scholars that "to fall away" (σκανδαλίζω = *skandalizō*), whether pre-resurrection or post-resurrection, *refers to the offense that results in the loss of salvation. Depending on whether or not a person already believes, it refers either to a falling away from or a rejection of faith.*[25]

The majority views take either one of two positions: that personal salvation is lost or the person was never "truly" saved. However, there is no explicit declaration in Scripture that a person who falls away forfeits personal salvation. While the Scriptures do speak of consequences for those who "fall away," nowhere in Scripture is the eternal lake of fire spoken of as one of them.

In Mark 14:27 (cf. Matt. 26:31), the Lord Jesus explicitly declares, "You will all fall away, for it is written, 'I will strike the shepherd, and the sheep will be scattered.'" All twelve disciples vehemently deny that this will occur (which is further described as denying the Lord). Yet soon enough, our Lord's prediction comes true. Mark 14:66–72 describes Peter's slow descent into apostasy, which concludes with the sad declaration, "He broke down and wept." All too often, modern definitions are forced back on the New Testament text without a good appreciation of the historical circumstance of the text. There is no evidence that Peter and his fellow contemporaries denied the deity of Christ. There is no evidence that they denied the existence of God or his promises. Because one proves to be a coward in the face of tribulation or persecution does not un-Christian a person.

To stumble at a tenet of the Christian faith or the fact that many Jews had a real problem with understanding how Jesus could be the Son of God did not nullify their belief in the God of Abraham, Isaac, and Jacob and/or the promises he made and that formed the basis of their daily expectation of seeing fulfillment.

Two thousand years have passed, and many New Testament saints still do not understand the nature of salvation, primarily because they do not understand the difference between the gospel from God and the gospel about Jesus Christ. Many, many disciples refuse to be progressively sanctified. Some refuse out of ignorance. Some refuse due to misinformation (false teachings). Others refuse out of fear of criticism. Still others refuse due to laziness. None of these conditions causes the loss of salvation. Rewards, on the other hand, are another matter altogether.

THE THIRD SOIL'S IDENTITY

"And others are the ones sown among thorns. They are those who hear the word, but the cares of the world and the deceitfulness of riches, and the desires for other things enter in and choke the word, and it proves unfruitful." (Mark 4:18–19)

The third type of response to the message of the sovereign administration of God is no different than the first and second in terms of the consequences. The difference is what causes a lack of production. When the word about the sovereign administration of God goes forth, disciples who follow Christ for different reasons are confronted with a choice. The offer to earn elite status in the coming rule of God on earth requires a level of devotion and commitment unparalleled in God's economy. To earn God's favor sufficient to be rewarded with the highest positions of honor in the coming rule of God on earth requires the abandonment of self-sufficiency, self-preservation, and self-exaltation. The longer one listens to

Christ, the more one understands the nature of the call and the challenges to faithfulness.

In the third soil, the word (of the sovereign administration of God) becomes unfruitful because it is choked out by "the cares of this world." The only close parallel to the phrase "the cares of the world" occurs in Luke 21:34: "cares of this life." The noun *merimna* (μέριμνα), according to Balz and Schneider, "refers to that which is existentially important, that which monopolizes the heart's concerns."[26] Matthew 6:25 defines the "cares of this life" as follows:

> *"Therefore I tell you, do not be anxious about your life, what you will eat or what you will drink, nor about your body, what you will put on."*

The problem being described here is a believer being overly concerned with these cares to the point that such concerns monopolize every waking moment and that the person no longer prioritizes earning elite status in the coming rule of God. You have to make a choice: God or money!

The second obstacle to successfully obtaining elite status in the coming rule of God on earth is "the deceitfulness of riches." The deceit of wealth is particularly dangerous because of the power of wealth's control over human nature (Matt. 19:23–24). Acquisition and control of wealth blind a person to God's priorities.

By "the desire for other things enter in," Mark makes room for the many other objections of the human heart that take priority over undiluted devotion to obtaining elite status in the coming rule of God. These three influences "choke the word." The word about the sovereign administration of God should move men and women to repentance and faith in the good news from God. Instead, the gatekeepers of men's hearts (i.e., the worries of life, the acquisition of wealth, and worldly desires) prevent men's hearts from full "followship" of Christ. The result: unfruitfulness.

The offer of the opportunity to earn elite status in the coming rule of God will prove unmotivating for many followers of Jesus Christ. Once personal salvation is obtained by faith in Jesus' death, burial, and resurrection for the forgiveness of sin, many will not advance in discipleship. Thus, what is absent in the first three soils is fruitfulness. None of the first three soils produced sustainable fruit.

THE FOURTH SOIL'S IDENTITY

"But those that were sown on the good soil are the ones who hear the word and accept it and bear fruit, thirtyfold and sixtyfold and a hundredfold." (Mark 4:20)

The last category of disciples is those whose reaction to hearing the word about the sovereign administration of God causes them to pursue the great honor of God with energy and effort. These are said to be "good soil." They are good in the sense that they produce fruit. There is no inherent goodness. To both hear and accept the word about the sovereign administration of God and to bear fruit that evidences this devotion characterize "good soil."

All soils heard the word. Three soils accepted the word, but only one soil bore fruit. Fruit production is not uniform. Thirty, sixty, and one hundredfold explains why kingdom rewards will differ. The Lord Jesus explains the distribution of rewards in the story of the talents. One, two, and five could become two, four, and ten, with additional rewards as described in the parable.

Notes

[1] G. R. Beasley-Murray, *Jesus and the Kingdom of God* (Grand Rapids: Eerdmans; Exeter: Paternoster, 1986), 71.

[2] Most scholars agree that the Gospel of Mark establishes two major points about the Lord Jesus. Mark 1:1–8:30 proves that he is the Son of God. Mark 8:31–16:20 proves that he is the Son of Man.[2] Mark fills the first half of the book with healings, demon extractions, and short controversies with the religious leaders to prove that Jesus is God's Son. The book ends with his disciples making this exclamation. Jesus exercises authority over demons, sickness, the forgiveness of sin, the Sabbath, and the ability to appoint men to exercise divine authority, authority over death, and authority over natural law.

[3] Horst Robert Balz and Gerhard Schneider, *Exegetical Dictionary of the New Testament* (Grand Rapids, MI: Eerdmans, 1990–), 135.

[4] Ibid.

[5] For a defense of Matthew 13 containing eight parables, see Mark L. Bailey, "The Parable of the Sower and the Soils," *Bibliotheca Sacra* 155 (1998): 173.

[6] How many parables Mark 4 contains is debated. We do not see Mark 4:21-25 as parables proper. Given the heavy emphasis on the parables of Jesus in the Gospel of Matthew, none of the expressions found in Mark 4:21-25 is identified as a parable by Matthew. This is also the case in Luke's Gospel.

[7] A. T. Robertson, *A Harmony of the Gospels* (Bellingham, WA: Logos Bible Software, 2009), John 4:43–45.

[8] Most students of the New Testament create more problems than they understand when Judas is set aside as a bad-guy unbeliever. Most people miss the fact that Judas demonstrated the same power and ability in ministry as Peter, James, and John. There is no indication that Judas did not perform just as the others did when they went out in groups of two to preach, heal, and cast out demons. See Mark 6:12-13; Matt 10:1ff.

[9] *Exegetical Dictionary of the New Testament*, 320.

[10] R. T. France, *The Gospel of Mark: A Commentary on the Greek Text, New International Greek Testament Commentary* (Grand Rapids, MI; Carlisle: W.B. Eerdmans; Paternoster Press, 2002), 196.

[11] Ibid., 193.

[12] Ibid.

[13] Douglas S. McComiskey, "Exile and the Purpose of Jesus' Parables" (Mark 4:10–12; Matt 13:10–17; Luke 8:9–10)," *Journal of the Evangelical Theological Society* 51, no. 1 (2008): 60.

[14] Douglas S. Mccomiskey, "Exile and Restoration from Exile in the Scriptural Quotations and Allusions of Jesus," *Journal of the Evangelical Theological Society* 53, no. 4 (2010): 680.

[15] Robert A. Guelich, Mark 1–8:26, vol. 34A, *Word Biblical Commentary* (Dallas: Word, Incorporated, 1989), 221. A check of many commentaries will confirm that Guelich's conclusion is shared by many scholars.

[16] The word about the kingdom of God.

[17] Horst Robert Balz and Gerhard Schneider, *Exegetical Dictionary of the New Testament* (Grand Rapids, MI: Eerdmans, 1990–), 189. Bock, also, interprets the ἵνα (*hina*) as a purpose clause. See Darrell L. Bock, Luke: 1:1–9:50, vol. 1, *Baker Exegetical Commentary on the New Testament* (Grand Rapids, MI: Baker Academic, 1994), 734.

[18] James L. Boyer, "The Classification of Subjunctives: A Statistical Study," *Grace Theological Journal 7*, no. 1 (1986): 8.

[19] "This should not be understood as an expression for full salvation in the immediate context; it refers only to the girl's healing." This is reflected in a footnote to this verse in the NET Bible. [Biblical Studies Press, *The NET Bible First Edition*; Bible. English. NET Bible; *The NET Bible* (Biblical Studies Press, 2005).]

[20] John A. Martin, "Luke," in *The Bible Knowledge Commentary: An Exposition of the Scriptures*, ed. J. F. Walvoord and R. B. Zuck, vol. 2 (Wheaton, IL: Victor Books, 1985), 225.

[21] Johannes P. Louw and Eugene Albert Nida, *Greek-English Lexicon of the New Testament: Based on Semantic Domains* (New York: United Bible Societies, 1996), 331.

[22] Ibid., 774.

[23] For a defense of this position, see Birger Gerhardsson, *The Testing of God's Son* (Eugene: Wipf and Stock Publishers, 1966), 25ff.

[24] (1) Self-sufficiency—make bread from rocks; (2) self-preservation—prove God will save your life from death; and (3) self-exaltation—the rule of earth does not have to go through the cross.

[25] Horst Robert Balz and Gerhard Schneider, *Exegetical Dictionary of the New Testament* (Grand Rapids, MI: Eerdmans, 1990–), 248.

[26] Ibid., 409.

CHAPTER 8

Other Secrets of the Kingdom of God

The parable of the sower (Mark 4:1–9) reveals *the* secret of the sovereign administration of God: that elite status in the coming rule of God on earth must be earned by faithful devotion to the commands of God. This status will not come by heredity. Nor will it come on the basis of favoritism. Self-sufficiency, self-preservation, and self-exaltation must be abandoned. It is trust in God's sufficiency, preservation, and exaltation that will ensure a disciple receives commendation, exaltation, and honoration at the Bema judgment.

Yet there are still many secrets yet to be revealed about the sovereign administration of God. Many of these secrets are revealed in the remainder of Mark 4: Jesus' discussion about the lamp (4:21:15), Jesus' parable of the growing seed (4:26:29), and Jesus' parable of the mustard seed (4:30:32).

Let's start by looking at Jesus' discussion about the lamp.

And he said to them, "Is a lamp brought in to be put under a basket, or under a bed, and not on a stand? For nothing is hidden except to be made manifest; nor is anything secret except to come to light. If anyone has ears to hear, let him hear." And he said to them, "Pay attention to what you hear: with the measure you use, it will be measured to you, and still more will be added to you. For to the one who has, more will be given, and from the one who has not, even what he has will be taken away." (Mark 4:21–25)

As we read this question, we must think about its context in the larger chapter. In this case, it is immediately preceded by the parable of the sower. Thus, the first question one must ask is, "Is there a relationship between our Lord's comments about the parable of the sower and the parable of the lamp? If so, what?" Many see both our Lord's comments about the lamp (Mark 4:21–23) and his comments about additions and deletions (Mark 4:24–25) as additional parables,[1] yet it may be better to see them as further insight on the parable of the sower instead.

The content of Mark 4:21–25 appears in several places in Matthew and Luke, as well.[2] Yet, nowhere is this material explicitly identified as a parable. Rather, our Lord's comments appear in his explanation of the parable of the sower. Thus, it is better to see Mark, not as recording a new parable, but as continuing our Lord's explanation of the significance of the parable of the sower for the insiders.

REVELATION OF KINGDOM REWARDS

The parable of the sower revealed the secret of the sovereign administration of God. Since leadership status in this administration must be earned, this will necessitate that the identity of the insiders be hidden until the appropriate time. At that time, revelation will come. Our Lord's illustration of this very point can be found in Mark 4:21–23. The purpose of bringing a lamp in is not to conceal it (put it under a basket or bed), but to put it on its stand. Just like a lamp, even that which is hidden or secret will eventually be exposed. Insiders will expose their purpose for all to see. This is part of God's plan.

As with the previous passage, to properly understand Mark 4:24–25, we must place it in its larger context. Here it follows the parable of the talents (Matt. 25:14–30). In this parable, the Lord explained that for faithful disciples, commendation, exaltation, and honoration await. But for unfaithful disciples, there will be denouncement, demotion, and divarication (Matt. 25:26–30). Not only will there be denouncement, demotion, and divarication, but these things will be meted out in proportion to the disciples' actions ("With the measure you use, it will be measured to you," Mark 4:24–25).

In Mark 4:24–25, we learn that both insiders and outsiders determine their destinies by their actions. For insiders, their rewards will be positive. For outsiders, their rewards will be negative. For insiders, their actions will determine the degree of their gain. For outsiders, their actions will determine the degree of their loss.

THE PARABLE OF THE GROWING SEED

Mark 4:26–29 lists the second of three kingdom parables in Mark's account in which we learn more about the secrets of the sovereign administration of the kingdom of God. The parable is unique to Mark's Gospel, but the central message is not. The text reads,

> *And he said, "The kingdom of God is as if a man should scatter seed on the ground. He sleeps and rises night and day, and the seed sprouts and grows; he knows not how. The earth produces by itself, first the blade, then the ear, then the full grain in the ear. But when the grain is ripe, at once he puts in the sickle, because the harvest has come."*

There is no consensus among scholars concerning how this parable is labeled. Guelich calls it "the parable of the seed's growth."[3] James A. Brooks labels it "the parable of the seed growing spontaneously."[4] Hendriksen and Kistemaker call it the "parable of the seed growing in secret."[5] The title of the parable is ultimately driven by what one sees as its central emphasis. "The sower," "the seed," "secret growth," and "the harvest" are all potential contenders.

Regardless of what we name the parable, the seed motif (which occurs in all three of the explicitly identified parables of Mark 4) appears. The seed is explicitly identified as "the word about the sovereign administration of God, i.e., "Repent, for the kingdom of heaven is at hand." In the parable of the sower, we discovered who will repent and bring forth fruit worthy of repentance. In this second "seed" parable, we discover that the growth of the sovereign administration of God will be natural.

In chapter one, Mark introduced the kingdom of God as the central core message of Jesus Christ. Jesus came shouting out loud that the sovereign administration of God on earth had begun. Until Jesus, the physical manifestation of the rule of God had been exercised from heaven through intermediaries (prophets, priests, and kings). With the arrival of the God-Man, that changed. Now, the physical manifestation of the sovereign administration of God—through the Messiah Jesus— began. Throughout Jesus' ministry, we see evidence of this sovereign authority as Jesus cast out demons and removed disease, death, and decay.

But for Jesus' listeners, one of the secrets of the sovereign administration of God was its development. Jesus' listeners were expecting God's physical rule on earth to be announced by cataclysmic disturbances in the sky and to result in political upheaval, leading to the people of God ruling from Jerusalem (Zeph. 1:14–18). As we learn from this seed parable, however, this is not how God's sovereign administration would begin. It would begin small and without much fanfare, then grow until all of the earth was under its authority. This parable tells us that disciples must not allow the kingdom's slow start to influence their confidence regarding its ultimate manifestation at the King's appearance to rule.

Note that the growth of the kingdom is not in the hands of the sower. The initial words of Mark 4:26 should be rendered: "The sovereign administration of God is like a man who scattered the seed on the ground." The introduction draws no special attention to the sower of the seed. Apart from the scattering and harvesting, the sower has little to do with its actual growth. Once sown, the farmer must wait for natural and unknown processes to work. He "sleeps and rises night and day." "The seed sprouts and grows; he knows not how" (v. 27). The most important aspects of the seed's growth remain outside the sower's knowledge or control. Germination and growth occur without the sower's help. "The growth process is summarized: "The earth produces by itself, first the blade, then the ear, then the full grain in the ear."

Once growth and production have occurred, harvest occurs. This kingdom parable illustrates the fact that God's ordained way of growth will occur regarding the sovereign administration of God. God will continue to grow the ranks of those who will be included in the kingdom's elite leadership. Once satisfied, God will initiate the harvest, which transitions the physical manifestation of ruling authority permanently on earth.

THE PARABLE OF THE MUSTARD SEED

And he said, "With what can we compare the kingdom of God, or what parable shall we use for it? It is like a grain of mustard seed, which, when sown on the ground, is the smallest of all the seeds on earth, yet when it is sown it grows up and becomes larger than all the garden plants and puts out large branches, so that the birds of the air can make nests in its shade." (Mark 4:30–32)

Mark's third and final kingdom parable is also a "seed" parable. The parable of the mustard seed is among the very few parables to occur in the Gospels of Matthew, Mark, and Luke. Most focus on peculiarities that exist between these three accounts. However, the point of the parable is not difficult to understand. A grain of mustard seed begins very small but ends larger than all garden plants. France correctly captures the point of comparison when he writes, "It is this contrast between an insignificant beginning and an impressive final size which is the point of the simile.[6]

In one sense, the sovereign administration of God began with the birth of the king. By all earthly standards, this birth was unremarkable. Even with the angelic accompaniment, few knew anything about it. Those who did were challenged in everything they had come to expect. With the birth of one child who, in the world's view, was unimportant, the sovereign administration or royal rule of God had begun.

For more than thirty years, nothing seemingly happened. Then after another three-and-one-half years, Jesus, the God-Man, began calling men and women to join him in pursuing the lofty goal of earning elite status in the coming rule of God on earth. Though then (as now), men overwhelmingly rejected God's offer, the ranks will grow. When God ultimately completes the court of his royal house leadership, a permanent physical manifestation of the rule of heaven will come to earth. At that time, God will have answered the prayer of the ages: "Thy kingdom come, thy will be done on earth as it is in heaven." The Lord Jesus will sit on his glorious throne, and those who earned the right to join him will do the same.

The whole world will submit to his rule. What was once a kingdom of one baby boy born into the dirt and grime of a stranger's stable will become the ruler of all creation. That is truly a mustard seed story if there ever was one!

Notes

1 John D. Grassmick, "Mark," in *The Bible Knowledge Commentary: An Exposition of the Scriptures*, ed. J. F. Walvoord and R. B. Zuck, vol. 2 (Wheaton, IL: Victor Books, 1985), 120.

2 Luke 8:16–18; Matt. 5:15 and Luke 11:33; Matt. 7:2 and Luke 6:38; Matt. 10:26 and Luke 12:2; Matt. 13:12; 25:29 and Luke 19:26.

3 Robert A. Guelich, "Mark 1–8:26," vol. 34a, *Word Biblical Commentary* (Dallas: Word, Inc., 1989), 237.

4 James A. Brooks, "Mark," vol. 23, *The New American Commentary* (Nashville: Broadman & Holman Publishers, 1991), 84.

5 William Hendriksen and Simon J. Kistemaker, "Exposition of the Gospel According to Mark," vol. 10, *New Testament Commentary* (Grand Rapids: Baker Book House, 1953–2001), 165.

6 R. T. France, "The Gospel of Mark: A Commentary on the Greek Text," *New International Greek Testament Commentary* (Grand Rapids, MI; Carlisle: W.B. Eerdmans; Paternoster Press, 2002), 216.

CHAPTER 9

Where Is My Seat?

I n the Gospel of Matthew, the mother of the sons of Zebedee comes to Jesus with a request for her two boys. The text records,

Then the mother of the sons of Zebedee came up to him with her sons, and kneeling before him she asked him for something. And he said to her, "What do you want?" She said to him, "Say that these two sons of mine are to sit, one at your right hand and one at your left, in your kingdom." Jesus answered, "You do not know what you are asking. Are you able to drink the cup that I am to drink?" They said to him, "We are able." He said to them, "You will drink my cup, but to sit at my right hand and at my left is not mine to grant, but it is for those for whom it has been prepared by my Father." (Matt. 20:20–23)

To many readers of the New Testament, this mother's question may be unsettling. Who would have the audacity to ask Jesus such a thing? But her question must not surprise us. Since our Lord began to shout out loud the good news from God, the most probative question on the minds of the Twelve was, "Who gets what?" Clearly, positions of honor in the coming kingdom were open. How one gets one of these positions must not have been clearly defined. The Lord Jesus' aunt, the mother of James and John of Zebedee, requested that her two boys sit "one at your right hand and one at your left." Would being seated in these positions be the highest honor possible?

Certainly, to be seated at the right hand of God is an exalted position. The book of Hebrews declares four times that Jesus, due to his faithfulness, received this honor: "He sat down at the right hand of the Majesty on high" (Heb. 1:3); "[Jesus] is seated at the right hand of the throne of the Majesty in heaven" (Heb. 8:1): "He [Jesus] sat down at the right hand of God" (Heb. 10:12); "[Jesus] is seated at the right hand of the throne of God" (Heb. 12:2). This is his reward for faithful service, which included his willingness to die on the cross.

The book of Hebrews reports Jesus taking this position as the fulfillment of messianic prophecy. Specifically, Hebrews 1:13 identifies Jesus as the fulfillment of Psalm 110:1, which a majority of scholars recognize as messianic.[1] Indeed, New Testament authors use Psalm 110 more than any other.[2] The verse states, "To which of the angels has he ever said, "Sit at my right hand until I make your enemies a footstool for your feet'"? This, the Hebrew writer says of the Son, Jesus Christ.

It is this, the very first verse of Psalm 110, that now draws our attention. Mark 12:35–37 states,

As Jesus taught in the temple, he said, "How can the scribes say that the Christ is the son of David? David himself, in the Holy Spirit, declared, 'The Lord said to my Lord, "Sit at my right hand, until I put your enemies under your feet."' David himself calls him Lord. So how is he his son?"

With his response, Jesus silenced the religious leaders. Mark 12:34 states, "After that, no one dared to ask him any more questions." Jesus had put the religious leaders in a time-out. So what is happening here?

In this passage, Jesus asked, "How can the scribes say that Christ is the son of David?" By this question, he is not denying Davidic parentage for the Christ. He is questioning the glass ceiling placed on him by the religious leaders of Israel. Logically, a son is inherently subordinate to his father. This is the normal, natural, customary way of thinking about a son. Yet, such thinking ignores another aspect of the Christ as presented in the Old Testament, one that the religious leaders were missing: his lordship.

There is no explicit reference in the Old Testament to the effect that Christ is a Davidite. While there may be a lack of explicit Old Testament scriptural basis to make this declaration, the same is not the case with his lordship. This is explicitly asserted in Scripture. It is to this very point that our Lord directs the scribes and others in the temple to consider. Our Lord asks, "How can the scribes say that Christ is the son of David?"

Since the scribes are the experts on the actual text of Old Testament Scripture (their job was to copy it word for word), who better to ask this question than them? We can assume that there is a pause after our Lord's question to allow the scribes to answer. After receiving no reply, Jesus reports, "David himself, in the Holy Spirit, declared...." What Jesus is about to articulate is from the inspired mouth of King David.

214 of CHARLES COOPER

By emphasizing that David himself wrote these words and that the Holy Spirit inspired them, Jesus gives no wiggle room for the scribes to reject what the text says. David himself declared, "The Lord said to my Lord."

The brilliance of Jesus to say a lot with so few words is on full display here. Every morning, the faithful practicing Jew rose to repeat the Shema: "Hear, O Israel: The Lord our God, the Lord is one," which Jesus referenced in Mark 12:29–31. Thus, every Jewish person would have recognized immediately without needing clarification that "The Lord our God" is the referent. Jesus understands the sentence to mean: "The Lord [God] said to my [David's] lord [the Christ]."

Jesus points out that David has recognized the lordship of Christ, which demands that Christ be more than a mere Davidite. In Mark 12:35–37, Jesus uses an explicit reference to Psalm 110:1 to make this point. The Christ is David's Lord. The uniqueness of Christ is evidenced by his invitation: "Sit at my right hand until I put your enemies under your feet." The exaltation of the Christ to "sit at my right hand" is far more significant than maybe first perceived.

THE RIGHT HAND: AN ELEVATED PLACE OF AUTHORITY

Most scholars recognize that an invitation to "sit at my right hand" suggests an elevation to a place of authority, power, and honor.[3] Used in Psalm 110:1, it connotes the unusual exaltation of David's Lord. By God's invitation, Christ assumes the most honored seat in all of creation, which speaks to his uniqueness. The implication is not subtle. When asked by the high priest at his trial, "Are you the Christ, the Son of the Blessed?" Jesus responded, "I am, and you will see the Son of Man seated at the right hand of

Power, and coming with the clouds of heaven." To this, the high priest tore his garments and said, "What further witnesses do we need? You have heard his blasphemy."

There are three declarative statements here: (1) "I am" the Christ; (2) "You will see the Son of Man seated at the right hand of Power"; and (3) "You will see the Son of Man ... coming with the clouds of heaven." Which of these three is a blasphemous statement? None. However, in the minds of the Jewish leadership, it was all three. Nothing about Jesus satisfied their expectation of what the Christ would do or say. They did not have a problem with the Christ being seated at the right hand of God. They had a problem with Jesus applying that claim—and that honor—to himself.

In neither the Old Testament nor the New Testament does anyone claim the honor of taking a seat at God's right hand, with one exception. Jesus! With honor comes authority. The Christ will exercise divine prerogatives (Rev. 2:26–27; 3:23), including being the divine cloud-rider. God as a cloud-rider is referenced several times in the Old Testament: Psalm 104:1–4; Daniel 7:13; Isaiah 19:1; and Psalm 18:9–15. Since God alone is the cloud-rider, for Jesus to claim this position was blasphemous indeed in the eyes of the religious leaders. Jesus was claiming to be God.

It is not clear how much the disciples understood about Christ's coming kingdom. However, it is apparent that they fully expected roles of honor to be given to them.

The mother of John and James requested that her two sons sit one at his right hand and one at his left in the coming kingdom. These positions of honor were available, but Jesus was not the one responsible for assigning them. Nor were those positions obtained by favoritism. Rather, Jesus answered, "You do not know what you are asking. Are you able to drink the cup that I am to drink?" "To drink the cup" implies that the honor of elite status in the coming kingdom of Christ is earned. Jesus had to earn it, and so must we.

For those who perhaps are still skeptical, Jesus' question is very insightful. Jesus obtained his seat by enduring pain and suffering that ended with death (Matt. 26:39, 42). The highest positions of honor in the coming kingdom must be earned by suffering, as well. Yet, even with a resume of suffering and death, it is the prerogative of the Father who gets the most honored seats.

It is unclear whether the disciples understood the metaphorical use of "drinking the cup." This cup that Jesus was about to drink involved both suffering and death, which he would request on several occasions that the Father "remove" from him. However, there is no indication that the disciples understood this and could contextualize our Lord's meaning.[4]

France identifies "the cup of suffering and judgment"[5] that blocks our Lord's path to glory. Evan calls it "the cup of wrath."[6] For Jesus, the metaphor of the "cup" is his death. There is no reason to believe that he did not have the fullest comprehension of what awaited him. On three previous occasions, Jesus warned the disciples that "the Son of Man would be delivered over to the chief priests and scribes, and they would condemn him to death and deliver him over to the Gentiles to be mocked and flogged and crucified." Jesus knew that his death would be painful and vicious, but he also knew that the crown of gold comes through the crown of thorns.

Thus, while the disciples might experience the same "cup" of death as Jesus did, he had no ability to assign them the two unique positions of honor they requested. He explained to his disciples that this prerogative is the exclusive domain of the Father: "To sit at my right hand

and at my left is not mine to grant, but it is for those for whom my Father has prepared it."

In Mathew 19:28, in response to the rejection of Jesus by the rich young ruler (the poster child for the third soil of the parable of the sower), Jesus gave the Twelve some very interesting news. He told them,

> *"Truly, I say to you, in the new world, when the Son of Man will sit on his glorious throne, you who have followed me will also sit on twelve thrones, judging the twelve tribes of Israel."*

Luke 22:28–30, which parallels Matthew's account, reports,

> *"You are those who have stayed with me in my trials, and I assign to you, as my Father assigned to me, a kingdom, that you may eat and drink at my table in my kingdom and sit on thrones judging the twelve tribes of Israel."*

Earning a kingship by suffering is modeled by Jesus' own life. It is compelling that he told the Twelve that their seats in the coming kingdom had already been determined. However, unlike the seats of greatest honor, their exaltation to the status of ruler during the Lord's reign is Jesus' prerogative. Here, the Lord answered Peter's question back in Matthew 19:27: "Then Peter said in reply, 'See, we have left everything and followed you. What then will we have?'" There is great irony here. If the rich young ruler had abandoned all his worldly goods and followed Christ, he would have gained far more than he had given up. He would have received the material blessings promised in this life, including elite status and rulership in the sovereign administration of God on earth, and the treasures stored up for him in heaven (Matt. 6:19–21), as well.

All of these promises are fulfilled "in the new world when the Son of Man will sit on his glorious throne." "The new world" is the expression chosen by the ESV to translate the Greek term παλιγγενεσία (*palingenesia*). The NET Bible prefers "in the age when all things are renewed." The KJV has "in the regeneration." The term is used twice in the New Testament.[7] In Matthew, it applies to the created order. In Titus 3:5, Paul applies it to men and women. In both cases, the dominant idea is new birth. New Testament scholars are not uniform in their convictions about the origin of this term as used by Matthew. Many are convinced that he borrowed it from Hellenism, where "it generally refers to the rebirth of the individual soul or the cosmos."[8]

Sim summaries Matthean scholars' view of Matthew 19:28 well when he writes,

> While all scholars accept that this term possesses eschatological import, there is no agreement on its precise meaning. One school of thought argues that the term reflects the common apocalyptic belief in the re-creation of the cosmic order after its prior destruction at the eschaton. Other scholars, however, dispute this interpretation and insist that παλιγγενεσία has basically temporal connotations; it refers merely to the new age which will succeed the present age.[9]

Few scholars believe the Lord Jesus actually spoke the word παλιγγενεσία during his ministry. Rather, most insist that "Matthew inserted" it.[10] Seemingly, a majority of scholars are so committed to their view of the compilation of the New Testament with respect to the Synoptic Gospels from written sources only that the role of the Holy Spirit is ridiculously minimized. Over a three-and-one-half-year period, the Lord Jesus taught on the subject of the gospel of God many, many times. What he said and how he said it are not detailed at every event.

With the Twelve, Jesus inaugurated the divine campaign to build his leadership constituency for the eventual physical manifestation of the divine rule of God on earth. All subsequent followers of Jesus are offered the opportunity to earn an elite position of leadership in his coming royal rule by suffering, as well. Therefore, it is critical that disciples understand when rewards will be given and exercised.

Matthew 19:28 explicitly tells us when in the sequence of end-time events this important transition will occur. As previously stated, Peter asks literally, "What then shall be to us?" Jesus explains, "Truly, I say to you all...." Jesus is speaking to the Twelve, which includes Judas. Jesus continues, "Truly, I say to you all that you all who have followed [aorist participle] me . . .." Notice the aspect highlighted here. First, Jesus is speaking only to the Twelve. There is no application beyond this because there are only twelve tribes of Israel.

Second, Jesus speaks of the history of the "followship" of the Twelve to this moment. He grants subordinate kingships to the Twelve based on their behavior: "You are those who have stayed with me in my trials, and I assign to you, as my Father assigned to me, a kingdom, that you may eat and drink at my table in my kingdom and sit on thrones judging the twelve tribes of Israel" (Luke 22:28–30).

Therefore, before their deaths, the Twelve knew that they would reign with Christ as kings. Ἐν τῇ παλιγγενεσίᾳ is the Greek phrase our Lord uses to explain when this will occur. In the παλιγγενεσίᾳ, when the Son of Man sits down on his glorious throne, is when this wonderful promise will be fulfilled.

It is our conviction that human history as we know it will end with the final week of Daniel's prophecy concerning the last seven years of Gentile dominance over the Jews and Jerusalem (Dan. 9:24–27). With the last blast of God's wrath against Satan, the beast, and the beast-marked worshippers in the form of seven bowl judgments, which devastate the physical earth, God will renew the earth for the reign of his Son, Jesus.

Notes

¹ For a defense of a messianic interpretation of Psalm 110, see Herbert W. Bateman, "Psalm 110:1 and the New Testament," *Bibliotheca Sacra* 149 (1992); Barry C. Davis, "Is Psalm 110 a Messianic Psalm?" *Bibliotheca Sacra* 157 (2000): 160ff.

² Ibid., 160; Psalm 110 is cited in Matt. 22:44; 26:64; Mark 12:36; 14:62; Luke 20:42–43; 22:69; Acts 2:34–35; Heb. 1:13; 5:6; 7:17, 21 and alluded to in Mark 16:19; John 12:34; Rom. 8:34; 1 Cor. 15:25; Eph. 1:20; Col 3:1; Heb. 1:3; 5:10; 6:20; 7:3; 8:1; 10:12–13; 12:2.

³ Robert G. Bratcher and Eugene Albert Nida, *A Handbook on the Gospel of Mark*, UBS Handbook Series (New York: United Bible Societies, 1993), 389; Craig A. Evans, "Mark 8:27–16:20," vol. 34b, *Word Biblical Commentary* (Dallas: Word, Inc., 2001), 273. John Aloisi, "Who Is David's Lord? Another Look at Psalm 110:1," *Detroit Baptist Seminary Journal*, vol. 10 (2005), 106.

⁴ See Psalm 11:6; 75:8; Isa. 51:17, 22; Jer. 25:15–17, 27–28; 49:12; 51:7.

⁵ R. T. France, "The Gospel of Mark: A Commentary on the Greek Text," *New International Greek Testament Commentary* (Grand Rapids, MI; Carlisle: W.B. Eerdmans; Paternoster Press, 2002), 585–586

⁶ Craig A. Evans, Mark 8:27–16:20, vol. 34b, *Word Biblical Commentary* (Dallas: Word, Inc., 2001), 413. As does James A. Brooks, "Mark," vol. 23, *The New American Commentary* (Nashville: Broadman & Holman Publishers, 1991), 168.

⁷ Matthew 19:28; Titus 3:5.

⁸ Burnett, F. W. (1983). Παλιγγενεσια in Matt. 19:28: "A Window on the Matthean Community?" *Journal for the Study of the New Testament*, 5(17), 60. https://doi.org/10.1177/0142064X8300501708 (last accessed 1/13/2024).

⁹ Sim, D. C. (1993). "The Meaning of παλιγγενεσία in Matthew 19:28," *Journal for the Study of the New Testament*, 15(50), 10. https://doi.org/10.1177/0142064X9301505001. (last accessed 1/13/2024)

¹⁰ Ibid., 3.

CHAPTER 10

Will There Be Crying at the Bema Seat?

The insistence by a majority of New Testament scholars of merging together the good news from God and the good news about Jesus Christ ensures that virtually every page of the New Testament results in confusion. Passages that speak of sanctification are confused with passages about salvation. For some, any suggestion of loss of salvation due to unfaithfulness only proves that the person was never saved in the first place. For others, it proves that a person can be saved for a while but eventually lose his or her salvation due to unfaithfulness.

The idea that one can lose his or her salvation due to unfaithfulness is often drawn from the three linked parables in Matthew 24 and 25 regarding the delayed return of the master. These parables address not only the master's delay, but also the consequences of being unprepared or not preparing appropriately for his return.[1]

The first of these parables concerns ten virgins (Matt. 25:1–13). Once the master appears, it is too late to get ready. In the other two, Jesus focuses, not on being unprepared, but on not preparing *appropriately* for the master's return (Matt. 24:45–25:30; 45–5²).

In the first of these two servant parables, Jesus says:

> *"Who then is the faithful and wise servant, whom the master has put in charge of the servants in his household to give them their food at the proper time? It will be good for that servant whose master finds him doing so when he returns. Truly I tell you, he will put him in charge of all his possessions. But suppose that servant is wicked and says to himself, 'My master is staying away a long time,' and he then begins to beat his fellow servants and to eat and drink with drunkards. The master of that servant will come on a day when he does not expect him and at an hour he is not aware of. He will cut him to pieces and assign him a place with the hypocrites, where there will be weeping and gnashing of teeth." (Matt. 24:45–51)*

In the parable of the talents, Jesus says, [3]

> *"For it will be like a man going on a journey, who called his servants and entrusted to them his property. To one he gave five talents, to another two, to another one, to each according to his ability. Then he went away.*

"He who had received the five talents went at once and traded with them, and he made five talents more. So also he who had the two talents made two talents more. But he who had received the one talent went and dug in the ground and hid his master's money.

"Now after a long time the master of those servants came and settled accounts with them.

"And he who had received the five talents came forward, bringing five talents more, saying, 'Master, you delivered to me five talents; here, I have made five talents more.' His master said to him, 'Well done, good and faithful servant. You have been faithful over a little; I will set you over much. Enter into the joy of your master.'

"And he also who had the two talents came forward, saying, 'Master, you delivered to me two talents; here, I have made two talents more.' His master said to him, 'Well done, good and faithful servant. You have been faithful over a little; I will set you over much. Enter into the joy of your master.'

"He also who had received the one talent came forward, saying, 'Master, I knew you to be a hard man, reaping where you did not sow, and gathering where you scattered no seed, so I was afraid, and I went and hid your talent in the ground. Here, you have what is yours.' But his master answered him, 'You wicked and slothful servant! You knew that I reap where I have not sown and gather where I scattered no seed? Then you ought to have invested my money with the bankers, and at my coming I should have received what was my own with interest.

"So, take the talent from him and give it to him who has the ten talents. For to everyone who has will more be given, and he will have an abundance. But from the one who has not, even what he has will be taken away. And cast the worthless servant into the outer darkness. In that place there will be weeping and gnashing of teeth." (Matt. 25:14–30)

Based on a superficial understanding, it is easy to see why many NT scholars hold the view that the worthless servants in both of these parables either lose their salvation or never had it in the first place. Typical of those holding to this view is Barbieri as reflected in *Bible Knowledge Commentary*: "Like the unworthy servant in

24:48–51, he [the servant who buried the talent] too would be eternally separated from God."[4] Thus, in Barbieri's view, the parable of the talents is about who will be spiritually saved and who will be spiritually lost.

Hagner comes to a similar conclusion. In his commentary on Matthew, he writes,

> The disciple who, on the other hand, fails to make productive use of what has been given faces the terrifying prospect of ultimate loss. The faithful will be further blessed; the unfaithful will lose all.[5]

R. T. France comes to a similar conclusion. He adds,

> In v. 30, as in 24:51, the story has been "invaded" by its application, and the traditional description of the fate of the wicked . . . makes explicit that the parable is to be understood . . . . in terms of the ultimate basis of salvation or condemnation.[6]

As long as there remains confusion about the good news from God and the good news about Jesus Christ, there will be this type of confusion and contradiction in interpreting New Testament Scripture. Salvation is a *faith* issue. Sanctification is a *faithfulness* issue. There is only one condition on which to receive personal salvation—faith—and we fail to see how unfaithfulness (a sin) in the life of a believer is not covered by the atonement of Christ. Yet there are countless conditions attached to receiving heavenly rewards as a result of one's continued *sanctification*.

There is a similar duality when it comes to consequences. The consequence of a lack of personal salvation is eternal punishment. The consequence of having lived a life of carnality is loss of rewards (1 Cor. 3:15). The gospel from God calls men to live sanctified lives in order to turn away God's coming judgment. The gospel about Jesus Christ calls men to believe in the death, burial, and resurrection of Jesus for the forgiveness of sin (Luke 24:47).

Understanding the difference between the two gospels is imperative for correctly interpreting the New Testament. Nowhere is this more important than in the gospels of Matthew, Mark, and Luke. There is no basis to see the death, burial, and resurrection of Jesus Christ for the forgiveness of sin controlling the meaning of these books. It is the good news from God that dictates the meaning of these texts.

WHO'S THE AUDIENCE?

In determining the appropriate interpretation of the three linked parables, the most probative question concerns the intended audience. Understanding the audience helps us determine the intent of the speaker—in this case, Jesus. Knowing whether Jesus is talking to believers only, to both believers and unbelievers or to unbelievers only greatly influences how one interprets the parables. It is our position that he is speaking to believers here. Thus, he is speaking to an audience made up of those who already believe and are committed to following him.

By way of reminder, Luke 8:9–10 states the purpose of parables. He records,

> When his disciples asked him [Jesus] what this parable meant, he said, "To you it has been given to know the secrets of the kingdom of God, but for others they are in parables, so that 'seeing they may not see, and hearing they may not understand.'"

Stated another way, the purpose of speaking in parables in the public arena was to keep outsiders (unbelievers)[7] ignorant and insiders (disciples) informed about kingdom operations and outcomes.

In Matthew 24:45–51, we have δοῦλος (a slave or servant) who can be either "faithful and wise" or "bad." In Matthew 25:1–13, we find ten virgins. Again, five of them are wise and five of them are foolish or bad. Finally, in Matthew 25:14–30, we find δοῦλος (slave or servant) again, who can be either "good and faithful" or "worthless and lazy."

Depending on one's theological presuppositions, who is represented in each parable is often predetermined before exegesis. Classical dispensational thinkers limit the text to national Israel. Barbieri's comments are typical when he writes,

> When the Lord returns "in His glory," He will judge not only the nation Israel (as in the Parable of the 10 Virgins [vv. 1–13] and the Parable of the Talents [vv. 14–30]) but also the Gentiles.[8]

Blomberg stands at the opposite extreme. He sees all humanity represented in this parable. He writes,

> The "three characters" are thus the master, the two good servants taken together, and the wicked servant. The final reckoning scene again refers to the final judgment that all people will undergo as they give account to God for what they have done with their lives .... Three points may again be discerned, one per the main character. (1) Like the master, God entrusts all people with a portion of his resources, expecting them to act as good stewards of it. (2) Like the two good servants, God's people will be commended and rewarded when they have faithfully discharged that

commission. (3) Like the wicked servant, those who fail to use the gifts God has given them for his service will be punished by separation from God and all things good.[9]

Between Barbieri's view that the parable's application is limited to Jews only and Blomberg's view that it extends to all mankind is Nolland, who gives an abbreviated analysis of the historical interpretation of the one-talent servant. Noting the different position of various authors, Nolland states:

Does the slave who buried the talent stand for those who fail to manifest the virtues of fidelity and effort (Jülicher), or those who preserve the Jewish tradition but make no profitable use of it for God (Jeremias), or the fearful legalists (Dupont), or those who will not make fruitful for God what Jesus brings (in various forms, Weiser, Weder, Didier), or the scribes and Pharisees, who see Jesus' God as too demanding (Lambrecht), or those who when faced with the challenge of the message of the kingdom of God, with its call to a bold readiness to risk all, take refuge in a sterile security (Puig i Tàrrech)?[10]

Where do we stand on these parables? We recognize that care must be taken not to force parables to say more than the author intended. At the same time, we maintain that their purpose was to enlighten insiders ("those around him with the twelve, Mark 4:10). Our view (and one that escapes most readers) is that the Olivet Discourse (Matt. 24–25) was given to Peter, James, John, and Andrew (Mark 13:3). These parables were spoken to insiders—believers in the kingdom message of Jesus. This is critical to understanding their meaning.

10 REASONS THE "SERVANTS" ARE DISCIPLES

In our view, ten reasons support the view that the servants in these parables are disciples (insiders). Thus, as parables spoken *to* disciples *about* disciples, the meaning of these parables cannot relate to the issue of spiritual salvation, but rather sanctification. We will take a look at the reasons for this here.

Matthew's parable of the talents is a kingdom parable, a fact to which the overwhelming majority of New Testament scholars agree. As such, it reveals a principle or principles of the kingdom of God. In the kingdom parables, the Lord Jesus teaches five things: (1) how the kingdom started; (2) how the kingdom grows; (3) how the kingdom transitions from the temporal phase to the eternal phase; (4) who the constituents of the kingdom are; and (5) how to earn rewards in the coming kingdom.

At this point, we are concerned with the identity of the constituents of the kingdom. In the parable of the talents, the master "called his servants and entrusted to them his property." Here are ten reasons that we believe all three "servants" represent disciples with spiritual salvation:

1. The Olivet Discourse was given to disciples who, if fortunate to be alive on the earth at the consummation, must live in constant readiness for the Son of Man's return (Matt. 24:3) to avoid negative consequences at the great harvest judgment. This is the same message John the Baptist preached during his earthly ministry.

2. Matthew 25:13 is a call for watchfulness. A second-person plural imperative is used here. The subject of our Lord's command is his disciples, both those sitting in front of him and those of us who would read his words later.

3. Matthew 25:14 identifies the servants as belonging to the master. It is inconceivable that the master would trust strangers or non-servants to manage his property. The call of the servants is to faithfulness in the discharge of their responsibilities while the master is away.

4. The purpose of parables was to limit "insider information"[11] to those who continued to walk with Jesus as disciples. Outsiders, who could be either disciples or critics, were kept ignorant of the secrets of the kingdom of God. How would an unbeliever be expected to be faithful to that that he is ignorant of?

5. The reason the one-talent servant hid the master's property until he returned was fear. Jesus exhorts his disciples not to hide their light (Matt. 5:14-15) and their faith (John 12:42; 19:38). The one-talent servant prepared for his master's return, but sadly, not correctly. This does not prove that the servant is lost, only that he is disobedient and unwise.

6. Upon the master's return, servants can expect a call to account for their service following the master's delayed return. Subsequent NT revelation reveals several judgments connected with this event. Theological presuppositions force this parable to apply to rapture positions. However, when during the end-time sequence the master's servants will give an account is not specified in the parable of the talents. We only know that an accounting will occur.

7. At no point is there any indication that the "servants" are anything other than servants. In other words, the master never doubted their identity. At issue is not who they are, but their faithfulness during his absence.

8. Each servant is explicitly stated to have been given talents "according to his ability." *Dynamis* (δύναμις = power, might) used in Matthew 24:15, Balz and Schneider suggest

means "ability or capability."[12] No unbeliever has the ability or capability to please God in service prior to salvation.

At the parabolic level, all three "talent" receivers are equal in the sense that they are servants. There is no indication that the servants are required to obtain something beyond what they already have to fulfill their mission. They already have everything they need. Therefore, the master knows enough about his servants to entrust them with his property. The idea that God entrusts kingdom knowledge to an unbeliever to carry to other unbelievers is unfathomable. There is no New Testament precedent for this notion. No unbeliever has the "ability" or "capability" to serve God faithfully prior to receiving the new birth.

Recognizing the need to exercise caution, we do not read the writings of the apostle Paul back into Matthew, but we do maintain doctrinal consistency across the whole of Scripture. Thirty-plus years after our Lord gave the Olivet Discourse to Peter, James, John, and Andrew, Paul makes explicit what is implied in Matthew 13:

> The natural person does not accept the things of the Spirit of God, for they are folly to him, and he is not able to understand them because they are spiritually discerned. (1 Cor. 2:14)

There is a consensus among New Testament scholars that the Greek Term *psychikós* (natural, human)[13] "means natural humanity without the eschatological gift of the *pneúma* (Spirit)."[14] Rather than accepting "the things of the Spirit of God" as truth, "they are folly to him." According to Paul, the natural person is not able (*dynamai*) to understand them. *Dynamai* is the verb form of the noun *dynamis*, which occurs in Matthew 25:15 and is translated as "ability." The natural person cannot understand the things of the Spirit.

Kistemaker and Hendriksen summarize 1 Corinthians 2:14 this way:

> The natural man belongs to the world, while the spiritual man belongs to God. The one is an unbeliever and the other a believer; the one lacks the Spirit while the other has the Spirit; the one follows natural instincts (Jude 19), the other follows the Lord.[15]

In our estimation, Paul's theology of man makes it impossible for any one of the servants in the parable of the talents to be an unbeliever. Why would God entrust spiritual truth to a man devoid of the Spirit, who, by definition, does not have the capacity to understand the very truth entrusted? Leon Morris is right when he states, "Anyone whose equipment is only of this world, who has not received the Holy Spirit, has no ability to make an estimate of things spiritual."[16]

Thus, in the parable of the talents, we can say that all three servants were truly *servants* in the fullest sense of the word. All three were entrusted with the master's property. All three had the requisite ability to fulfill his or her obligation. All three will be judged by the same standard—production. All three will face the possibility of reward or punishment.

9. Matthew 25:28 indicates that the one-talent servant will suffer loss at the master's reckoning. The talent is actually taken away from him. If the one-talent servant is lost, then he was never saved. Thus, what is taken away cannot be spiritual salvation. If the person is lost and was never saved, then what does he have to lose? Arminians would say that this person lost his salvation due to

unfaithfulness. However, the loss of salvation would have occurred long before the judgment. If this were the case, it would seem (tragically) that the one-talent servant would have no clue that he or she had become lost until the reckoning. This scenario points more towards the loss of rewards than the loss of spiritual salvation. Particularly given that the talent is taken and given to another person. If the five- and two-talent servants represent those who are saved, giving them additional salvation at this point makes no sense. This alone in our estimation rules out any possibility that the one-talent servant was saved and then lost. Or that the "talent" has anything to do with spiritual salvation. To give the talent to the servant who has ten makes no sense if the talent is spiritual salvation.

10. It is possible for believers to suffer loss for unfaithfulness. The apostle Paul makes this point abundantly clear in 1 Corinthians 3:10–15. He says outright, "If anyone's work is burned up, he will suffer loss, though he himself will be saved, but only as through fire." While some insist that rewards are lost but no other negative consequences will follow, we warn all men to abandon this notion. The negative consequences detailed in Matthew 25:28–30 are intended for believers.

DO THE TALENTS REPRESENT KNOWLEDGE OF THE KINGDOM?

Clearly, Jesus, the Son of Man, is the master who calls his disciples to behave while he is away, with the expectation of rewarding their faithfulness or punishing unfaithfulness upon his return. The single most consistent element of Matthew 24–25 is the return of the Son of Man. His return marks a defining turn in human history. This is a key doctrine in the kingdom parables.

Matthew, Mark, and Luke have been very careful to draw a distinct line between those who are insiders and those who are outsiders relative to our Lord's teachings about the kingdom. All can hear the parables, but only the insiders get the correct interpretation.

If Jesus limited kingdom understanding to insiders, why would he entrust kingdom assets to unbelievers? Why would he expect faithfulness from an unbeliever? If unbelievers have no knowledge of the kingdom, why would Jesus entrust them with kingdom assets? No unbeliever is rewarded with salvation for faithfulness to God's law. There is no evidence that "chaff" ever becomes "wheat." There is no evidence that "not my sheep" becomes "my sheep." Yet, there are those who insist that Jesus gives unbelievers kingdom assets and holds them responsible for faithfulness.

That this is not true can be proven by understanding what the "talent" represents in this parable. Parabolically speaking, a "talent" is a certain amount of money. Does it have a specific counterpart in the spiritual arena? Ben Chenoweth argues that our Lord did intend significance with respect to "talent." After surveying different interpretive conclusions about the underlying referent, Chenoweth argues that the talents are "the knowledge of the secrets of the kingdom of heaven"[17] that Jesus entrusts to his disciples.

We agree that the parable of the talents is a kingdom parable.[18] Therefore, we expect to see truth(s) of the sovereign administration of God as with other parables. However, we disagree with Chenoweth about the identity of the talents. There is no indication anywhere in Matthew, Mark, or Luke that insiders have limitations on their knowledge.[19] Nor does Chenoweth explain how knowledge can be taken away once understood. How can taking away knowledge at the end of human history as we know it be a punishment? Since the judgment in view happens at the Lord's return, it must include those resurrected. How can resurrected saints have limitations imposed on their knowledge of the kingdom they now experience as resurrected saints?

Five facts about the nature of a "talent" seem to limit their intended meaning. First, a talent is a managed asset. Second, it is given according to a servant's ability. Third, a talent can be multiplied. Fourth, a talent can be taken from one servant and given to another. Fifth, the talent never belongs to the servant. These facts seem to rule out Chenoweth's conclusion. Taking away knowledge is not a punishment in the face of the beginning of the Lord's earthly kingdom.

Rather, we see the talent(s) as the opportunity all insiders have to earn elite status in the coming sovereign administration of God. In the coming kingdom, disciples can earn positions of honor that include (1) kingships (Matt. 19:28), (2) inheriting eternal life (Matt. 19:29),[20] (3) a hundredfold inheritance (Matt. 19:29), first-place status (Matt. 19:30), eating bread in the kingdom of God (Luke 14:15), and kingdom fellowship (Luke 13:26).[21] These are rewards for faithfulness. Unfaithfulness results in the loss of kingdom privileges.

We are firm in our conviction that Carson goes too far in his conclusion:

> *Attempts to identify the talents with spiritual gifts, the law, natural endowments, the gospel, or whatever else, lead to a narrowing of the parable with which Jesus would have been uncomfortable.*[22]

If, as we maintain, every kingdom parable conceals a secret(s) of the sovereign administration of God, then the parable of the talents must convey an essential secret. Our position is that a talent represents the opportunity to earn status or positions of honor in this royal rule. The essential question does not concern who is ruled over, but who rules. All disciples are assured opportunities to earn elite status in the coming kingdom. Faithful disciples will receive opportunities to serve the master during the kingdom, but unfaithful disciples will lose their opportunities to live and work with the master during that time.

DISCIPLES' SINGULAR FOCUS

The essential goal of disciples relative to the coming kingdom (i.e. elite status) should be the singular focus of our lives. All disciples should be committed to the singular goal of ruling and fellowshipping with Christ in this kingdom. Ruling with Christ must be earned. Every disciple has the opportunity. The depth of one's devotion will be evidenced by one's production. Maximum production will receive the highest awards. No production will result in loss of kingdom status and isolation.

The kingdom principle regarding rewards is expressed in Matthew 25:29, which states,

> *"For to everyone who has will more be given, and he will have an abundance. But from the one who has not, even what he has will be taken away."*

With very minor changes, this verse is the same as Matthew 13:12. This saying appears in a parallel section of Mark 4:25 and Luke 8:18, 19:26. This kingdom principle is an important insight for insiders and is first enunciated by the Lord Jesus in connection first with the parable of the sower and then with the parable the talents. In both parables, this enigmatic saying occurs in connection with judgment. It explains why the faithful will be given more responsibility during our Lord's kingdom rule and the unfaithful will be reduced to worthlessness (no fellowship with the King). Faithfulness will be rewarded. Unfaithfulness will be punished with loss of kingdom status and the freedom to travel.

The punishment for unfaithfulness is expressed in Matthew 25:26a, 28, 30. Together, these verses say,

> *"But his master answered him, 'You worthless and slothful servant . . . So take the talent from him and give it to him who has the ten talent . . . And [he] cast the worthless servant into the outer darkness. In that place there will be weeping and gnashing of teeth.'"*

It is these three statements that lead many Bible students to conclude that the one-talent servant is not a believer. However, the reasoning is faulty. Instead of the positive commendation given to the previous servants, the one-talent servant has criticism to look forward to: "You worthless and slothful servant." In an overwhelming majority of modern translations, the term πονηρός, is translated as either "wicked" or "evil." Louw-Nida suggests four possible nuances of this term: (1) wicked; (2) worthless; (3) guilty; and (4) be sick.[23] The first nuance BADG suggests is "pertaining to being morally or socially worthless, wicked, evil, bad, base, worthless, vicious, degenerate.[24] Coupled with the adjective oknēros (lazy, idle); we support the nuance "worthless." Worthless and lazy captures the sense of the criticism. The one-talent servant produced nothing.

This better explains the master's evaluation of his servant. Clearly, the master would not have entrusted his talent to a servant who, by nature, was wicked or evil. To expect anything other than the resulting outcome would have shown a lack of wisdom on the part of the master. In our opinion, to condemn an evil man for being evil offers no new insight into this parable.

The second negative consequence for the unfaithful one-talent servant is the loss of opportunity to serve in the Lord's kingdom. Instead of exaltation to greater responsibility, he receives a demotion. The text says, "So take the talent from him and give it to him who has the ten talents" (Matt. 25:28). This verse alone should be sufficient evidence that salvation is not in view here. No person will appear before Christ saved only to lose salvation because of insufficient funds in his or her account.

The fact that the "talent" can be given, taken back, and transferred to another significantly limits what the talent is. Old Testament history is filled with accounts demonstrating the transfer of inheritance rights due to misbehavior. Both Esau and Ruben are poster children for this. Hebrews 12:15–17 says of Esau:

> See to it that no one fails to obtain the grace of God; that no "root of bitterness" springs up and causes trouble, and by it many become defiled; that no one is sexually immoral or unholy like Esau, who sold his birthright for a single meal. For you know that afterward, when he desired to inherit the blessing, he was rejected, for he found no chance to repent, though he sought it with tears.

The writer of the Book of Hebrews expresses Esau's reaction with the phrase, "he sought it with tears." Genesis

27:34 offers a more graphic depiction. Notice, "As soon as Esau heard the words of his father, he cried out with an exceedingly great and bitter cry." At the critical point, repentance and weeping were insufficient to restore Esau's firstborn inheritance status. Esau never lost his sonship, but he did lose the rights and privileges of the firstborn.

Similarly, Ruben, Jacob's firstborn, lost all rights and privileges of being the firstborn son, as well. 1 Chronicles 5:1–2 reports:

> *The sons of Reuben the firstborn of Israel (for he was the firstborn, but because he defiled his father's couch, his birthright was given to the sons of Joseph the son of Israel, so that he could not be enrolled as the oldest son; though Judah became strong among his brothers and a chef came from him, yet the birthright belonged to Joseph).*

All the honors, privileges, and rights of a firstborn son were lost to Ruben due to his misbehavior (Gen. 35:22).

"SONS OF THE KINGDOM"

Despite chastising them for misbehavior, Jesus is speaking to believers. Both audiences—disciples and Jews—are identified as "sons of the kingdom." Thus, Jesus is rebuking those who are already "in the family." It is in this context that he rebukes Jewish leaders for their failure to display a faith similar to some Gentiles:

> *"I tell you, many will come from east and west and recline at table with Abraham, Isaac, and Jacob in the kingdom of heaven, while the sons of the kingdom will be thrown into the outer darkness. In that place there will be weeping and gnashing of teeth."*

A Handbook on the Gospel of Matthew identifies sons of the kingdom as follows: "a Semitic idiom meaning 'people (We would add here, the Jewish people) who belong to the kingdom.'"[25] Nolland identifies them as "natural heirs of the kingdom."[26] The natural heirs will suffer loss identified as the same as the one–talent servant, being "thrown into the outer darkness," where "there will be weeping and gnashing of teeth." The contrast between the faithless Jewish heirs of the kingdom and the Gentiles of faith is clear.

The transfer of talent signals a loss of rights and privileges as a son of the kingdom. Regarding Matthew 8:11-12, Hagner writes:

> The allusion is to the eschatological banquet (J. Behm, TDNT 2:34–35; Str-B 4:1154–56), a great festival of rejoicing and feasting in celebration of the victory of God, anticipated in both the OT and NT (see, e.g., Isa 25:6; Matt 22:1–14; 25:10; Rev. 19:9; Luke 14:15–16; b. Pesaḥ; 119b; Exod. Rab. 25, 10).[27]

The right to sit and sup with the Lord Christ in his kingdom will be lost to those who failed to behave appropriately during his absence.

The second occurrence of the phrase "sons of the kingdom" occurs in Matthew 13:38. As Jesus is explaining the meaning of the kingdom parable of the weeds of the field, he identifies "the good seed" this way. Jesus, the Son of Man, sows the good seed (sons of the kingdom) in the world until the end of the age when there will be a separation in which the sons of the evil one will be removed. "Sons of the kingdom" are disciples (insiders) whose inheritance depends on their behavior.

The third and final negative consequence of the one-talent servant's unfaithfulness is restricted access to the King and his rule. Instead of gaining elite status in the sovereign administration of God, with all the rights and privileges that come with it, unfaithful sons will be restricted to observance only. Instead of ruling with Christ, unfaithful disciples will be ruled over with no joy.

WHAT IS MEANT BY "OUTER DARKNESS"?

The parable of the talents concludes with a most horrifying statement: "Cast the worthless servant into the outer darkness." The adjectival descriptor *achreios* (useless, worthless, unsuitable)[28] suggests the one-talent servant no longer has any value for the master. He has nothing that shows glory or honor. He or she has no work and no rewards. Thus, his or her destiny is "the darkness outside."

The casting of the one-talent servant "into the outer darkness" has led some students of Scripture to conclude that this servant must be an unbeliever. We are disappointed in *A Handbook of the Gospel of Matthew* because the authors write, "*The outer darkness*, obviously [is] a reference to hell."[29] The phrase "outer darkness" occurs three times in Matthew's Gospel: 8:12, 22:13, and 25:30. Contra Balz and Schneider, who conclude: "Here σκότος refers to the eschatological place of punishment,"[30] i.e., the destiny of unbelievers.

There are three primary reasons we see Balz and Schneider drawing a wrong conclusion here. First, in the three passages of Matthew where the phrase is used, there is no mention of fire, furnace, or hell associated with "outer darkness." Of the three occasions where this phrase occurs, only those *expected to produce* for the kingdom are cast there, i.e., the sons of the kingdom who are improperly "wedding attired" or who proved worthless. On the other hand—and this is critically important—fiery punishment is only associated with those who could *never produce*, i.e., chaff, weeds, trees that produce bad fruit, goats, and evil men.

In each case, only those whose nature is consistent with their behavior are assigned to the fiery punishment. It is also worth noting that there is no change in the nature of these sons. Wheat never becomes chaff or vice versa. Good trees never become bad trees or vice versa. Sheep never become goats or vice versa. A fiery destiny is the result of one nature.

The phrase "outer darkness" does not occur with any mention of fire associated with it. "Outer darkness" is the choice of most modern translations. However, the NIV suggests a slight modification. Instead of "will be thrown into outer darkness," it suggests "will be thrown outside, into the darkness." The Greek phrase τὸ σκότος τὸ ἐξώτερον (the darkness outsidest [superlative]) taken literally would have the sense "the darkness farthest out." This view recognizes the superlative function of the adjective τὸ ἐξώτερον.

Hagner suggests:

> The expression τὸ σκότος τὸ ἐξώτερον, "the outer darkness," here refers to the greatest possible contrast with the brilliantly illuminated banquet hall (cf. 22:13; 25:30; for darkness as judgment generally, see 2 Esdr 7:93; 1 Enoch 63:10; Pss. Sol. 14:4; 15:10).

Hagner uses the two other New Testament occurrences and intertestamental references to support his conclusion, which he sees as ultimately referring to the place of eternal damnation. The most exhaustive study of the phrase "outer darkness" is Marty Cauley's study *The Outer Darkness*.[31] Cauley's conclusion is probably close to Dillow, who concludes:

> By using the phrase "the darkness outside" rather than "outer darkness," we are freed from traditional usage that might color our thinking, enabling us to more easily discern what the phrase means in context. When we do that, it becomes highly probable that this phrase refers to the darkness outside the relative light of the banquet hall.
>
> Presumably, in the story, this is a local area immediately outside the banquet hall. The phrase is a metaphor for an experience of exclusion from the joy. . . . Matthew, therefore, leads us to imagine a feast of great rejoicing. All the faithful Christians of the church are there to celebrate their wedding feast with their King. This joyful banquet is portrayed by the Lord as occurring in the evening in a brightly lit banquet hall. Outside the banquet, where the shining lights of the feast are not present, in that place, the evening darkness prevails. This is a metaphor for the relative physical darkness. This darkness is not literal, but is a metaphor for the exclusion of the carnal Christian from the glorious reign of the Metochoi. It is not the darkness of eternal exclusion from heaven.[32]

Instead of seeing the one-talent servant as an unbeliever cast into the eternal lake of fire, Dillow and Cauley see a carnal Christian restricted from the sweet fellowship of the Lord Jesus and faithful disciples for a period of time. Dillow and Cauley divide, however, on when during the eschatological future the Bema Seat Judgment occurs and how long the carnal disciples will be restricted from this sweet communion.

The result of the one-talent servant being cast into the darkness outside is "weeping and gnashing of teeth."

This expression occurs seven times in the New Testament (Matt. 8:12; 13:42, 50; 22:13; 24:51; 25:30; and Luke 13:28). There is one sure commonality that exists between these passages: "Weeping and gnashing of teeth" comes in response to divine judgment. Contrary to Rodney K. Duke, who states that both Matthew and Luke use this clause "in final-judgment texts,"[33] we see his comments as overly simplistic. The object of judgment and when in the sequence of the return and rule of the Son of Man a particular judgment occurs must be contextually determined. To assume or attempt to defend only one eschatological judgment requires the abandonment of the consistent hermeneutic necessary in light of progressive revelation. At a minimum, Revelation 20:4–6 and 11–15 demand a one-thousand-year separation between the judgment of the righteous dead and the wicked dead.

"WEEPING AND GNASHING OF TEETH"

An oversimplified eschatology creates more problems than solutions for the overall end-times sequence. Jesus explicitly promises to return to earth and rule with his disciples. Thus, there is significant evidence in Matthew, Mark, and Luke that the wicked living at that time will be removed from the earth. These judgments are pronounced upon the living. In order for them to apply to the wicked, the wicked would need to have been resurrected. Yet in not a single parable of the kingdom is there an explicit basis for the claim that the wicked dead will experience resurrection before their judgment leading to eternal fire as reflected in the White Throne Judgment of Revelation 20:11–15.

In the seven passages that use the idiom "weeping and gnashing of teeth," those suffering are alive and judged.

Again, we see no evidence of an immediate resurrection associated with any judgment scene in these passages.

There is nothing uniquely Christian or unchristian about the idiom "weeping and gnashing of teeth" (Matt. 8:12; 13:42, 50; 22:13; 24:51; 25:30; and Luke 13:28). Matthew 13:42,50 applies it to unbelievers, while Matthew 8:12; 22:13; 24:51; 25:30; and Luke 13:28 apply to disciples. The phrase in and of itself is a reaction to the sentence of judgment. Once the sentence is completed, the one-talent servant reacts with "weeping and gnashing of teeth."

The term for weeping (*klauthmos*) occurs twice in the New Testament outside of the eschatological passages under review. Matthew 2:8 speaks of Rachel weeping for her children, which refers to Jeremiah's record of events connected with the Babylonian captivity. Clearly, slaughtering innocent babies would cause moms to wail over the death of their children.

A second, more interesting occurrence occurs in Acts 20:37. During the occasion of Paul's farewell to the Ephesian elders, the text reports:

> *And there was much weeping on the part of all; they embraced Paul and kissed him, being sorrowful most of all because of the word he had spoken, that they would not see his face again.*

The cause of "much weeping" is "being sorrowful most of all that they would not see" Paul's face again. The Ephesians experienced great anxiety concerning Paul's departure. Their sorrowful regret was on display for all to see.

In many cases, "loud laments" are paired with the "gnashing of teeth." There is no scholarly throughout Scripture. We are inclined to agree with McComiskey, who argues that the rare appearance and usage of this phrase in secular Greek and Jewish literature should cause New Testament interpreters to seek a precise meaning from each passage and its immediate context.[34]

While the individual words are important, the significance for our study is the idiom itself. Whether this idiom is an invention of the Lord Jesus or a common speak of his day is unknown. Erdey and Smith, in their article "Weeping and Gnashing of Teeth: The Nature of the Suffering of the Wicked in Matthew," conclude as follows:

> The three concepts associated with the phrase "weeping and gnashing of teeth," namely, "outer darkness," "fiery furnace," and "dismemberment" . . . may help to provide the essential context required for understanding such a unique Matthean passage, without verbal or conceptual precedent on which to rely for accurate interpretation.[35]

We believe that "darkness outside" refers to the abode of unfaithful disciples during the thousand-year rule of Christ on the earth. It is the punishment for those who refuse to live repentant lives before our Lord's return. These will lose all rights and privileges of sonship.

The "fiery furnace" refers to the abode of the living wicked once judged at the return of the Son of Man. In the parable of the wheat and weeds, the destiny of the weeds (those who belong to Satan) is removal from the earth and being thrown alive into the fiery furnace. The weeds were never wheat nor vice versa.

The third group, identified as those who will weep and gnash their teeth, is seen in Matthew 24:51: "He will cut the servant to pieces." This describes the result for those who are found unfaithful at the Lord's return. Taken at face value, many scholars automatically see dismemberment as a judgment that results in eternal damnation. Duke uses this verse to bolster his claim that those thrown out of the kingdom are not the ones who weep and gnash their teeth. Duke calls for restraint when considering what conclusions, one should draw from metaphorical language in these passages.[36]

Yet, Duke violates his own rule here in that he does not restrain himself from drawing a conclusion that needs a better defense. To cut the servant into pieces can just as easily be taken metaphorically as literally. If literal death by dismemberment is the punishment for unfaithful servants, this passage alone teaches such a conclusion. Rather, we are better to interpret this as metaphorical since nowhere else in Scripture is physical death the eternal punishment of the wicked. Those judged and thrown into the eternal fire in Matthew 25:41 never experience physical death, but are thrown into the fire alive.[37]

WHAT ABOUT 'NO MORE TEARS'?

If, as we insist, unfaithful believers will suffer profound regret after receiving their punishment, then we must explain Revelation 7:17, which affirms, "God will wipe away every tear from their eyes." Likewise, Revelation 21:4 also promises, "He will wipe away every tear from their eyes, and death shall be no more, neither shall there be mourning, nor crying, nor pain anymore, for the former things have passed away."

Of the two, the less difficult text to explain is Revelation 21:4. If one accepts, as we do, the chronological development of Revelation 19–21:8, the promises contained in Revelation 21:4 find fulfillment once the thousand-year reign of Christ has finished and the eternal future of mankind begins (following the creation of a new heaven and earth [Rev. 21:1]). Once humanity is past the temporal reign of Christ on earth, the Sovereign of all glory will rule over the totality of creation. For those who are righteous in his eyes, all characteristics and reminders of this fallen world will pass away. Thus, the tears that are wiped away are those associated with death, mourning, and pain. Yet, one must agree that these are not the sole producers of tears in believers' lives. Believers will also experience tears of joy and tears shed over the loss of loved ones who did not make it into the camp of the saved.

Our understanding of Revelation 7:17 is more nuanced. Without dealing at length with the chronology of the book of Revelation and whether there is a recapitulation in some sections, we see Revelation 7 preceding the physical manifestation of the sovereign administration of God on earth. The context limits the audience to those "coming up out of the great tribulation," where persecution, murder, violence, and pain have ruled for several years.

Scholars recognize, whether directly or indirectly, that in verse 17 John alludes to Isaiah 25:8. The promise to "wipe away tears from all faces," must be contextually defined. In both Isaiah 25:8 and Revelation 7:17, the promise of no more tears is connected with the alleviation of physical death and suffering. After promising those "coming up out of the great tribulation" that they will hunger or thirst no more, Revelation 7:17 adds the promise that the Lamb "will guide them to springs of living water." Thus, this must refer to spiritual water or the endless supply of eternal life because the text just informed the reader that there will be no need to drink water or eat food. Yet, during the Lord's temporal kingdom on earth there will be eating and drinking (see Mark 14:25).

Thus, we must limit the cessation of tears associated with death and dying only. Tears associated with shame, regret, joy, and powerful aesthetic experiences like the sudden appearance of the Lord Jesus, the glorious throne of the Father, or the New Jerusalem are not removed.

We see no necessity to include in this promise tears of joy, tears of relief, or tears of accomplishment. Contextually, to see a blanket ban on tears of any kind seems unwarranted and overly simplistic.

Notes

[1] John Nolland, *The Gospel of Matthew: A Commentary on the Greek Text, New International Greek Testament Commentary* (Grand Rapids, MI; Carlisle: W.B. Eerdmans; Paternoster Press, 2005), 1012.

[2] John Nolland, *The Gospel of Matthew: A Commentary on the Greek Text, New International Greek Testament Commentary* (Grand Rapids, MI; Carlisle: W.B. Eerdmans; Paternoster Press, 2005), 1012.

[3] Matthew 24:45-51 is not explicitly identified as a kingdom parable by Matthew; however, Luke does explicitly identify it this way (Luke 12:41). The next parable in this trilogy (the ten virgins) explicitly begins, "Then the kingdom of heaven will be like . . ."; thus, there is an explicit identification as a kingdom parable. The parable of the talents does not have such an explicit identification. However, Matthew 25:14 begins with grammatical indicators that signal the relationship between the parable of the ten virgins and the parable of the talents. Contra Holland and others who connect the linking γάρ ('for') "to the preceding parable," as a whole, we see Matthew 25:14-30 explaining the command for watchfulness in Matthew 25:13 alone. The adverbial comparative conjunction *hōsper* introduces the point of the comparison between the parable of the talents and the need for watchfulness. Prepared watchfulness is the only way to ensure a pleasing life for the returning master. As well, depending on one's view of the relationship between Matthew's parable of the talents and Luke's parable of the pounds, Luke identifies his material as a parable (Luke 19:11-27).

[4] Louis A. Barbieri Jr., "Matthew," in *The Bible Knowledge Commentary: An Exposition of the Scriptures*, ed. J. F. Walvoord and R. B. Zuck, vol. 2 (Wheaton, IL: Victor Books, 1985), 80.

[5] Donald A. Hagner, "Matthew 14–28," vol. 33b, *Word Biblical Commentary* (Dallas: Word, Incorporated, 1995), 737.

[6] R. T. France, *Matthew: An Introduction and Commentary*, vol. 1, Tyndale New Testament Commentaries (Downers Grove, IL: InterVarsity Press, 1985), 357.

[7] By "unbeliever," we intend those who refuse to believe the message of Jesus concerning the kingdom of God.

[8] Louis A. Barbieri Jr., "Matthew," in *The Bible Knowledge Commentary: An Exposition of the Scriptures*, ed. J. F. Walvoord and R. B. Zuck, vol. 2 (Wheaton, IL: Victor Books, 1985), 80. See John F. Walvoord, "Christ's Olivet Discourse on the End of the Age," *Bibliotheca Sacra* 129 (1972): 210; also Samuel L. Hoyt, "The Judgment Seat of Christ in Theological Perspective Part 1: The Judgment Seat of Christ and Unconfessed Sins," *Bibliotheca Sacra* 137 (1980): 33.

[9] Craig L. Blomberg, *Interpreting the Parables, Second Edition* (Downers Grove, Il), 222-223 https://www.mybibleteacher.net/uploads/1/2/4/6/124618875/interp reting the parables by craig l. blomberg z-lib.org .epub.pdf (last accessed, 6/17/22).

[10] John Nolland, "The Gospel of Matthew: A Commentary on the Greek Text," *New International Greek Testament Commentary* (Grand Rapids, MI; Carlisle: W.B. Eerdmans; Paternoster Press, 2005), 1020.

[11] Ben Chenoweth, "Identifying the Talents: Contextual Clues for the Interpretation of the Parable of the Talents (Matthew 25:14–30)," *Tyndale Bulletin* 56, no. 1 (2005): 70.

[12] Horst Robert Balz and Gerhard Schneider, *Exegetical Dictionary of the New Testament* (Grand Rapids, MI: Eerdmans, 1990–), 356.

[13] Johannes P. Louw and Eugene Albert Nida, *Greek-English Lexicon of the New Testament: Based on Semantic Domains* (New York: United Bible Societies, 1996), 694.

[14] Gerhard Kittel, Gerhard Friedrich, and Geoffrey William Bromiley, *Theological Dictionary of the New Testament, Abridged in One Volume* (Grand Rapids, MI: W.B. Eerdmans, 1985), 1352.

[15] Simon J. Kistemaker and William Hendriksen, "Exposition of the First Epistle to the Corinthians," vol. 18, *New Testament Commentary* (Grand Rapids: Baker Book House, 1953–2001), 91.

[16] Leon Morris, *1 Corinthians: An Introduction and Commentary*, vol. 7, Tyndale New Testament Commentaries (Downers Grove, IL: InterVarsity Press, 1985), 64.

[17] Ibid., 70.

[18] Leon Morris, "The Gospel According to Matthew," *The Pillar New Testament Commentary* (Grand Rapids, MI; Leicester, England: W.B. Eerdmans; Inter-Varsity Press, 1992), 626–627.

[19] While we cannot say that Matthew, Mark, and Luke contain all of the parables our Lord spoke (since this is unknowable, since we cannot know what was not recorded), we can study all of the parables that *were* recorded in Scripture.

[20] "To inherit eternal life" is not the same as receiving spiritual salvation which one receives as a result of faith in Jesus Christ's death, burial, and resurrection for the forgiveness of sin. As evidenced in the account of Jesus and the rich young ruler, to inherit eternal life is the result of one's works. Inheriting eternal life speaks to the quality of one's life and not the longevity of life.

[21] Matthew 5 contains what is traditionally called "the Beatitudes," which list rewards based on the lifestyle of disciples.

[22] D. A. Carson, "Matthew" in *The Expositor's Bible Commentary*, vol. 8 (ed. Frank E. Gaebelein; Grand Rapids: Zondervan, 1984): 516.

[23] Johannes P. Louw and Eugene Albert Nida, *Greek-English Lexicon of the New Testament: Based on Semantic Domains* (New York: United Bible Societies, 1996), 202.

[24] William Arndt et al., *A Greek-English Lexicon of the New Testament and Other Early Christian Literature* (Chicago: University of Chicago Press, 2000), 851.

[25] Barclay Moon Newman and Philip C. Stine, *A Handbook on the Gospel of Matthew*, UBS Handbook Series (New York: United Bible Societies, 1992), 230.

[26] John Nolland, "The Gospel of Matthew: A Commentary on the Greek Text," *New International Greek Testament Commentary* (Grand Rapids, MI; Carlisle: W.B. Eerdmans; Paternoster Press, 2005), 357.

[27] Donald A. Hagner, Matthew 1–13, vol. 33a, *Word Biblical Commentary* (Dallas: Word, Incorporated, 1993), 205.

[28] Horst Robert Balz and Gerhard Schneider, *Exegetical Dictionary of the New Testament* (Grand Rapids, MI: Eerdmans, 1990–), 186.

[29] Barclay Moon Newman and Philip C. Stine, *A Handbook on the Gospel of Matthew*, UBS Handbook Series (New York: United Bible Societies, 1992), 231.

[30] Ibid., 256.

[31] Marty A. Cauley, *The Outer Darkness: Its Interpretations and Implications* (Sylva, NC: Misthological Press, 2012).

[32] Dillow, Joseph C. *Final Destiny: The Future Reign of The Servant Kings Revised Edition*, 790, 792. Grace Theology Press. Kindle Edition.

[33] Rodney K. Duke, "The Idiom of 'Weeping and Gnashing of Teeth' in the Gospels: A Funerary Formula," *Perspectives in Religious Studies* 47 (2020), 283.

[34] Douglas S. McComiskey 1976. In Brown C (ed.), *The New International Dictionary of New Testament Theology*, vol. 2 (Grand Rapids, MI: Zondervan), 421.

[35] Zoltan L. Erdey and Kevin G. Smith, "'Weeping and Gnashing of Teeth'—the Nature of the Suffering of the Wicked in Matthew," *Conspectus 2013*, vol. 15, 156.

[36] Rodney K. Duke, "The Idiom of 'Weeping and Gnashing of Teeth," 293.

[37] To be thrown alive into the lake of fire is a form of death in that death is a separation. The separation of men from God's presence and possible forgiveness is called the second death in Revelation 20:14.

CHAPTER 11

Training to Reign: Suffer Well!

By recognizing the fundamental distinction between the gospel from God and the gospel about Jesus Christ, we have demonstrated how many problematic passages in the Synoptic Gospels are resolved. Instead of seeing at least one offer of spiritual salvation on every page, we see our Lord focused on the coming rule of God on the earth and the unique opportunity disciples have been given to participate in the ruling cabinet.

The gospel of the kingdom of God not only announces God's intent to grant his Son authority to rule over the earth but also announces God's invitation to the disciples to share in that kingdom's rule. It also announces that judgment awaits those who refuse to live a repentant life. The sovereign administration of God will consist of the Lord Jesus and the men and women who *earn* the right to rule with him. Ruling with Christ is a reward. The primary avenue that will lead to this reward is *suffering!*

SUFFERING—THE DIVINE IMPERATIVE

Every man, woman, boy, or girl who hopes to take part in the coming rule of God upon the earth must acquire that honor through suffering. There are no exceptions. In this, Jesus Christ was our model. The suffering of our Savior was not theoretical nor limited to the spiritual arena. He predicted "that he must go to Jerusalem and suffer many things from the elders and chief priests and scribes, be killed, and on the third day be raised" (Matt. 16:21, ESV, emphasis added). Jesus predicts that he, himself, must (δεῖ) suffer. Δεῖ (*dei*), often translated in the New Testament as "must," is generally understood to indicate a divine imperative. Balz and Schneider summarize that,

> *Δεῖ designates an unconditional necessity; sentences with this vb. have fundamentally an absolute, unquestioned, and often anonymous and deterministic character... In the NT statements with δεῖ are normally understood more or less as divine decrees.*[1]

In essence, the suffering of Jesus was the explicit and unalterable will of God. W. J. Bennett, Jr. concludes that *dei* is a circumlocution for "God wills it."[2] The suffering of the Lord Jesus is explicitly predicted in the Old Testament Scripture—thus the necessity of its fulfillment (Luke 24:46).

The probative question is why? Why was it an absolute necessity that the Son of God suffer in the flesh? A passage that speaks to this issue explicitly is Hebrews 2:10. The writer states, "For it was fitting that he [God the Father], for whom and by whom all things exist, in bringing many sons to glory, should make the founder [Jesus Christ] of their salvation perfect through suffering." What does the writer mean by "perfect through suffering?" We categorically affirm that the Lord Jesus had no moral imperfections (2 Cor. 5:21). Yet, Scripture affirms that Jesus grew in wisdom, knowledge, and favor with God and man (Luke 2:52).

Our Lord's growth in "wisdom, knowledge, and favor" helps us understand what the writer of Hebrews means by "perfect through suffering." We agree with Silva that the focus is "two successive stages in" the Lord's "human-messianic existence."[3] The writer of Hebrews makes a critical point regarding the significant difference between the pre- and post-resurrection Jesus. Silva highlights that Hebrews 1:4 tells us that

> God's Son has inherited a name superior to that of the angels. But when we ask what is the name that this Son has inherited, the answer is, oddly enough, Son again (verses 5ff.). It is, I think, surprising that very little has been made in the past of the apparent fact that the author uses the word Son in two different senses in these verses. In verse 2 it indicates what Jesus is, and has always been, by divine nature; in verses 4ff. it is the Messianic title He receives in connection with some type of change in his human nature. Surely this temporal distinction—that after completing his work Jesus became something he was not before—accords naturally with the context.[4]

The writer of Hebrews distinguishes two phases of our Lord's life by stating, "We see him [Jesus] who for a little while was made lower than the angels, namely Jesus, crowned with glory and honor because of the suffering of death" (Heb. 2:9). For Jesus, perfection was the attainment of the status and statue that were the intent of his incarnation. His resurrection finalized his human experience. Suffering unto death fulfilled the experiential necessity of the God-Man knowing the fullest sense of both sides of his nature, i.e., God and man.

The verb used in Matthew 16:31 is πάσχω = paschō, to *suffer* (death).[5] *Paschō* occurs no less than 42 times in the New Testament, with 35 of those occurrences referring to either the Lord Jesus or his followers. On two subsequent occasions, the Lord will describe the type of suffering he will endure at the hands of the Jewish leadership in Jerusalem. *Paschō* is the only explicit term for suffering used in connection with Jesus in the Synoptic Gospels. (See Matthew 16:21, par. Mark 8:31/Luke 9:22; Matthew 17:12, par. Mark 9:12/Luke 17:25; Luke 22:15 and 24:26, 46.)

The depth of physical suffering our Lord endured is hard to grasp. The Synoptics seem to go out of their way to portray his physical suffering in the most graphic way possible. It is to this end that all disciples of Jesus Christ are called. The Lord Jesus states in Matthew 16:24: "If anyone would come after me, let him deny himself and take up his cross and follow me." A cross has only one purpose—to inflict pain and suffering that leads to physical death.

DISCIPLES MUST SUFFER

The Lord Jesus explicitly tells his disciples, "In the world you will have tribulation" (John 16:33). He reserves *thlipsis* to describe their future experience. The same verb is used by the apostle Paul in Acts 14:22, where he declares that "through many tribulations we must enter the kingdom of God." It is as much the will of God that disciples endure "many tribulations" as it was for Jesus. Δεῖ (*dei*) occurs here as it does in connection with the

THAT OTHER GOSPEL • 259

Lord's prediction in Matthew 16:31. Both Jesus' suffering and his disciples' tribulation are divine requirements.

Paul's term to describe the type of suffering all disciples are called to endure is "tribulation" (θλῖψις = *thlipsis*). Balz and Schneider state, "The noun θλῖψις is always (45 NT occurrences) used in the fig(urative) sense in the NT."[6] Louw and Nida define *thlipsis* to mean "trouble involving direct suffering—'trouble and suffering, suffering, persecution.'"[7] John 16:21 illustrates *thlipsis* when it states,

> When a woman is giving birth, she has sorrow because her hour has come, but when she has delivered the baby, she no longer remembers the anguish [thlipsis], for joy that a human being has been born into the world.

As with Jesus, we ask the question, "Why is suffering necessary?" Previously, we demonstrated that in Acts 14:22 Paul's point referred to participating in the divine leadership of God's coming rule. This is confirmed in his letter to the Romans. In the clearest presentation of the theological basis for the gospel of God (Rom. 1:1), Paul reminds his readers:

> For you did not receive the spirit of slavery to fall back into fear, but you have received the Spirit of adoption as sons, by whom we cry, "Abba! Father!" The Spirit himself bears witness with our spirit that we are children of God, and if children, then heirs—heirs of God and fellow heirs with Christ, provided we suffer with [συμπάσχω = sympaschō] him in order that we may also be glorified with him. (Rom. 8:15–17 ESV, emphasis added)

Again, if we assume that at every turn the New Testament is always referencing spiritual salvation versus damnation, then Romans 8:15–17 is but another of many passages caught up in the fight between Calvinism and Arminianism because of the apparent necessity of works to be saved. Is our salvation dependent on our suffering? What is the relationship between suffering and spiritual salvation? How much suffering is necessary to pass the test? By insisting that every New Testament pericope must accord with the notion that spiritual salvation or damnation are the only two options, students must wrestle with how to reconcile the unreconcilable. Otherwise, salvation must ultimately be obtained by works. This is an untenable conclusion for those who insist that spiritual salvation is obtained by faith alone. Rather, we see Jesus offering men and women a "talent" (opportunity) to earn elite status in the ruling class of his coming kingdom.

Regarding Romans 8:15–17, *The Bible Knowledge Commentary* claims that Paul's statement in verse 17 is salvific in nature. It states,

> *Since Christians are God's children, they are His heirs (cf. Gal. 4:7), and they are co-heirs with Christ. They are recipients of all spiritual blessings (Eph. 1:3) now, and in the future they will share with the Lord Jesus in all the riches of God's kingdom (John 17:24; 1 Cor. 3:21–23). Sharing with Jesus Christ, however, involves more than anticipating the glories of heaven. For Jesus Christ it involved suffering and abuse and crucifixion; therefore being co-heirs with Christ requires that believers share in His sufferings (cf. John 15:20; Col. 1:24; 2 Tim. 3:12; 1 Peter 4:12). In fact believers do share in His sufferings; if indeed translates eiper, which means "if, as is the fact" (cf. Rom. 8:9). Then after the suffering they will share in His glory (2 Tim. 2:12; 1 Peter 4:13; 5:10).*[8]

Sadly, the BKC creates more questions than are answered here. If we adopt that *eiper* means "if, as is the fact," as the proper sense Paul intends, then we must conclude that all believers share in Christ's suffering. How can this be possible? Is suffering in this case limited to the spiritual arena only? Is Paul speaking metaphorically? Similarly, we must conclude that all believers will share in his glory. Really? For this to be true, how a disciple lives his or her life has no bearing on rewards.

The grammatical basis that drives the BKC's conclusion is clearly stated by the authors of the NET Bible. In the NET Bible, Romans 8:17 reads: "And if children, then heirs (namely, heirs of God and also fellow heirs with Christ)—if indeed we suffer with him so we may also be glorified with him."

The NET Bible offers the following explanation regarding this translation: "On the one hand, heirs of God; on the other hand, fellow heirs with Christ." Some prefer to render verse 17 as follows: "And if children, then heirs— that is, heirs of God. Also fellow heirs with Christ if indeed we suffer with him so we may also be glorified with him." Such a translation suggests two distinct inheritances: one coming to all of God's children, the other coming only to those who suffer with Christ. The difficulty of this view, however, is that it ignores the correlative conjunctions μέν . . . δέ (*men . . . de*, "on the one hand . . . on the other hand"). The construction strongly suggests that the inheritances cannot be separated since both explain "then heirs." For this reason, the preferred translation puts this explanation in parentheses.[9]

The grammatical conclusion that forms the basis of the NET Bible's claim is not true. The correlative conjunctions μέν . . . δέ can function to either indicate comparison or contrast between two or more objects. The correct technical terms are disjunctive or conjunctive. Is Paul's intent to show that "heir of God" and "co-heir of Christ" are disjunctive = contrast (i.e., a difference), or is his intent to show a conjunctive relationship = comparison (i.e., equality)? The correlative conjunctions μέν ... δέ occur in 13 passages in the book of Romans.[10] Setting aside Romans 8:17, the remaining passages are all contrastive (disjunctive, indicating a difference) and not conjunctive.

Now, this alone does not prove that Romans 8:17 is contrastive. However, one must show that this one passage is distinct from all the others. The point of contrast seems to be that the difference between being an heir of God and being a co-heir with Jesus Christ is that co-heirship with Christ must be earned by suffering.

Paul is not teaching that believers share in the Lord's suffering in a symbiotic sense. While it is true that believers benefit from the death of Christ, Paul calls upon all believers to physically suffer to earn the right to join him in the administration of the coming kingdom. In Acts 14:22, Paul teaches "that through many tribulations [thlipsis] we must enter the kingdom of God." Equally, Paul adds in 2 Timothy 3:12: "Indeed, all who desire to live a godly life in Christ Jesus will be persecuted [diōkō]." Is Paul stating an explicit prophecy here? Or is this a generalization that may or may not apply to every single believer throughout all time?

George W. Knight is representative of those who believe that the phrase, "all who desire to live godly in Christ Jesus" is not a designation of a subgroup of Christians who desire a more godly life but rather a description of real Christians in distinction from those who follow false teaching.[11] In contradistinction, we believe that the key to Paul's intent is the phrase, "in Christ Jesus." Paul is not saying that all believers will be persecuted just because they are believers. Rather, his emphasis is on living a godly life in Christ Jesus.

Mounce concludes, "Paul is saying that everyone wishing to live a godly life, specifically Christian godliness, will be persecuted."[12] Thus, it is a subgroup that can count on persecution. Consequently, we see Romans 8:17 in perfect accord with Acts 14:22b and 2 Timothy 3:12.

Therefore, we separate "heir of God" and "co-heir with Christ." Being an heir of God is obtained by faith in the promise, which brings God's righteousness to a sinner. In Galatians 4:7, Paul states, "So you are no longer a slave, but a son, and if a son, then an heir through God." Notice the absence of conditionality. There is agreement among NT scholars that Galatians 4:7 is a direct parallel with Romans 8:17. Thus, the absence of the reference to the conditional co-heirship with Christ is significant. In Galatians 3:29, Paul argues that "if you are Christ's, then you are Abraham's offspring, heirs according to promise." Paul is referring to spiritual salvation. For Paul, being "in Christ" makes a believer an adult son of God, and so, an heir of God. Heirship to God has only one condition, i.e., faith in the promise of God, just as we see in Abraham.

However, co-heirship with Christ is multi-conditional, not on faith alone, but on suffering. Revelation 3:21 informs us, "The one who conquers, will sit with Christ on his throne."[13] The conditionality is stated more forcefully in Revelation 2:26, which states, "The one who conquers and who keeps my works until the end, to him I will give authority over the nations." Notice the multi-conditionality!

Romans 8:17 protects salvation by faith and rewards by faithfulness by separating God's heirship and Christ's co-heirship. Rather than the unfortunate conclusion drawn by the NET Bible, the ESV maintains a theologically accurate translation of the verse. We see no less than two reasons to maintain two distinct heirships in Romans 8:17—heirs of God by faith and co-heirs of Christ by faithfulness. First, recognizing the separation between God's heirship and Christ's co-heirship removes the unnecessary appearance of a works-based salvation. Second, recognizing the separation emphasizes how disciples live after putting their initial faith in Jesus Christ for spiritual salvation.

WHAT SUFFERING BRINGS ETERNAL REWARDS?

If co-heirship with Christ requires suffering (*páschō*), we must show what type of suffering is required. Of the 45 occurrences of *thlipsis* in the New Testament, none includes a list of examples of tribulation. The closest examples of what can be potentially labeled "tribulation" occur in Hebrews 10:32-34. Here the writer details a difficult season his audience experienced. The text states,

> But recall the former days when, after you were enlightened, you endured a hard struggle with sufferings [pathēma], sometimes being publicly exposed to reproach and affliction [thlipsis], and sometimes being partners with those so treated. For you had compassion on those in prison, and you joyfully accepted the plundering of your property, since you knew that you yourselves had a better possession and an abiding one.

The author of Hebrews recounts that "you [the Hebrews] endured a hard struggle with sufferings." In essence, they endured a "contest" consisting of sufferings = πάθημα (*pathēma*). Notice that the term is plural. The Hebrews were in a contest with multiple sufferings. They were publicly exposed to reproach and affliction (*thlipsis*). The Greek term for reproach is also plural and could be translated "insults." Louw and Nida suggest, "to speak disparagingly of a person in a manner which is not justified—'to insult, insult.'"[14]

The verbal insults are accompanied by *thlipsis*, which is also plural. These were not one-offs, but systematic patterns. If these were not enough, the writer continues, "For you had compassion on those in prison, and you joyfully accepted the plundering of your property." There is no reason not to conclude that their (the Hebrews') imprisonment was unjustified. Lawlessness ruled.

Unlike so many who attempt to limit the New Testament depiction of tribulation to that final generation just before the beginning of the eschatological kingdom of God, we see every generation as having many who endure both physical and spiritual persecution because of their unwavering commitment to Jesus Christ.

THE NARROW WAY

In 1979, A. J. Mattill, Jr. published an article entitled "The Way of Tribulation." His article is unique in that he argues that "the meaning of *thlibō* in Matt 7:14b is the same as that of the related word *thlipsis* in Acts 14:22."[15] Mattill seeks "to establish that Matt 7:14, like Acts 14:22, is concerned with entrance into the kingdom of God; and that *thlibo* in Matt 7:14b means the end-time tribulation, as does *thlipsis* in Acts 14:22. In other words, the last obstacle to entering the kingdom of God is the great tribulation detailed in Matthew 24, Mark 13 and Luke 21. Thus, Jesus and Paul are not teaching that every individual disciple must suffer, but that a final generation of disciples will face the great tribulation, which will give way to the inauguration of the Kingdom of God."

At the outset, we fundamentally object to Mattill's ultimate conclusion. First, he assumes the traditional meaning of "enter the kingdom of God." As we have shown, "entering the kingdom of God" refers to participation in the sovereign administration of God. Suffering is rewarded with elite status in the ruling council of God's coming kingdom. Thus, for Mattill, Paul is not calling upon individuals to recognize their responsibility to suffer in order to participate in the sovereign rule of God, but rather the writer emphasizes the group as a whole. Put another way, Paul is not calling upon every single individual Christian to suffer, but the body of Christ in general will suffer, i.e. a few suffer for the masses.

Second, Mattill, like so many others, assumes a limited apocalyptic significance of the New Testament references to tribulation. Thus, he concludes, "Given this apocalyptic meaning, Matt 7:14b would then refer to the end-time tribulations, including persecution, on the way leading to eternal life in the kingdom of God."[16] Adopting this conclusion, only the final generation faces "the great tribulation." That generation will face the actual deeds of the Antichrist. All other generations may pass with little difficulty.

If we put aside these errors in judgment, is it possible to see a connection between Matthew 7:14 and Acts 14:22? Can the concept of tribulation found in Acts 14:22 be attached to Matthew 7:14? "The way is hard [*thlibō*] that leads to life." *Thlibō* is the verb, which relates to *thlipsis*, the noun. Both the verb and the noun used in the New Testament are primarily limited to the figurative sense: to afflict (the verb) or affliction (noun).[17]

Unfortunately, as previously stated, most New Testament students see every page of the NT containing the offer of spiritual salvation versus damnation. Matthew

7:13-14 is consistently interpreted in a salvific sense. Is Jesus describing how a person obtains spiritual salvation? Can it be said that men and women must "find" salvation? Are only a "few" people going to be saved? Are these words meant for unbelievers? Some see no problem with this passage presenting the gospel of Christ. However, at the end of the day, it must be agreed that "finding" the way is work. Staying in "the way" is hard work. One can only know potential success after death. All of these questions rule out a salvific intent, in our opinion. If one adopts the view that "the way" is Jesus Christ and that unbelievers must "find" him, then we would offer that "hard" is not a correct descriptor of the task. A better descriptor would be "impossible." Paul states unambiguously that "no one seeks for God" (Rom. 3:11).

It is our view that Matthew 7:14 is not salvific, but rewardific. As we have argued from the beginning, co-heirship with Jesus is conditional. Suffering is necessary and commanded for those who hope to "obtain the prize of the high calling of Jesus Christ." The road (way) to reigning with Jesus Christ in his coming kingdom is hard. Jesus said, "The way is hard that leads to life." The way is not life. It *leads* to life. The rewardific road is hard (*thlibō*). The grammatical language used in Matthew 7:14 is difficult to replicate in English. The perfect passive participle of *thlibō* emphasizes the state of the action. The sense of this verbal aspect is that the effect, once begun, continues without interruption.

Since the verb *thlibō* means "to press hard" and figuratively "to afflict," most NT students see the literal sense in Matthew 7:14, thus the common translation "hard" or "difficult."[18] To obtain the best quality of life possible in the coming rule of God, one must consistently fight the afflictions of the righteous.

In John 16:33, our Lord predicted "that in this present world, you will have affliction [*thlipsis*]." Given the repeated emphasis on affliction for following Jesus, there is no need to limit our Lord's prediction to the original Twelve. In the parable of the sower, affliction is a reason given for many disciples' failings to produce fruit (Mark 4:17). Matthew records that one category of "commendables" in the coming kingdom will be those who chose to "rejoice and be glad" in the face of those "who revile and persecute, and utter all kinds of evil against" them (Matt. 5:11–12).

Repeatedly, Paul warns his converts that affliction is the constant companion of those who are serious in their "followship" of Jesus Christ. Notice how Paul intermingles Greek terms in his second letter to the Corinthians. He writes,

> *Blessed be the God and Father of our Lord Jesus Christ, the Father of mercies and God of all comfort, who comforts us in all our affliction [thlipsis], so that we may be able to comfort those who are in any affliction [thlipsis], with the comfort with which we ourselves are comforted by God. For as we share abundantly in Christ's sufferings [pathēma], so through Christ we share abundantly in comfort too. If we are afflicted [thlibō], it is for your comfort and salvation; and if we are comforted, it is for your comfort, which you experience when you patiently endure the same sufferings [pathēma] that we suffer [paschō]. Our hope for you is unshaken, for we know that as you share in our sufferings [pathēma], you will also share in our comfort. For we do not want you to be unaware, brothers, of the affliction [thlipsis] we experienced in Asia. For we were so utterly burdened beyond our strength that we despaired of life itself. Indeed, we felt that we had received the sentence of death. But that was to make us rely not on ourselves but on God who raises the dead. He delivered us*

*from such a deadly peril, and he will deliver us. On him we
have set our hope that he will deliver us again. (2 Cor. 1:3–10)*

That which causes suffering and the result of this
suffering were evident in the lives of Paul and the
Corinthians, and it will be the same for those who desire to
reign with Christ in his coming kingdom. As if to
underscore the reality of suffering for all believers, Paul
repeats the conditions of his life as he fulfills his charge.
Again, he writes:

*But we have this treasure in jars of clay, to show that the
surpassing power belongs to God and not to us. We are
afflicted [thlibō] in every way, but not crushed; perplexed, but
not driven to despair; persecuted, but not forsaken; struck
down, but not destroyed; always carrying in the body the
death of Jesus, so that the life of Jesus may also be manifested
in our bodies. (2 Cor. 4:7–10)*

Similarly, Paul offers the same hope to those living in
Thessaloniki. He writes,

*Therefore we ourselves boast about you in the churches of
God for your steadfastness and faith in all your persecutions
[diōgmos] and in the afflictions [thlipsis] that you are
enduring. This is evidence of the righteous judgment of God,
that you may be considered worthy of the kingdom of God,
for which you are also suffering [paschō]— since indeed God
considers it just to repay with affliction [thlipsis] those who
afflict [thlibō] you, and to grant relief to you who are afflicted
[thlibō] as well as to us, when the Lord Jesus is revealed from
heaven with his mighty angels in flaming fire, inflicting
vengeance on those who do not know God and on those who*

do not obey the gospel of our Lord Jesus. They will suffer the punishment of eternal destruction, away from the presence of the Lord and from the glory of his might, when he comes on that day to be glorified in his saints, and to be marveled at among all who have believed, because our testimony to you was believed. (2 Thess. 4–10)

We have quoted at length from the writings of the apostle Paul to encourage you not to be frightened, but to count it all joy if and when the avenues of your life run through neighborhoods of affliction. It is but your *talent* (opportunity) to train to reign with Jesus Christ in the coming rule of God. No greater calling exists in the life of those who follow Jesus Christ than this:

Train Today to Reign Tomorrow!

Notes

[1] Horst Robert Balz and Gerhard Schneider, *Exegetical Dictionary of the New Testament* (Grand Rapids, MI: Eerdmans, 1990–), 279.

[2] W. J. Bennett, Jr., "The Son of Man Must..." *Novum Testamentum*, vol. XVII (1975), 128.

[3] Moisés Silva, "Perfection and Eschatology in Hebrews," *Westminster Theological Journal 39*, no. 1 (1976): 64.

[4] Ibid., 63.

[5] Horst Robert Balz and Gerhard Schneider, *Exegetical Dictionary of the New Testament* (Grand Rapids, MI: Eerdmans, 1990–), 51. All three Synoptic Gospels utilize the same verb, *paschō*, to describe our Lord's prediction.

[6] Horst Robert Balz and Gerhard Schneider, *Exegetical Dictionary of the New Testament* (Grand Rapids, MI: Eerdmans, 1990–), 152.

[7] Johannes P. Louw and Eugene Albert Nida, *Greek-English Lexicon of the New Testament: Based on Semantic Domains* (New York: United Bible Societies, 1996), 242.

[8] John A. Witmer, "Romans," in *The Bible Knowledge Commentary: An Exposition of the Scriptures*, ed. J. F. Walvoord and R. B. Zuck, vol. 2 (Wheaton, IL: Victor Books, 1985), 471.

[9] The NET Bible (Biblical Studies Press, 2005), Ro 8:15–17.

[10] See Romans 2:7-8, 25; 5:16; 6:11; 7:25; 8:10, 17; 9:21; 11:22, 28; 14:2, 5; 16:19.

[11] George W. Knight, *The Pastoral Epistles: A Commentary on the Greek Text, New International Greek Testament Commentary* (Grand Rapids, MI; Carlisle, England: W.B. Eerdmans; Paternoster Press, 1992), 441.

[12] William D. Mounce, "Pastoral Epistles," vol. 46, *Word Biblical Commentary* (Dallas: Word, Incorporated, 2000), 560.

[13] Being a conqueror in salvation (1 John 5:4) is not the same as being a conqueror in sanctification. Salvation is a reality now; however, whether we will be included among those proclaimed in Revelation 3:21, we must wait to see.

[14] Ibid, p. 432.

[15] A.J. Mattill, Jr., "The Way of Tribulation," *JBL* 98 (1979), 531.

[16] Ibid., 531.

[17] Horst Robert Balz and Gerhard Schneider, *Exegetical Dictionary of the New Testament* (Grand Rapids, MI: Eerdmans, 1990–), 152.

[18] ESV, NET, CSB, NLT, NRSV, RSV.

Kingdom Alive Bible Studies

If you would like to join a live online
Bible Study with Charles Cooper concerning:
The Gospel of the Kingdom of God.

Email:
Coop@kingdomalive.us

Indicate the
The day of the week –
Time of day –
Time Zone
That would be best for you.

Find a Bible Study Near You:

www.ingramcontent.com/pod-product-compliance
Lightning Source LLC
Chambersburg PA
CBHW011227120626
46549CB00008B/3181